SOUTH AFRICA IN FOCUS

Editor drs Willem Drechsel
Translation from the Dutch by drs Jacky Meijer
Photo editing Peter Homan
Overall final editing drs Christine Waslander

KEGAN PAUL INTERNATIONAL
London and New York

COUNTRY OF MANY FACES

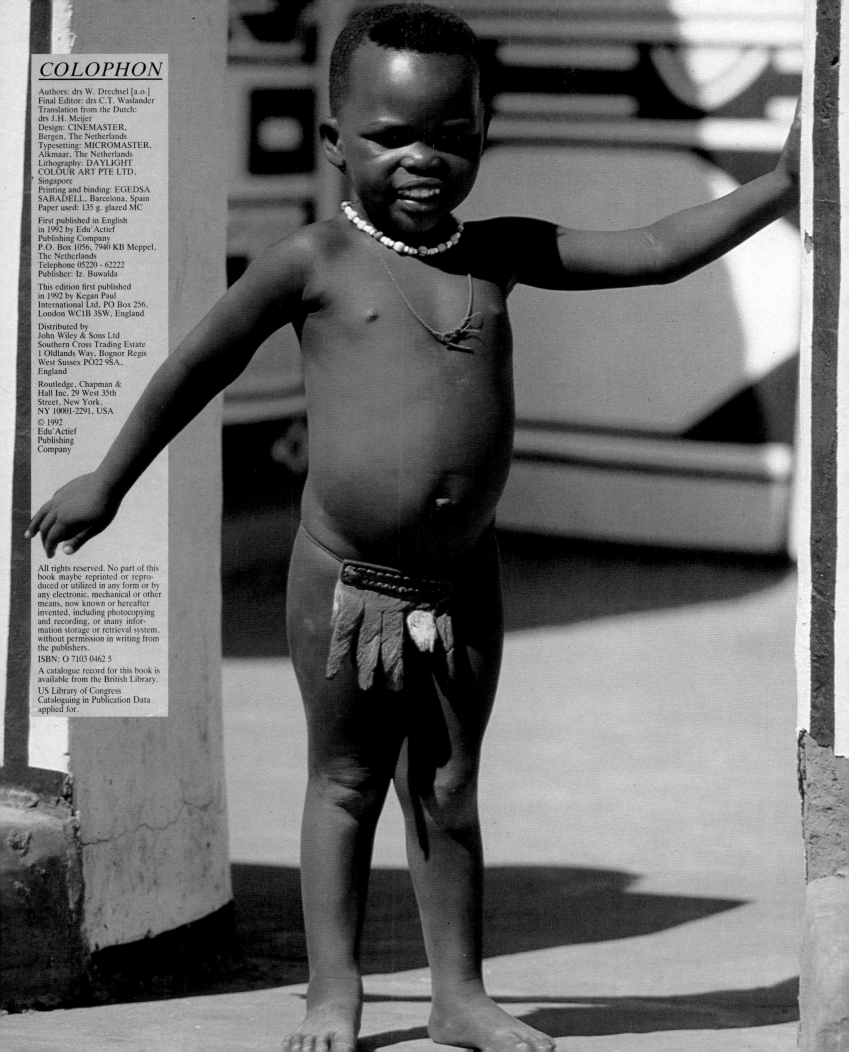

COLOPHON

Authors: drs W. Drechsel [a.o.]
Final Editor: drs C.T. Waslander
Translation from the Dutch:
drs J.H. Meijer
Design: CINEMASTER,
Bergen, The Netherlands
Typesetting: MICROMASTER,
Alkmaar, The Netherlands
Lithography: DAYLIGHT
COLOUR ART PTE LTD,
Singapore
Printing and binding: EGEDSA
SABADELL, Barcelona, Spain
Paper used: 135 g. glazed MC

First published in English
in 1992 by Edu'Actief
Publishing Company
P.O. Box 1056, 7940 KB Meppel,
The Netherlands
Telephone 05220 - 62222
Publisher: Iz. Buwalda

This edition first published
in 1992 by Kegan Paul
International Ltd, PO Box 256,
London WC1B 3SW, England

Distributed by
John Wiley & Sons Ltd
Southern Cross Trading Estate
1 Oldlands Way, Bognor Regis
West Sussex PO22 9SA,
England

Routledge, Chapman &
Hall Inc, 29 West 35th
Street, New York,
NY 10001-2291, USA

© 1992
Edu'Actief
Publishing
Company

ISBN: O 7103 0462 5

A catalogue record for this book is
available from the British Library.

US Library of Congress
Cataloguing in Publication Data
applied for.

SOUTH AFRICA IN FOCUS

CONTENTS

PREFACE

Not since Harold MacMillans Winds of Change envisaged the African continent in the 1960's, has South Africa been so near to becoming a full participative member of the southern African economic community.

For well over 40 years I have advocated that this is where South Africa belongs, because we have the infrastructures, the national resources, management expertise, technical skills and the knowledge of Africa to fulfil our role as a catalyst for development.

However, our acceptance as an economic member has, to the detriment of all in the sub-continent, been temporarily delayed by a political ideology which has now failed, like many other ideologies elsewhere.

Because ethnicity, in the words of an American banker, is built into the genes of man, there are still deep-seated cultural, political and ideological differences in southern Africa. In my opinion, however, the biggest binding factor is our economic interdependence and the region's yearning for peace and prosperity.

Our economic interdependence is a given reality. We use the same banking system, legal and insurance systems, the same infrastructure of railways, which cross the region like steel arteries, and the same harbours. Furthermore, we are joint together by a power network spanning the whole of southern Africa, by trade links, tourism, the exchange of knowledge as well as medical and veterinary services, and by a world language which facilitates communication.

As a link between Africa and Europe, South Africa is the logical road for western aid programmes directed toward Africa; it is the locomotive for growth in the sub-continent.

This is endorsed by the fact that South Africa generates more than two thirds of the electricity used in sub-Saharan Africa; that is moves more than three quarters of the rail freight in the region; that it consumes 72 percent of Africa's steel, 40 percent of the continent's cement and has more than half of its telephones.

Now that the international community has abandoned sanctions and that the negotiating process is underway, albeit still very fragile, our biggest challenge is to meet the economic aspirations of a population of 37 million people, 28 million of whom are black, many without jobs, homes and, for far too long, without hope.

I believe that peaceful coexistence and shared prosperity are possible once consensus has been reached on a constitution to accommodate the aspirations and the diversity of all our peoples. Personally I am positive that goodwill, good sense and good faith will prevail. Through there positive attitudes, confirmed support, long-term investments and by sounding the alarm whenever it is necessary, the international community can help us to chart a safe course through the present troubled waters of economic recession.

Hopefully this book will contribute to this.

Dr A.E. Rupert

Dr A.E.Rupert, honorary president of the South African-Dutch Chamber of Commerce.

I gladly subscribe to what my friend Anton Rupert has stated in his preface.

South Africa is very active in the field of nature protection. The parks in this beautiful country are exemplary and a joy for everyone who is so fortunate as to be able to pay them a visit. I myself hope to do this soon again.

His Royal Highness Prince Bernhard of The Netherlands

Prince of The Netherlands

◄ *The giant protea (Protea cynaroides), the national flower of South Africa, has a diameter of 25 centimetres.*

1 MINI ATLAS

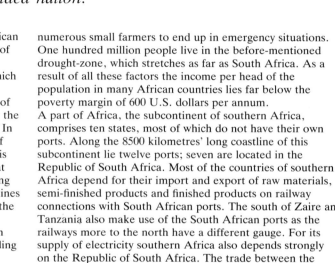

South Africa, a country with an overwhelming natural scenery, a turbulent history and a challenging future. Cultures have to be melted down into a new democratic, multiracial society. Rich, natural resources and an advanced technology can be at the basis of a favourable economic development, provided a number of social and political conditions are met.
'South Africa in focus, country of many faces', a fascinating exploration of a many-sided nation.

South Africa, the southern tip of the gigantic African continent, is mainly located south of the tropic of Capricorn. It comprises the Republic of South Africa and four territories denoted as national states, which were called 'Homelands' for a long time: Transkei, Bophuthatswana, Venda and Ciskei. The independence of these so-called T.B.V.C.-countries is only recognized by the Republic of South Africa and the territories themselves. In this book these territories are also reckoned to be part of South Africa. Introducing the 'country of many faces' this first chapter presents a collection of noteworthy facts that provide a general picture of South Africa. In the following chapters the 'many faces' are revealed. Chapter two outlines the historical development, which is deeply engraved in the consciousness of all population groups. Chapter three provides a review of the cultural variety of South African society. In the subsequent chapters four up to and including seven, the major touristic sights are described in a combination of background information and travel reports. Finally, in chapter eight, the economic perspective of South Africa is outlined.

Africa, southern Africa and South Africa

The African mainland covers 22 percent of the global surface. Six hundred million people live on this continent, representing twelve percent of all the inhabitants in the world. The annual population growth is among the highest on earth. Due to the fact that an equivalent increase in means of support seriously lags behind, many people in several states are threatened in their future existence.
The insufficient economic growth is the result of a number of causes with mutually reinforcing adverse effects. Unfavourable factors are, amongst others, the inadequate infrastructure and a failing industrialization. Practising agriculture on too small family-run farms, with limited technological knowledge and experience, also impedes an optimal development. Moreover, crops that are liable to strongly fluctuating, generally low, world-prices are often cultivated. Besides this there is the political instability of several regions, such as in the Sudan, Eritrea, Ethiopia, Somalia and Moçambique, which has led to disastrous wars causing innumerable people to be deprived of their homes. Finally Africa is harassed by lengthy periods of drought, which now and again afflict millions of people in large areas of the continent. In a broad zone, south of Tanzania, Zaire and South Angola, harvest failures occurred in 1992, causing

numerous small farmers to end up in emergency situations. One hundred million people live in the before-mentioned drought-zone, which stretches as far as South Africa. As a result of all these factors the income per head of the population in many African countries lies far below the poverty margin of 600 U.S. dollars per annum.
A part of Africa, the subcontinent of southern Africa, comprises ten states, most of which do not have their own ports. Along the 8500 kilometres' long coastline of this subcontinent lie twelve ports; seven are located in the Republic of South Africa. Most of the countries of southern Africa depend for their import and export of raw materials, semi-finished products and finished products on railway connections with South African ports. The south of Zaire and Tanzania also make use of the South African ports as the railways more to the north have a different gauge. For its supply of electricity southern Africa also depends strongly on the Republic of South Africa. The trade between the above-mentioned neighbouring countries and South Africa has recently increased. About half of the South African export to African countries (with a total value of almost one billion dollars) takes place within the Southern African Customs Union between Botswana, Lesotho, Swaziland, Namibia and the Republic of South Africa. In recent years more than a million labourers from the adjoining countries have found work in South Africa. Moreover, many investments in the neighbouring countries are brought about

◄ *The eagle (Polemaetus bellicosus) is the largest bird of prey in Africa. Circling over the steppes and savannas he hunts, among others, for birds, dwarf antelopes and badgers (Mellivora capensis).*

and financed by the South African private sector. In the field of Public Health there are also intensive contacts. Most vaccines and other medicines, which are used in the prevention and treatment of contagious diseases in southern Africa, are produced in South Africa.

Geography and geology

More than 100 million years ago Australia, South America, Antarctica and India broke away from the giant Gondwanaland. The detached parts slowly drifted apart to their present positions far from their motherland Africa. On the remaining African continent an animal and human world started to develop, which has attracted numerous explorers and travellers over the years.

With a surface area of 1.3 million square kilometres South Africa is five times larger than Great Britain and just as large as Germany, France and Italy together. Along the 3000 kilometres' long coastline run two main oceanic currents: the warm Agulhas current in the south-east and the cold Benguela current in the west. The narrow coastal strip is formed by a plain, which is of a desert-like dryness in the west, has a mediterranean climate in the region around Cape Town, and via a region with a temperate climate ends in a subtropical zone in the east.

Average days of sunshine			
	Per year	Maximum per month	Minimum per month
Johannesburg	263	26	18
Durban	197	21	12
Cape Town	245	24	17

▲ One of the more than 100 erica species on the Cape peninsula. The vegetation along the south-west coast of the Cape Province, the so-called fynbos, consists, among others, of several kinds of ericas, proteas, reed-like plants and a large group of bulbous and tuberous plants.

Population

South Africa has a population of around 38 million people, 56 percent of whom live in the big cities. The population density, fourteen persons per square kilometre, is considerably lower than the world-average or that of Africa. The South African population, however, is strongly concentrated in the eastern half of the country. As a result of historical development a large diversity of population groups live within South Africa. The annual increase of the black part of the population is much bigger than that of other groups, which is why the percentage that the former group constitutes within the total population will increase considerably. Around the turn of the century the number of inhabitants of South Africa will have exceeded that of 50 millions. The expectation for the year 2000 is that of the inhabitants 78 percent will be black, 11.5 percent white, 8 percent coloured and almost 2.5 percent Asian.

The black population divides into a variegated mosaic of groups, which clearly reveal differences in language and culture. They are distinguished in four language sections: Nguni, Sotho, Tsonga and Venda. These, in their turn, are divided into sub-language divisions, which are spoken by several population groups.

The Nguni language group is divided into four sub-language sections: Zulu, Swazi, Xhosa and Ndebele. The Zulu speaking population, circa 7.6 million people, live in KwaZulu in Natal and in a number of urban areas. The Swazi speaking population, about 1.2 million people, mainly live in KaNgwane (East Transvaal). The Xhosa speaking population, about 3 million people, predominantly live in Transkei, Ciskei, the eastern Cape Province and the big cities. Within this sub-language group, however, are many groups who speak a dialect that is not clearly related to

Climate

Due to the location of South Africa at a latitude of between 22 and 35 degrees South the country generally has a moderate climate. The gulfstreams along the coast strongly influence the temperatures. The cold Benguela current has a cooling effect along the west coast during its course to the north. The warm Agulhas current causes higher temperatures in the eastern coastal regions.

On the West Cape the winters are cool and humid and the summers sunny and dry. In the rest of the country there is regular rainfall during the warm summers. These rains often pour down during heavy thunderstorms in the interior. The winters are generally dry and mild. In the mountainous regions periods of intense cold weather occur now and then.

In general the country has its most pleasant temperatures at the end of the South African summer during the months of April and May. For certain regions, such as the coast of Natal and the north and east of Transvaal, June and July are considered to be the best months.

Cape Point, the most southern
▼ tip of the Cape peninsula, better known as the Cape of Good Hope. Here the warm Agulhas stream and the cold Benguela stream meet.

Xhosa, on which the written language is based. The South Ndebele form a small group in Central Transvaal. Finally the North Ndebele have, for a major part, been assimilated with the Sotho.

The Sotho speaking population, 7.6 million people, consists of three almost equally large population groups: the North Sotho, who used to have their domain in Lebowa in North Transvaal; the South Sotho in Lesotho and Orange Free State; and the Tswana in Bophuthatswana.

The Tsonga speaking population, 1.5 million people, originally lived in GazanKulu in North-East Transvaal. They are also often denoted as Shangaan-Tsonga.

The Venda speaking population, some hundreds of thousands of people, mainly live in Venda. The Lemba, who are of Semitic origin, also belong to this language group.

In addition to the above-mentioned facts, it has to be noted that nearly half of the black population lives in or in the neighbourhood of urban conglomerates and often has few cultural ties with the population groups just cited.

Afrikaans and English are the languages spoken by the circa five-and-a-half million white people. Afrikaners are descendants from the former Cape colonists: Dutchmen, Germans and Frenchmen. Afrikaans developed from the seventeenth century 'Cape Dutch', that started to differ strongly from Dutch. Many words have been adopted from KhoiKhoi, Portuguese. Malay, German, French, English and the indigenous languages of the black Africans. However, Dutchmen can still understand and read Afrikaans well. Most of the whites, 57 percent, speak Afrikaans.

The English speaking population, 38 percent of the whites, for a small part descend from the first *settlers*, who set foot ashore at Port Elizabeth in 1820. For the majority, though, they belong to the descendants of the group of English speaking immigrants, who flowed into South Africa at the end of the nineteenth century after the discovery of diamonds and gold.

The majority of the coloured population, 85 percent of whom live in the Cape Province, mostly speak only or preferably Afrikaans. The Asians, finally, nearly all speak English. Some groups from India still use native Indian languages. A respectable number of, mainly English, newspapers circulate in South Africa. Radio and television broadcasts are transmitted in English, Afrikaans and in several indigenous African languages.

Health care

Compared to the average expenditure in the world, 4.6 percent of the Gross National Product, health care expenses in South Africa are high (5.6 percent in 1990/91). The quality of most services is excellent. The lower income groups, irrespective of race and origin, obtain free medical help on all levels or for very low fees.

The quantity of the services rendered is very high in comparison with other African countries. The number of doctors in South Africa amounts to 1 per 1300 inhabitants, while in entire Africa it is 1 per 1700 inhabitants. For 1 out of every 200 inhabitants one hospital bed is available, for entire Africa that average is 1 out of 700.

Many patients from other African countries go to South Africa for medical treatment. In the field of medical research South Africa renders assistance to a large number of African countries. In comparison with western countries, where the average life expectancy is nowadays more than 70 years, the figure for South Africa (63) can be called low. Yet compared with Africa as a whole, with an average life expectancy of 53 years, the South African figure can be considered high again. Despite this there is a backlog in health care of blacks in relation to whites, coloured people and Asians. However, the figures do closely approach the standard of the World Health Organization.

▲ *The Ndebele population-group lives in Mid and North Transvaal. The women wear characteristic copper rings and broad bands of beads around their necks.*

Population groups in South Africa				
	Numbers in 1990 in millions	Percentage in 1990	Growth in percentages 1980-1988	
			Per annum	In the period
Blacks	28,2	74,2	2,39	20,8
Coloured *	3,3	8,7	1,89	16,1
Asians **	1,0	2,7	1,78	15,1
Whites	5,5	14,4	1,14	9,1
Total	38,1	100	2,1	18,1

* denotation of multi-racial people.   ** mainly Indians.

Soweto from the air. In this district the original schematic structure of the
▼ *'township' is clearly recognizable. In the background the big Baragwanath Hospital.*

Education

Due to the cultural diversity education in South Africa faces large problems. Equal rights in schooling have not been reached by far. At the moment there is compulsory education up to sixteen for whites and coloured people and up to fifteen for Indians. A phased introduction of compulsory school attendance for the black population has been started. Between 1986 and 1990 government expenses relating to education were increased from sixteen to twenty percent of the entire government budget. Put in percentages of the Gross National Product the expenditure increased from 4.2 percent to 5.5 percent. Compared to the percentages in the United Kingdom (5), The Netherlands (6.8), the United States (6.7), Japan (5) and Germany (4.5) this can be considered high.

Although the expenses for education to blacks have revealed a relatively strong increase in recent years, they lag behind considerably per head of the population compared to other groups in South African society. It is obvious that the process of 'levelling' will still demand a lengthy period of time. If an equal amount of money would be spent on education for blacks as on education for whites, the total costs would be 37 billion rands. An amount equivalent to thirteen percent of the Gross National Product. At this moment one fifth of

Expenditure on education in South Africa		
	Per head 1989/90 in rands *	In total 1990/91 in million rand
Blacks	930	6504,5
Coloured	1983	2025,4
Indians	2659	824,4
Whites	3739	5533,5

Source: 'South Africa 1992' of the South African Foundation.
* In 1991 the rate of the rand was 0.39 US dollar.

all blacks older than sixteen never attended school. Of the others 25 percent did not complete primary school, nineteen percent followed secondary education and merely one percent obtained a university degree. Fifty percent of the adult population is illiterate.

In 1990, 5.6 million pupils out of the 6.9 million pupils attending one of the 25,805 primary schools belonged to the black part of the population. Of the 2.7 million pupils following state secondary education 2 million were black. Among the total number of students at the Teachers' Training College (72,174) were 42,429 blacks. The students at the 21 universities totalled 302,041, of whom 111,202 belonged to the black population.

Infrastructure

Electricity production in South Africa has increased during the past decades with almost eight percent per year. The country produces more than half of all electricity generated on the African continent. Coal-fuelled power stations provide ninety percent of the need for energy. The remaining electricity is generated at nuclear, hydro-electric and gas-turbine power stations. The Republic of South Africa has guaranteed that nuclear technology will only be applied for peaceful purposes.

In the beginning of 1990 the State Companies of the South African Transport Services (SATS) were privatized into Transnet, comprising of five companies. The eight commercial sea-ports of South Africa are controlled by Portnet. Petronet provides the transportation of 85 percent of all oil-fuels via pipelines from the refineries, across a distance of more than 3000 kilometres. 'Spoornet' controls the 20,000 kilometres long railway network. The firm 'Autonet' is responsible for the construction and maintenance of motorways, which connect the urban and country centres over a distance of about 180,000 kilometres. About 82,000 kilometres of the road network is asphalted and is in excellent condition. The national airline company SAL and several smaller companies take care of domestic air transport.

Tourism

The South African Tourism Board (Satour) plays a central role in promoting South Africa as a tourist destination. The agency has thirteen international offices at its disposal, with seats in the capitals of the West European countries, America, Taiwan, Japan, Israel and Zimbabwe. The main office in South Africa is situated in Pretoria; furthermore there are ten regional offices, divided over the main cities.

In the tourist guide published by Satour – on the back of a map of South Africa – all kinds of practical data in connection with tourism are mentioned. Besides this Satour has recently made a concise travel guide available. In it the main tourist areas and major cities are described, followed by an enumeration of the sights. Finally, some suggestions are made for trips by touringcar or (rented) car. Travel-agencies from several countries make use of these

Map legend:
- desert and semi desert
- forest belt and palm belt
- mediterranean
- savanna
- moderate grasszone

north
400 km

- main road
- railway
- state boundary

Water supply

A good 30 percent of all the rainwater in the world is transported to the sea via rivers. Due to the abundant sunshine and the resulting high degree of evaporation this percentage is a mere 9 for South Africa. As the average annual rainfall only exceeds 500 millimetres in 40 percent of the country, the major part of South Africa is unsuitable for agriculture without irrigation. Extensive investments in all kinds of waterworks were therefore necessary. The majority of the surface water is put to use via an elaborate system of dams and irrigation canals. The largest waterworks are part of the Orange-, Vaal-, Drakensberg- and Lesotho-projects. Besides this, in many regions water is pumped up.

The South African rivers are nearly all unnavigable and there are hardly any natural lakes. The water surfaces denoted as lakes, are in fact lagoons or have been formed by the above-mentioned artificial dams in rivers.

suggestions when compiling their programmes.
In the course of the nineties the travel-world was quick to sense that South Africa had a potential to become an ideal holiday country after having abolished apartheid. The unequalled scenery, the varied flora and fauna, the historical sights, the cultural diversity, the favourable climate and the good amenities, even in remote nature reserves, vouch for this. After the 'silent period' of ten years, during which there was hardly any increase of international tourism, the number of visitors grew steadily from 1986 onwards. In 1991 foreign visitors numbered over 1.7 million, 66 percent more than in 1990. Of these guests 521,000 came from overseas and circa 1.19 million from Africa, the majority from Zimbabwe, Lesotho and Swaziland. The African visitors mainly came to visit relatives, to do shopping and to search for jobs. The overseas visitors chiefly came from Great Britain, Germany, the United States, France, Finland, Switzerland, Taiwan, The Netherlands and Belgium. For the next decade an increase of international tourism of dozens of percents on an annual basis is reckoned with. It is expected that, in the year 2000, at least four times as many overseas visitors a year will visit this fascinating new destination.
South African authorities do not stimulate mass tourism. Accommodation and travel possibilities are especially offered to the so-called 'eco-tourists', who are attracted by the splendid nature reserves, and also to people who are interested in the historical and cultural sights. For 'vulnerable' nature reserves, in particular popular wildlife areas such as the Krugerpark, a daily maximum of visitors is introduced during the high season.
Both for groups and individual travellers the accommodations and amenities are good. Capacity is, except during some peak periods, amply available in most places. Some tour-operators organize 'combination' journeys, including both transport and accommodation. These journeys consist of routes by bus, rented car, plane, train and safaris in wild parks.

The economic development

Of all the states on the African continent South Africa has by far the strongest economy, which is, among other things, expressed in the height of the Gross National Income (more than 80 billion U.S. dollars in 1989).

Gross National Income in 1989		
	in billion US dollar	population in millions
Egypt	32	52,5
Nigeria	29	11
Zaire	10	35
Kenya	9	8
Tunisia	7	25
Zambia	5	7,8
Zimbabwe	5	10
Moçambique	1	16
Great-Britain	718	57
The Netherlands	222	15

The historical, sociological and economic accounts incorporated in several chapters of this book, are also intended to provide a closer insight into a number of topical issues. For South African and foreign business this information can be of importance. Especially for foreign companies who, now that South Africa is on its way to join the democratic multi-racial societies in the world, are considering setting up business relations or expanding already established relations.

▲ *The chalets in the main camp of the Londolozi Game Reserve are provided with balconies offering a view of the surrounding lush vegetation.*

Accommodation

Generally speaking the hotels are comfortably furnished and service is good. The hotels are distinguished according to the star-system, varying from ordinary (one star) to excellent (five stars). Well-known hotel chains are: Protea Hotels and Inns, Southern Sun Holiday Inns and Sun International. In the popular tourist areas there are also motels, holiday apartments, bungalows, town and country-houses, game-lodges, holiday farms and youth hostels, besides caravan parks and camping-sites. The so-called 'time-share units' form a new type of accommodation which is booming. Private persons are also quite willing to provide lodgings to tourists.
The efficiently and beautifully designed 'Portfolio of Country Places' is a publication by Tony and Liz Westby-Nunn. This brochure provides important information concerning a large number of country-houses, hotels and game-lodges in South Africa, including some hotels in the cities. Besides this, the Portfolio 'Town and Country Retreats' is published, a guide dealing with smaller accommodation possibilities.
Drinking water is of an excellent quality throughout South Africa. There are no special vaccination regulations, but visitors to East Transvaal and northern Natal are advised to take anti-malaria tablets. Furthermore it is not advisable to swim in the rivers and lakes in the east and north of the country, as the bilharzia-parasite may be present in the water.

▲ *The diamond industry forms a significant pillar of the South African economy.*

After the recent positive developments concerning the political reforms many Dutch, English and other foreign companies have changed into a higher gear in order to expand existing contacts in South Africa and to come to new initiatives in the field of trade and investments. In this book the final chapter will present an analysis of these problems and a perspective for the future.

2 A LIVING PAST

An outline of South Africa's history: from the times when European ships passed Africa's southern point en route to the east, to the beginning of the 1990s. Moreover a sociological retrospect on the Apartheid period and a prospect of the future now that South Africa is on its way to a democratic society.

In South Africa the past is a visible part of the present. People from Africa, Europe and Asia, representing many different nations and cultures, provide regions and cities with their own characters. There are numerous topographical references in the languages of South Africa's black population. Some, such as Gariep, Outeniqua and Kei (river) have been derived from the language of the old hunters and collectors, today indicated by the name Khoisan and formerly known as Hottentots and Bushmen. Other names refer to the colonists from the days of the Dutch East Indian Company – in Dutch: Vereenigde Oost-Indische Compagnie (V.O.C.) – who gave good Dutch sounding names to their new surroundings: Stellenbosch, Witsenbergen, Hottentots-Holland! Later generations of Dutch colonists named their settlements after their place of origin: Ermelo, Utrecht, Amersfoort, Amsterdam. Thus English colonists, *setlaars*, also left their traces after 1820: King William's Town, East London, Somerset West. Unfortunately there are numerous names that bear witness of the conflicts between the various population groups: Vegkop, Weenen, Blood River. More hopeful moments were fortunately also recorded geographically: Avondrust, Behulpsaam, Broedersput to mention a few, or more well-known: Genadendal, Botshabelo, Rehoboth.

Place-names like Sharpeville and Soweto have a worldwide significance. They are symbols of the political and social contrasts in South Africa, known by a loan-word, adopted by all languages and taken from Afrikaans: apartheid. In everyday topicality more historical names resound: Van Riebeeck and Kruger, Shaka and Dingaan (Dingane). Besides all this dates have their special place in that controversial, but vivid past: 1652, 1838, 1881, 1902, 1910, 1912, 1948, 1990. In this chapter they will be discussed.

Strongly different, sometimes completely opposite, are the images of the past among the various South African population groups. Images that determine their self-image and their view of others to a very high degree. Present and past can not be understood separately in South Africa.

Professor dr Gerrit Schutte will discuss this past in more detail; the sociological contribution is made by professor dr Jacques van Doorn.

Settlement of a colony

From the late fifteenth century European ships rounded the southern tip of Africa en route to the riches of the Orient, China, Japan, India, the Moluccas, or homewards from those

◄ *The Voortrekkers' monument at Pretoria keeps the memory alive of the Boer past in South Africa. The wildebeests in the façade symbolize the warriors of Zulu king Dingaan and also the 'barbarism' that had to yield to 'civilization'. The buffalo head symbolically defends the monument against attacks from outside.*

regions, laden with spices, silk, cotton, tea and other much coveted items. Since the end of the sixteenth century an increasing number of those ships came from the Low Countries, from 1602 onwards adorned with the flag of the Dutch East Indian Company (V.O.C.). This company had been founded to end the cut-throat competition between the various Dutch Companies and to form a strong union with other European and Asian traders. After half a century the V.O.C. had grown into a mighty and flourishing company, the largest multinational of The Netherlands, employer of many thousands of seamen, merchants and soldiers. The company owned a series of fortresses, factories and establishments in ports and trading cities in almost every part of Asia: from the Arabian Mocha to Deshima in Nippon (Japan), a region otherwise forbidden territory for Europeans. Batavia, the capital of the V.O.C. in the Orient, was at an eight or nine months' sailing distance from Europe. On their long journeys the crew of the Company ships were exposed to numerous dangers. Insufficiently protected against wind and rain, packed together in far too great numbers, they had to withstand the changes of climate; their food was not at all varied, often went rotten and was insufficient in quantity. Diseases and ailments afflicted the sailors; on average ten percent of them died during the journey. Small wonder therefore that Governors of the V.O.C. hoped to find a remedy in the form of a settlement half-way, at the Cape of Good Hope. On 6 April 1652 Jan van Riebeeck set foot ashore in the Table Bay in order to found a maritime station and staging post for the Company. According to seventeenth century European views the right to do this was indisputable. International law prevailing in those days allowed colonization in uninhabited regions. Van Riebeeck was sent with the assignment to live in peace with the neighbouring nomadic Khoisan and to respect their freedom.

The Cape settlement experienced difficult first years. Adapting to local conditions took effort and time and was not without set-backs. The issue of land, in 1657, to the first free burghers was of utmost importance. As independent entrepreneurs they could cultivate the land and breed cattle and sell the proceeds to the Company. In order to solve the shortage of labourers a second significant event took place in 1658: the first groups of slaves were imported. Gradually the Cape settlement extended. Farmers settled further and further from the Castle situated near Table Bay. Especially during the days of governor Simon van der Stel, who founded Stellenbosch in 1679, the expansion got well under way.

The Cape was at many places far more suited to intensive cattle breeding than to crop-farming or horticulture; the distance to Cape Town, which was then and remained the only consumers' market, promoted that orientation to cattle breeding. In the course of the eighteenth century colonists settled in the interior, north and east of Cape Town. The climate and the quality of the grazing land again and again forced them to keep looking in new regions for means of existence for their herds. They were now called 'Trekboeren', semi-nomadic cattle breeders who led

Jan van Riebeeck, founder of the Cape colony. Painting from the collection of the
▼ *Rijksmuseum at Amsterdam.*

a lonely life far from the centres of civilization and administration. Once every three months they might have gone to the nearest village to attend a church service; once a year they visited Cape Town, sometimes as remote as a 40 day-journey, to sell their cattle and cattle breeding products and to make the necessary purchases. It was almost an Old Testament biblical-patriarchal existence, with large families, a number of Khoikhoi servants and shepherds and perhaps some slaves. And the Trekboer penetrated the country further and further.

The expansion of the Cape settlement was not without conflicts with the semi-nomadic Khoisan, who lived from all that their cattle, hunting and the veld yielded. Conflicts of interests soon arose about grazing land and water-places, and there were misunderstandings about game and cattle. As early as in 1659, shortly after the settlement of the first free burghers, the Khoikhoi tried to expel the Europeans. After that time conflicts repeatedly occurred as well. However, they could not impede the growth of the settlement. Khoi society was divided and weak, a part of them soon being willing to profit from the Europeans and to co-operate with them. Some joined the expanding settlement, others withdrew into the interior. The San people offered far more resistance. Hardy and agile hunter-collectors as they were, they proved far less adaptable and more capable of strong opposition. In the course of the eighteenth century a mutual extermination war developed, which blocked the expansion of

the Trekboer northwards for dozens of years. Eventually, however, the San also had to bend and withdraw.

Thus a new society developed at the Cape during the first century and a half of colonisation. A settlement, similar to the ones arising in North America and Australia. An increasing number of people of European descent found a new existence here: Dutchmen, Germans, Frenchmen (in 1688 a few hundreds of Huguenots, who had fled their mother-country for religious reasons, arrived with the Company's assistance) and all kinds of other people. In due course the colony got its own, Cape-Dutch character. It was mainly an agrarian society. Around Cape Town, which slowly extended into a port and a centre of administration, the wine and grain farmers dominated; in the interior cattle breeding provided the means of livelihood. That is why the inhabitants obtained the name Boers: Afrikaner Boers, because they soon felt at one with Africa, their home country. Of course the ties with Europe remained, via the Board of the V.O.C., the economy, family relations, the church and culture. The Cape people built houses with Cape-Dutch gables and read from the Authorized Version of the Bible. Yet their vernacular language proved that a new identity was gradually developing, as their life-style and customs clearly started to reveal features of their own.

The development of that specific character was rooted in the colonial structure and composition of the Cape population. For they did not merely consist of European colonists. The Cape also housed a large non-European population group. Slaves for instance, from several parts of Africa, but especially from South and South-East Asia; liberated ex-slaves and others who formed the group of the 'free blacks'; free Khoikhoi. There were all kinds of contacts between these population groups, including sexual ones. Thus a racially and culturally pluriform society developed at the Cape.

Colonial social patterns

Cape society possessed a typical colonial structure and had a dominant dichotomy. On the one hand there was a group of European descent, life-style and culture; relatively rich, educated and well-respected. The other group was of non-European or mixed origin, had no or merely limited knowledge of European culture (including Christianity), was poor and not distinguished, some were even slaves. The dichotomy was not everywhere as clear or unbridgeable. The dividing line was not so much determined by race as by culture and religion. Already during the first years of the settlement a certain 'Eva de Hottentottin' was allowed inside the European group after having been baptized and married. The latter group itself, for that matter, increasingly revealed signs of social diversification. There was a great social distance between the elite of the high Company employees and the wealthy land-owners from Cape Town and its immediate vicinity and the ordinary Company soldiers, the poor free burghers or the semi-nomadic cattle farmers in the remote interior. The latter adopted quite a few customs from their surroundings. All the poor, regardless of their origin, resembled each other as far as their living conditions were concerned. In due course groups arose, uniting their own, indigenous and European cultural elements, such as the 'free blacks' and the slaves, the Griqua and the Basters. In this way the original tri-partition of the colonial population based on origin, juridical status and culture in Europeans, slaves and Khoikhoi had been replaced by the end of the eighteenth century by a multi-layered and differentiated, yet coherent pattern.

At that time hardly any independent Khoikhoi lived within the boundaries of the Cape colony any more. They now worked as shepherds and servants with the white Boers. They constituted the Cape labourers' class, together with the slaves and free blacks, who were a considerable part of the skilled craftsmen in Cape Town and the surrounding area. At the beginning of the nineteenth century they had to a large extent exchanged their own culture and language for the culture and language of their masters. Except a small group, who remained loyal to the Islam

Reproduction of a drawing by Johannes Rach: View of the town hall at Cape Town. In 1764 Cape Town was still a simple village, where the colonial contrasts became clearly visible though. In the front, right, a palanquin, left a slave with his hands tied behind his back. Typical is also the man with the pikolan: an oriental influence.

Groot Constantia, the mansion that governor Simon van der Stel had built in 1685.

Old picture of the Drostdy at Tulbagh.

(the Cape Malayans), they also embraced the Christian faith; Genadendal near Baviaanskloof was the first permanent missionary post among the Khoikhoi in 1792.

The class division of the population was not identical to the racial diversity. In the eastern Cape border region, for instance, the colonial Khoikhoi took part in the commandos together with Trekboers against free Khoisan and Xhosa, as allies in the battle for cattle and grazing land. But although the division was not rigid or without exceptions, the dividing lines in the Cape society in the second half of the eighteenth century mainly ran parallel to the contrasts between white and non-white, rich and poor, master and servant, European and non-European, Christian and non-Christian.

At the end of the eighteenth century the Cape colony already had a certain vastness: about 25,000 slaves, 20,000 European colonists, 15,000 Khoikhoi and 1,000 free blacks lived there. Due to the fact that the inhospitable natural environment and the fierce resistance of the San arrested the expansion in north-westerly and northern directions respectively, the main development took place in an eastern direction. In the third quarter of the eighteenth century, however, the Trekboers came upon the Xhosa, Nguni speaking shepherds and agrarians, organized in clans and tribes, in that region. In 1799 the first in a series of Frontier wars took place between Xhosa and Trekboers, who disputed grazing lands and water-finding places in the Suurveld between the rivers Sunday and Fish. The Cape government tried in vain to separate both parties by proclaiming an agreed border. The inhabitants of the Frontier area (white and black) would not be told what to do. In 1796 the Boers in the remote interior near Graaff-Reinet even refused to acknowledge the authority of the Company any longer.

The rebellion of the Frontier farmers happened at a time, when the authority of the Company was no longer effective: in September 1795 the Cape government had to surrender to the British. There were great revolutions in Europe during those years. The old Dutch Republic was not immune to them and fell in 1795. Great Britain, at war with revolutionary France and therefore with its satellite state the Batavian Republic, had sent a fleet in order to take over the Dutch colonial possessions. That is how the Cape colony came under British rule, first on a temporary basis but in the end definitively (Convention of London, 1814).

Although British rule and annexation into the British empire brought certain advantages, a part of the Cape people reacted negatively to the take-over from the very beginning. Besides socio-economic factors, the authoritarian administration and the Anglo-Saxon influence of language and culture were important arguments. The eastern Frontier remained a region full of tensions and repeated conflicts. The settlement of British colonists in 1820, precisely in the contested area, did not provide the calming buffer against the Xhosa that was hoped for, but intensified the contrasts. Again and again the conflicts resulted in new wars. The British colonial administration was not very popular among the western Cape Boers either due to its measures to ensure the legal status and freedom of action of the coloured (Khoikhoi) population in 1812 and 1828, and subsequently by proclaiming the emancipation of slaves in 1833. The Cape people considered those regulations as a violation of their rights and property (emancipation of slaves without sufficient compensation), their security of existence (they depended on slave- and coloured-labour) and their way of life (which was based on the distinction between master and servant). Feelings of uncertainty, insecurity and dissatisfaction therefore played a part in the start of the Great Trek in the years following 1834, although overpopulation and a lack of land were the two main reasons for this drastic migration.

▲ Genadendal; colour lithograph by George French Angas. From: 'The Kafirs illustrated' (1849).

Extremely difficult ascent of the Drakensberg Mountains at Cradock's Pass during the Great Trek in ▼ 1840; engraving by Charles Cornwallis Mitchell. Collection South African Museum.

STATE OF CRADOCK'S PASS IN 1840

The Great Trek

▲ *The voyage of the Voortrekkers across the Drakensberg Mountains is depicted on one of the panels in the Voortrekkers Monument in Pretoria.*

▲ *Sarel Cilliers (1801-1871), one of the leaders of the Great Trek.*

Klaas Smits River - Waggon broke down, crossing the drift. Colour lithograph by Thomas Baines. From: 'Scenery and ▼ *events in South Africa' (1852).*

Between 1834 and 1840 about 15,000 people migrated from the Cape colony in order to build a new subsistence in the interior. They called themselves emigrants; later terms such as *Voortrekkers* and Great Trek were introduced. Discontentment about the conditions in the colony, in particular in the eastern border regions, formed the background. The people were not completely unfamiliar with the situation across the border. There were accounts of hunters, traders and missionaries and reports from exploratory committees. The *Voortrekkers* travelled in groups under self-chosen leaders, accompanied by their cattle and servants, their furniture laden on ox-carts. There were different opinions about the final destination. The early *Voortrekker* leaders Louis Trichardt and Hans van Rensburg migrated through the Transvaal Lowveld and Portuguese East Africa right up to Lourenço Marques (the present-day Maputo). Hendrik Potgieter ousted the mighty Ndebele monarch Mzilikazi from West Transvaal, pursued him far into present-day Zimbabwe and subsequently lived alternately in West, Central and North Transvaal. Piet Retief cast his eye on the Natal coastal plain. At the beginning of 1838 he and 100 men – 70 *Voortrekkers* and 30 servants – rode to Mgungundlovu, the capital of the powerful Zulu king Dingaan in order to talk with him about surrendering those parts of Natal. On the sixth of February 1838 a treaty between the Zulu and the *Voortrekkers* was signed, but subsequently Piet Retief and his men were unexpectedly attacked and killed. During attacks on Boer *laagers*, another 500 people were killed and many thousands of cattle were seized by the Zulu *impis* (regiments). The Great Trek had reached a very critical stage. However, on 16 December 1838 the new *Voortrekkers'* leader Andries Pretorius managed to turn the tide of chance near the Blood River. Independent *Voortrekkers'* republics were founded in Natal, Transoranje and Transvaal. The course and the result of the Great Trek are unexplainable without knowledge of the battle and migration that had afflicted southern Africa during the decades preceding the Great Trek. From the late eighteenth century some tribal chiefs of the North Nguni had been occupied with extending their rule by subjecting and annexing surrounding tribes. Shaka, since 1816 chief of the Zulu, resumed that thread with full vigour and founded a rule that was feared far and wide. Aided by his very disciplined army and some technical and tactical innovations, such as shield and stabbing assegais, half-moon formation of his army during attacks, age-groups and a standing army, he expelled and subjected neighbours

▲ *Shaka, 'King of the Zoolus'; lithograph by W. Bagg. From: 'Travels and adventures in Eastern Africa...' by Nathaniel Isaacs (1836).*

Shaka

Shaka (1781-1828) is the most renowned and most disputed king of the Zulu. He was the son of the Zulu chief Senzangakhona and Nandi, the daughter of a Langeni tribal chief. He is supposed to have had a difficult youth, but despite this had developed into a strong and inventive military leader. After his father's death in 1816 he had his successor killed and took over leadership. A period of expansion began, which made the Zulu kingdom great and formidable in the wide surroundings and caused a period of war and migrations in southern Africa, the *Mfecane*.

Shaka's rule was based on centralized military power; young men, divided into age-groups, were turned into heavily trained regiments, despite their tribal backgrounds. They lived in barracks, in strict celibacy and were severely disciplined. In combination with the introduction of the stabbing assegai and the shield Shaka turned the Zulu *impis* into a cruel, hard war machine. Simultaneously they formed the kernel of the political structure of the Zulu people and were the bearers of tribal pride and tradition.

Shaka's personality is disputed; his significance for the Zulu and for South African history is however unmistakable. Shaka was murdered by his half-brothers Dingaan and Mhlangane, especially because of his excessive behaviour after the death of his mother Nandi. Shaka honoured her with mourning ceremonies during which thousands of people perished; with extravagant sacrifices, a prohibition to cultivate the land and to have sexual intercourse, and with lamenting forced by military display from the surrounding tribes. Shaka's grave lies near his *kraal* Dukuza, where a monument rises in his commemoration.

▲ *Etching of Thaba Bosiu. From: 'A narrative of a Visit to the Mauritius and South Africa' by James Beckhouse (1844).*

Moshesh

Moshesh, founder of the Basotho nation, was born around 1786 as the son of a village chief. At the time of the *Difaqane* he was forced to flee with his men from his town Butha-Buthe and thereupon settled on top of the mountain Thaba Bosiu. In that almost unassailable fortress fugitives of all origins, fleeing the then prevalent violence, were welcome; from among them Moshesh formed the people of the Basotho. As a skilful diplomat and administrator he managed to maintain his position.

In 1833 Moshesh welcomed French missionaries, who founded a missionary post on Morija. Moshesh probably saw a means to strengthen his position even further by their presence and to obtain knowledge, especially with regard to associating with Griqua and whites.

For a long period of time he succeeded in maintaining his independence against obtrusive *Voortrekkers*, Griqua, Korana, Zulu, Ndebele and other enemies, who he tried to play off against one another with success. Notably in order to create a counterbalance against the neighbouring Orange Free State, he accepted a British protectorate in 1868, two years before his death.

'Moshesh en 1833'; woodcutting signed by C. Roux and
▼ *Delangle. From: 'Les Basoutos ...' by E. Casales (1861).*

and adversaries. Shaka caused a chain-reaction creating turmoil in southern and Central Africa. The disruption and the loss of lives caused by the *Mfecane* (devastating total war, Nguni) or *Difaqane* (forced migration, Sotho) were inconceivable. Entire regions were depopulated and destroyed; people withdrew into inhospitable and almost inaccessible areas, and were sometimes forced to commit cannibalism. It is clear that the *Voortrekkers* profited from the weakness and incapacity of several black tribes and could settle without much resistance in almost deserted regions, where they were greeted as allies against the dominant Zulu and Ndebele. Mzilikazi and his Ndebele (Matabele) were driven across the Limpopo River by them and the Zulu from Natal under Dingaan were beaten; yet the Zulu remained a force the *Voortrekkers'* states had to reckon with. The same held good for political units that had arisen due to *Difaqane*, such as, for example, the Basotho kingdom of chief Moshesh, who had managed to maintain his power since 1824 on Thaba Bosiu in the present-day Lesotho.

The years of the Great Trek were of fundamental significance for the further history of South Africa. Although not at all a political unity as yet, the arisen conglomerate of British colonies, Boer republics and black states in southern Africa already revealed the outline of the current Republic of South Africa. The settlement of whites up to far into the interior also laid the foundation for the plural composition of the population. Furthermore it signified the opening up of that interior for future economic processes of change.

Trekboers and *Voortrekkers* had crossed the border to continue their traditional patterns of life. But there was no question of a purely geographical extension of their society. The cultural differences and numerical ratio between white and black caused the subordination of one group to the other in the *Voortrekkers'* states. So two forms of society telescoped in South Africa: the settlement colony and the exploitation colony. The latter comprised a dominant western top layer beside a subordinated indigenous majority, a black population group serving as a labour reservoir for those sectors of the economy that were dominated by the whites.

As a result of the Great Trek South African politics were determined by the triangular relationship between Bantu, Boer and Briton for more than a century. To safeguard her world dominion, England annexed the colony of Natal in 1842 and thus ended the experiment of the independent Boer Republic of Natalia. However after some hesitation, acceptance of the Boers' independence in the Overvaal and Transvaal regions seemed to London to be the cheapest and safest way to avoid too much involvement in the turbulent interior. The Sand River Treaty of 1852 recognized the independence of the Transvaal, the Convention of Bloemfontein (1854) that of the Orange Free State.

The Boer republics

Both Boer republics were initially poor, under-developed, sparsely inhabited and internally divided. The striving for a union of both states, of which the Transvaal president M.W. Pretorius was an advocate, stranded due to mutual differences (and a British veto). In the Orange Free State the contrasts faded away the quickest. Unity was needed in view of the tense relationship with the Griqua and especially the Basotho, resulting in a series of wars. This situation only really ended after Moshesh had put his country and people under British protectorate in 1868. Greater unanimity was also brought about by the British pressure to give up the Free State claims on the area around Kimberley, where diamond was discovered in 1867. Under the careful leadership of president J.H. Brand (1863-1888) the Orange Free State developed into a well-governed, democratic Boer republic.

Discord also characterized the early history of the Overvaal

▲ *Signing of the 'Sandrivierkonvensie' in 1852, in which the English recognize the independence of Transvaal. When the treaty was violated in 1877 by the English annexation of Transvaal, war with the Boers was inevitable.*

Mpande

Mpande (1798-1872) was a son of the Zulu king Senzangakhona and a younger half-brother of Shaka and Dingaan. Unlike his brothers he showed little military interest or talent; as he was not considered to be a dangerous competitor, he stayed alive. Dissatisfied about his part in the battle against the *Voortrekkers*, Dingaan decided to eliminate Mpande in 1839. Only by fleeing and concluding an alliance with the *Voortrekkers* in Natal was Mpande able to maintain his position. In 1840 Mpande sent his armed forces, accompanied by a commando of Afrikaners to Zululand; Dingaan had to flee to Swaziland and died there. Mpande became king of the Zulu and settled in Nodwengu. He pursued a less expansive policy than his predecessors and also tried to maintain peace with the Afrikaners and subsequently with the British in Natal. After a vehement conflict about succession rights between Mpande's sons Cetshwayo and Mbuyazi, Cetshwayo actually took over command of the Zulus in 1857. On the instigation of Theophilus Shepstone, who hoped to found a British protectorate over Zululand in an informal manner, Cetshwayo had himself appointed as his father's successor in 1861.

'Umpanda the King of the Amazulu'; colour lithograph by George French Angas.
▼ *From: 'The Kafirs illustrated' (1849).*

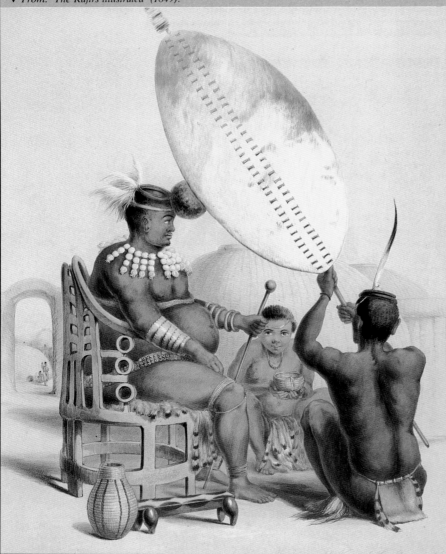

The Vicissitudes of Sekhukhuni

After the death of his father in 1861 Sekhukhuni caused the fall of his half-brother and became chief of the BaPedi. He strived to expand his territory from the unassailable mountain fortress behind the Steelpoort River across this same river. In 1867 president Burgers of Transvaal – for lack of a suitable army leader – had to take charge of a commando himself, which however was no match for the war tactics of Sekhukhuni. Thereupon Burgers had a number of fortresses built in East Transvaal, who were manned by well-paid volunteers. Under pressure of the resistance that these fortresses offered, Sekhukhuni concluded a peace-treaty, which he shortly afterwards violated again. In 1877 the British annexed Transvaal. After a terrible fight against 8,000 Swazi, who fought side by side with some British regiments, Sekhukhuni's warriors were defeated in 1879. He himself was captured in his *kraal*. At the restoration of the independence of Transvaal Sekhukhuni was set free, yet not long afterwards he was murdered in his own *kraal*.

South African Republic. The contrasts between the various regions and leaders repeatedly increased and led to civil wars and the proclamation of independent regional republics. The weakness of this republic appeared in 1871, when president Pretorius could not resist the British pressure to part with the diamond regions in the west. It was also repeatedly obvious from the conflicts with the black tribes in the border regions. Thus the Boers were actually forced to withdraw from the Soutpansberg Mountains in the north (where villages such as Schoemansdal and Ohrigstad belonged to the oldest white settlements) and did not succeed in ending the war with the BaPedi under the leadership of Sekhukhuni in 1876 and the successive years. Criticism on his policy had forced Pretorius to vacate his function as president. An outsider was chosen as his successor, the reverend T.F. Burgers of the Cape. On starting his post on 1 July 1872 he found an administrative chaos. Burgers began his job energetically, reorganized finances and education, improved the relations with the Free State, established diplomatic connections with a number of European states, attracted (especially Dutch) civil servants and teachers, and took measures to effectuate a railway connection with the port of Lourenço Marques. However, the railway project became a costly failure; as was the case with the war against the BaPedi. Burgers, according to some of the Transvaal people too much of a liberal anyhow, lost his final credit among the population. England made use of this situation.

British Imperialism

Lord Carnarvon, the British minister of Colonies, wanted to unite entire southern Africa, including the Boer republics, in a confederation under British supremacy. Profiting from Burgers' weak position he sent Theophilus Shepstone as a special governor to the Transvaal. On 12 April 1877, on Church Square in Pretoria, Shepstone read aloud the proclamation, with which Great Britain annexed the South African Republic. The motives given were the desperate financial situation and the incapacity of the Transvaal government to guarantee peace and safety in relation to the black inhabitants. Shepstone himself soon also experienced the difficulties arising from the relations with the black peoples. Sekhukhuni could not be forced to surrender until 1879. The British confederation plans also necessitated the subjection of the Zulu, who strongly resisted this under the leadership of king Cetshwayo. At the beginning of 1879 an English army invaded Zululand. On 22 January 1879 an army-column was almost completely annihilated near Isandlwana: 858 British officers and soldiers lost their lives, together with 471 black soldiers; the Zulu counted more than 1,000 dead. In May 1879 a second invasion took place; this time the Zulu army was defeated at Ulundi. Cetshwayo was forced to accept peace and to resign. However, it remained turbulent in Zululand, which was annexed in 1887 and thereupon incorporated with Natal. Around that same time the last independent black communities in the surrounding area were forced to yield to British imperialism. In 1894 Pondoland was incorporated with Natal. The Xhosa resistance against the obtrusive whites had lasted more than half a century, little by little they had been forced to give up their independence. The Gcaleka reacted with the well-known chiliastic act of despair in 1857. They complied with the vision of the prophetess Nongqawuse to slaughter all their cattle and destroy the harvest, as a sacrifice to the ancestors. A disastrous famine followed. Not until a full generation later had the Xhosa recuperated. In 1877 a war between the Gcaleka and the Mfengu led to a new Frontier war. It marked the beginning of a period of conflicts, battle and subjection. The black communities did not merely loose their political independence in those years: much land fell into white hands and traditional and economic structures were partially lost. More or less successful incorporation into the colonial society followed.

Afrikaner Nationalism

The British annexation of 1877 roughly awakened the Transvaal Boers. They would not accept the loss of independence, but buried the old differences of opinion and chose new leaders, of whom Paul Kruger (commander-general and vice-president under Burgers) was the most important one. Some deputations travelled to London in vain to plead for a re-establishment of independence. A general assembly at Paardekraal charged a triumvirate consisting of Paul Kruger, general Piet Joubert and former president Pretorius with the task of restoring independence. On 16 December 1880 the four-coloured flag was hoisted at Heidelberg. Boer commandos inflicted several defeats on the British army divisions, among others at Laingsnek and Majuba. Before the end of March 1881 England signed a peace treaty. The independence of the South African Republic was restored. This first Transvaal war of Independence – as the Anglo-Boer War of 1880-1881 is preferably called by the Afrikaners – has been of great significance for the developments in South Africa. It stimulated the Afrikaners' national feelings and strengthened his self-confidence.

In 1875 the 'Genootskap van Regte Afrikaners' (Society of True Afrikaners) was founded in Paarl (Cape colony). It aimed 'te staan ver ons taal, ons nasie en ons land' (to stand up for our language, our nation and our land). Members of this 'Genootskap' established the first Afrikaans newspaper 'Di Afrikaanse Patriot' (1876), a 'Geskiedenis van Ons Land in die Taal van Ons Volk' (History of Our Country in the Language of Our People) (1877) and some Afrikaans literature. One of the leaders, reverend S.J. du Toit advocated a united South Africa under Afrikaner government; he was involved in the establishment of the Afrikaner Bond, which played an important role in Cape politics from 1881 onwards.

The Afrikaner nationalism found well-prepared fertile ground in both Boer republics as well. Their inhabitants experienced the continuous emphasis of the British hegemony as an annoying interference, contrary to their recognized independence. The annexation of the diamond fields, of Transvaal and of many parts of Betsjoeanaland (Botswana) (1885) made the aversion to the British adversary even more rigid. In 1886 gold was discovered on the Witwatersrand. That discovery changed South Africa fundamentally in a short space of time. People came flocking in from everywhere: within a couple of years Johannesburg was the biggest city of southern Africa. The economic centre shifted from the Cape colony to Transvaal, up till then a backward, underdeveloped agrarian state. The South African Republic saw its income sevenfolded in three years' time. A rapid modernization followed, naturally not without problems. The large mining companies wished to have more freedom of action and the 'Uitlander' population who (probably unjustifiably) considered themselves more numerous than the Transvaal Boers, wanted to have more influence in affairs. They found president Paul Kruger and his government opposing them. Kruger was adamant about the republican independence. For this purpose he sought support in an alliance with the Orange Free State, established economic ties with countries such as The Netherlands, Germany and France, and strived for an access-road to the sea that was not dominated by England. That is why he awarded the concession for the construction of a railway connection between Transvaal and the port of Lourenço Marques to the Nederlandsche Zuid-Afrikaansche Spoorwegmaatschappij (NZASM) in 1887. Again and again Paul Kruger had to experience that he was being thwarted by the British. He was especially opposed by Cecil John Rhodes. The eighteen-year-old Rhodes had emigrated to South Africa in 1870 for health reasons. Ten years later he had amassed a fortune, had founded the De

Paul Kruger

Stephanus Johannes Paulus Kruger was born on 10 October 1825 into a family of Trekboers, who joined the Great Trek party headed by Hendrik Potgieter ten years later. From 1851 onwards Paul Kruger was involved in the foundation of the Transvaal state and all the conflicts it brought along. One month before the British annexation of the South African Republic in 1877 Kruger was appointed vice-president. He could not avert the loss of independence, but took a central position in the movement trying to restore it. With this aim in mind he travelled to England in 1877 and 1878; following this he also visited The Netherlands. After he had become part of the triumvirate that conducted the Transvaal liberation war, he became state president of the restored Suid-Afrikaansche Republiek in 1833.

Paul Kruger became the symbol of the inflexible and independent Afrikaner Boer, especially when, during the Anglo-Boer War, he departed as a refugee to Europe in 1900, where he tried in vain to get support for the Republic from the governments. As an exile he stayed in The Netherlands; he died at Clarens, Switzerland in 1904. His remains were later interred in Pretoria. 'Uncle Paul' is one of the remarkable figures of South African history, subject of numerous stories and anecdotes, symbol of the Afrikaners' struggle for independence. While drinking coffee and smoking a pipe he held the reins of a patriarchal presidential government. He received visitors, guests and citizens on the steps of his house, invariably wearing a top hat on these occasions. Opposite the Kruger House in Church Street in Pretoria is the Reformed Church, of which he had been one of the fellow-founders and where he sometimes spoke some edifying words.

Beers Company and had gained a seat in the Cape parliament. Rhodes was convinced of the superiority of the Anglo-Saxon 'race' and its culture; at the end of 1895 he had the administrator of his British South Africa Chartered Company, dr Jameson, invade Transvaal from Betsjoeanaland. However, the Jameson-raid was an ignominious failure, also due to the fact that a revolt of the Uitlanders on the Witwatersrand did not take place. Despite this, the undermining of the South African Republic

Cecil Rhodes (1835-1902), one of the founders of the British Empire, premier of the Cape colony from 1890 ▼ to 1896.

▲ *Piet Joubert, the besieger of Ladysmith, during the Anglo-Boer War.*

▲ *General Louis Botha (1862-1919), victor on the Mauchs Mountain on 10 September 1900 during the Anglo-Boer War, owing to the Long Toms.*

Blockhouse at Prieska in the north of the Cape Province. These defensive works were built by the British during the ▼ *Anglo-Boer war.*

continued and on 11 October 1899 the second Anglo-Boer War broke out.

It was a fight between very unequal parties. Two small Boer republics boasting no more than 60,000 adult male civilians between the ages of 16 and 60, took a stand against the, in those days almighty, British Empire. However, the Boers were determined, well-armed, excellent marksmen and knew the territory. Initially therefore they had the initiative. The arrival of more and more British troops forced them into the defensive. In that position the Boer armies acquired their greatest glory, time and time again they managed to ward off the attack of an enemy outnumbering them by far: Magersfontein, Colenso, Spioenkop are just a few examples. Yet after the initial successes the tide turned for the two Boer republics: the Boer armies could not withstand the superior strength of regular British troops. The occupation of the republican capitals (May-June 1900) and the proclamation of the incorporation of both republics into the British Empire did not signify the end of the war, however. The Boer leaders changed their tactics and reverted to guerilla warfare. With small commandos they continued the battle, even extending it to large parts of the Cape colony. In various places they inflicted defeat and damage to the enemy, broke through the abounding fortified blockhouse lines and remained elusive, even though the British supreme command deployed a quarter of a million men against them. They managed to hold on for nearly another two years. The British army tried to break the opposition by means of the scorched earth tactic. There was a high death-rate among women and children, who were housed in concentration camps by the British. Only fear of a complete annihilation of the country and the physical end of the Afrikaner people, and concern about the increasing hostile attitude of the black population, persuaded the Boer generals and their tough *bitterenders* to end the war. On 31 May 1902 they signed the Vereeniging Peace Treaty. Despite worldwide sympathy for the Afrikaner Boers and their fight for freedom and justice, they had to give up the ideal of the independent Afrikaner Boer republics. South Africa was British.

'Volkseenheid'

The Afrikaner people were powerless, subjected, poor and divided in 1902. The Afrikaner felt humiliated and embittered. His position seemed hopeless: his farm buildings were destroyed, his cattle killed, his land unkempt. Moreover he was jeopardized as regards his identity and prospects: his language and culture hardly seemed to have any future at all. Leading generals such as L. Botha, J.C. Smuts, J.H. de la Rey and J.B.M. Hertzog understood that although the war was lost, peace could possibly be won:

owing to their numerical superiority the Afrikaners could regain in the ballot-box what they had lost on the battlefield. Having thus acquired political dominance, they could win back control over their own fate, and safeguard their own identity and social position. Besides a clear aim, this policy also had an explicit condition: in order to succeed, co-operation of all Afrikaners was necessary, an ethnic unity, a 'volkseenheid'. There was no place for discord and contrasts between *bitterenders* and *hensoppers*, between Republicans and Cape loyalists. Therefore these contrasts were obscured, suppressed, smoothed away. Emphasis was laid on joint ethnicity, on 'volkseenheid' and ethnic mobilization. The names of the political parties after 1902 already denote this: Het Volk (The People), Orangia Unie; later the Suid-Afrikaanse Partij and the Nationale Partij. Moreover, in the first half of the twentieth century South African politics were dominated by generals from the Boer war, who were held in great esteem and exercised a strong personal leadership. Leadership and docility, 'saamstaan' (togetherness) and unity, subordination of the individual to the group came to characterize the Afrikaner national movement.

In 1907 the liberal British government granted the former South African Boer republics and colonies self-government, in 1910 they formed the Union of South Africa. General Louis Botha, previously commander-in-chief of the Transvaal in the Anglo-Boer War, became Prime Minister. The Union was a compromise between the English speaking whites, who were determined to retain the tie with the British Empire, and the Afrikaners who wanted to be their own masters. The Suid-Afrikaanse Partij, in power until 1924, embodied that compromise. Leaders like Botha and Smuts attempted to have all white South Africans merge into one bilingual nation, despite the differences in background, interests and ideology. Whoever considered South Africa to be his home, could call himself a South African.

However, for others the notion of nationality was based on tribal kinship, joint cultural experience, language, tradition and history. Within a couple of years after 1910 the unity in the Afrikaner ranks was therefore broken. A group of nationalists led by general Hertzog and dr D.F. Malan rejected the options and strategy of Botha and Smuts. Hertzog recognized the legitimacy of the Union. Yet he wanted it to develop into a separate and independent identity within the British Empire. And within the South African state the Afrikaners should be able to retain their own unique nationality: a two-stream policy therefore instead of one stream. Hertzog and Malan used the Afrikaans language and culture to mobilize the Afrikaners. They considered language to be the soul and characteristic of a nation. They devoted themselves to making Dutch the official language and to developing Afrikaans both as a spoken and a written language. In their view Botha's one-stream policy in practice amounted to neglect of equal rights for Afrikaans. Hertzog's two-stream policy aimed at expansion of the cultural lives of the two population groups in strict equality. For many Afrikaners reconciliation with the English was inconceivable, however. Only emphasizing their collective ethnical identity allowed the Afrikaners to deal with the defeat and the display of superiority by the English.

One of the problems that advocates of the process of ethnic mobilization had to face, was the social and economic position of the Afrikaners. Already before the Anglo-Boer War the economic differences among the Afrikaners were demonstrable. There was an increasing group of 'bywoners': landless Boers, without much education or perspective. The development of mining after 1886 had offered new chances to some of them, but not to many. The Anglo-Boer War brought general impoverishment, and not everyone proved to get the opportunity to recuperate afterwards. The economic revolution caused by mining and industrialization, forced the Afrikaner to migrate to the city. Within one

▲ *The first Union Ministry. Standing (from left to right): Hertzog, Burton, Moor, O'Grady Gubbin, Smuts, Malan and Sir David Graaf. Sitting: Sauer, Botha and Fisher.*

generation a traumatic social shift took place: at the end of the nineteenth century ten percent of the Afrikaners had settled in cities and villages, in 1911, 1926 and 1936 this number was 29, 41 and 50 percent respectively. In the city the Afrikaner's position was hardly better than that of the black proletariat. Around 1934 (at the height of the worldwide economic depression) a quarter of the Afrikaners belonged to the 'armblanken' (poor whites); as 'bywoners' in the countryside or as a supported group in the city they led a miserable existence.

Although the distinction between the Afrikaner proletariat and the black working class was less than that between the Afrikaner 'armblanken' and the English labourers (let alone the dominant English group of entrepreneurs), the Afrikaner labourers identified themselves with their ethnic group, not with the labour class as such. A feeling of superiority, which had developed among the whites in South Africa and elsewhere since the eighteenth century, resisted the realization of such an alliance of white and black proletarians: the centuries' old dominant pattern of social stratification along racial lines. An important phenomenon in relation to this was the existence of a separate labour market. White labourers, who were expected to keep up a certain standard of living, could not compete with blacks who were not subject to such demands. Therefore they protested, whenever blacks threatened to compete with them, not because those blacks were black, but because they could accept an income on which it was impossible for a white person to sustain himself. Besides the racial feelings and the separate labour market the political system hampered the development of a joint front of the white and black labour proletariat. Since 1910 the white men had the right to vote. Through using their right to vote and by means of political action the Afrikaner labourers envisaged the best possibilities to achieve their material desires. Many joined the Unions of their English colleagues and supported the Arbeiderspartij (Labour Party); the nationalist movement and the Christian-national Unions deriving from it did not really appeal to them. Gradually, however, that changed. The Afrikaner workman learned to view the Arbeiderspartij as an ally of British imperialism and the Unions as organisations dominated by foreigners; at the same time a clear anti-capitalistic mentality started to become apparent in Afrikaner nationalist circles. The history of the Afrikaner identity and the process of ethnic mobilization entered into a new phase.

Discord and Resistance

The economic world crisis, which started with the crash on Wall Street in 1929, also threw the South African economy into deep depression. In order to be able to bear its consequences, the two large political parties formed a coalition government with Hertzog as premier and Smuts as vice-premier. A year later the two parties even merged and became the Verenigde Partij (United Party). This merger of 1934 drastically changed the South African political landscape.

The desire for unity and self-government, which had dominated South African politics in the years of the Union around 1910, had soon disappeared. Unionists devoted to England and the Arbeiderspartij had taken an independent stance from the beginning. Hertzog left the Suid-Afrikaanse (Nasionale) Party as early as in 1912 and became one of the leaders of the National Party. For the time being the NP was a small opposition party and Botha and Smuts ruled. Both proved that they wanted to be loyal to the British empire. South Africa fought on the side of the English in the Great War. For several veteran soldiers of the Anglo-Boer War this was unacceptable. Various well-known figures participated in the rebellion of 1914: the death of the famous general Koos de la Rey and the imprisonment of several others caused a deep cleft in the Afrikaner ranks. However, Botha and Smuts kept a level head and personally led the attack on the German colonies in south-west and south-east Africa (after the war the League of Nations was to have South West Africa/Namibia governed by South Africa as a mandate). Moreover, Smuts was a member of the British War cabinet and was closely involved in the Peace Treaty of Versailles and the foundation of the League of Nations. In 1919 Louis Botha died unexpectedly; Smuts succeeded him as Prime Minister of the Union of South Africa.

The Botha-Smuts government was also controversial in the socio-economical field. The growth of the militant unions and the Arbeiderspartij repeatedly led to protests against labour conditions and to strikes, especially in the mines. Repeatedly the army was deployed to put an end to the industrial unrest: in July 1913 to end a miners' strike, at the beginning of 1914 to break a general strike. During the Great War a decreasing import and an increasing demand resulted in industrial growth; a short economic boom immediately afterwards made pay-rises possible. Agriculture, though, was afflicted by drought, the sales of coal stagnated, inflation increased and the price of gold dropped: at the end of 1921 South Africa was ensnared in an economic crisis. Unemployment and decrease of earnings led to a big strike on the Witwatersrand in 1922. Partly due to the influence of radical leadership there were serious clashes, resulting in dozens of dead and wounded. Again Smuts opted for a confrontation: thousands of strikers were seized, hundreds convicted for committing violence, four 'ringleaders' sentenced to death and hanged.

The industrialization and the growth of the labour movement compelled the introduction of a legislation improving the labour conditions. Numerous stipulations were introduced to protect the white labourers at the expense of the black ones. Unequal legal status, lower pay and forbidden access to skilled labour positions were the share for the latter group. In conformity with traditional practice and the prevailing mentality, the *naturelle* policy revealed the features of colonial distinction and subordination. A clear example was the Naturellen Landwet (Land Law) of 1913, which in principle limited landownership of blacks to the traditional tribal regions, at the time somewhat less than eight percent of the entire South African territory.

In accordance with a tacit agreement between both parties, the Anglo-Boer War was to be a whiteman's war, coloured inhabitants of South Africa would not be involved. Except of course for the fact that the closure of the mines brought

▲ *General J.C. Smuts (1870-1950).*

them unemployment. However, nearly 150,000 blacks were taken to British concentration camps during the war, where they were put to work and where no less than ten percent of them died. Tens of thousands worked as unarmed labourers, grooms or supplied other services in both armies. After some time blacks also played a role in military actions. The British in particular enlisted them as scouts, guards or soldiers.

The hope of the South African coloured population that their

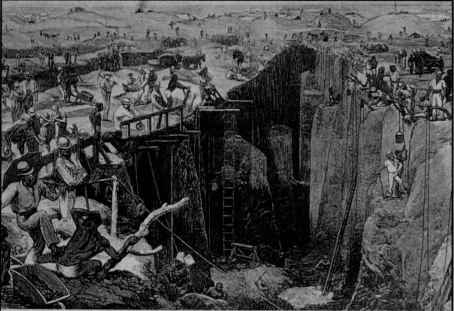

▲ The Kimberley mine in 1876. From: 'Illustrated London News'.

Gold and the Socio-economical Structure of South Africa

After the big gold finds in Witwatersrand around 1885, Johannesburg became the main city of South Africa. However, it was soon discovered that the gold veins were lying very deep in the earth and that the alloy was slight. After some years therefore it appeared that individual gold-seekers, who dug at a shallow depth, had to stop their activities. Only very substantial companies were capable of making the necessary investments, which became a condition for gold winning. The small companies were soon swallowed up by the bigger ones, who finally started to co-operate and formed some powerful monopolies.

For the black communities in the surroundings of Johannesburg the consequences were drastic, a situation which had also occurred at the diamond mines of Kimberley. The gold industry in Johannesburg was actually only profitable if the production costs could be kept low. The influx of numerous black workers enabled a systematic use of their cheap labour. This caused white miners to be ousted from their positions. The many small farmers were also unable to keep up with the rapid economical and social revolutions that took place and joined the growing army of 'poor whites'.

At a depth of 225 metres in the old Crown Mine. In the East Rand Proprietary Mine just outside
▼ Johannesburg gold is won nowadays at a depth of more than 5,000 metres.

loyalty to the British Empire would be rewarded after the war, soon proved to be idle. At the peace negotiations extension of their civil rights was not a subject of discussion. After 1902 several organisations drew attention to the position and rights of the black, Indian and Coloured population, but without result. At the Convention that discussed the making of the Union and drew up a constitution, it was decided that, as regards the suffrage, each province would retain its own system. In fact that limited the right to vote for blacks and Coloureds to the Cape province, where a qualified franchise system held good and where they comprised some percentage of the electorate. The Cape Provincial Council was open to coloured members, but only whites could be elected to a seat on the Volksraad and the Senate. In London in 1909 a delegation of representatives of several organisations of coloured people had pleaded in vain against the acceptance of these constitutional regulations. Following tradition and comparable situations in other colonies, only the whites, 21,5 percent of the entire population, were considered as the South African 'pays légal' in 1910.

It should be added, that a large majority of the blacks was poor, lived in the countryside or in their own 'reserves' and had no western development. In 1911 only thirteen percent of the four million blacks lived in the cities. Political organisations and unions were small and divided among themselves. The South African Native National Congress for example, which was founded in 1912 and has been known since 1923 as the African National Congress (ANC), had merely a few thousand members. It was not the only black movement, whereas Coloureds and Indians mostly concentrated on their own organisations, such as the African Political (later 'Peoples') Organisation, founded in 1902 by dr Abdullah Abdurachman. There was not even complete unanimity in resistance to the Naturellen Landwet of 1913, against which the ANC protested in vain in London.

The Great War strengthened black political consciousness. In the years after the war the Industrial and Commercial Workers Union (ICU) was the most important movement, which reflected the increasing significance of black labour and also the leadership of Clements Kadalie (1896-1951). Several strikes and protest actions took place, for instance against the pass legislation, which limited the blacks' freedom of movement. The ICU was initially positive about Hertzog's Pact government of Nationalists and Arbeiders (Labourers) (1924), but fiercely resisted Hertzog's naturellen legislation of the 1920s. Radicalization, among other things by communistic influences, and internal discord caused the ICU, which at its height numbered at least 100,000 members, to fall apart and lose its significance in 1929.

From Pact to Fusion

The elections of 1924 provided a majority for the coalition of the National Party and the Labour Party. They had agreed on a Pact in 1923, opposing Smuts, whose conduct against the strike at the Witwatersrand in 1922 was considered as being in league with the British mine owners. There was no question of labourers' solidarity across the colour bar: the white labourer wanted to be protected against the competition of their black contestants. The Pact government therefore set out energetically to promote industrial development. The foundation of the steel works Yskor, in 1928, serves as an example. This was to create employment. Employment, in which 'civilized labour' for a 'civilized tariff' was distinguished from unskilled labour for coloured labourers. The 'colour bar', provision of work for unskilled labourers on railways and other state services and all kinds of other measures had to meet with the growing problem of the 'armblanken'. At the same time, Hertzog tried to get a grip on the *naturelle* issue by creating an extensive system of legislation. His proposals were characterized as an attempt to standardize the rights of the coloured population, which on the one hand brought an extension of their chances, and on the other hand curtailed them even more.

However, neither race policies nor economic policy were the most important theme of the National Party. That was the Afrikaner nationalism. Hertzog's main objectives were to obtain equality for the Afrikaners compared to the English speaking people within South Africa and constitutional independence of the Union from England.

In 1925 Afrikaans was declared to be the official language of the Union of South Africa alongside English (and Dutch). Afrikaans quickly started to replace Dutch in administration, education, church and culture. In 1929 the Federasie van Afrikaanse Kultuurvereniginge (FAK) was founded and a beginning was made with the publication of the 'Woordeboek van die Afrikaanse Taal' (Dictionary of the Afrikaans Language). In 1933 an Afrikaans Bible translation was published. The 'Generation of Dertig', which produced poets such as N.P. van Wyk Louw, Elisabeth Eybers and D.J. Opperman, proved that the young Afrikaner literary culture had vigour and quality. The equality of English and Afrikaans and the demand for bilingualism opened up career perspectives for the Afrikaners in civil service and in business.

At an imperial conference at London in 1926 Hertzog also successfully put forward the issue of the equalization of the dominions to Great Britain within the British Commonwealth. The introduction of a South African Ministry of Foreign Affairs and the implementation (1928) of a national flag besides the Union Jack served as a confirmation of the new sovereignty. In Hertzog's view the ideals of the National Party had been achieved to a considerable extent: the constitutional objectives had been realized and the equal status of the Afrikaner and his culture had been gained. More radical nationalists, however, wanted complete realization of the old republican ideal and therefore resignation from the Commonwealth. They preferred dominance of the Afrikaner group above equality with the English speaking people. The economic world crisis and its results, aggravated from 1932 onwards by a lengthy and serious drought, caused many problems. Hertzog's leadership was challenged in his own circle and outside. In 1933 he formed a coalition government together with Smuts. At the end of 1934 there was a merger of their two parties, which were joined in the United (South African National) Party. According to Hertzog the foundation of the United Party expressed the realisation of the ideals that he had been propagating since 1912 concerning a two-stream policy: equality of Afrikaners and English people, self-determination of the Union within the Commonwealth and segregation of white and black. Smuts thought that the fusion would be the means to create a larger unity between both white population groups and was satisfied with the dominion status within the Commonwealth.

A small group of nationalists did not want to be absorbed by the United Party. Headed by the Cape leader dr D.F. Malan they formed the Gesuiwerde Nasionale Party (Purified National Party); only nineteen of the 75 NP members of parliament joined this movement. Again a new phase in the struggle for the Afrikaner identity and unity commenced.

The Gesuiwerde Nasionaliste

Malan and his Gesuiwerde Nasionaliste considered the fusion to be a threat for the Afrikaner people. Their rejection of the United Party had a socio-economic background besides a cultural one. The impoverishment of the countryside and the trek of the Afrikaners to the city demanded an active industrialization policy and protection of the white labourers. However, they feared that capitalists and especially the mine owners would dominate the United Party. This would divide the whites in a propertied and a

labour class, resulting in entrepreneurs replacing the half-skilled and unskilled Afrikaner employees by cheaper black labour. Moreover, it would increase the economic independence from the British Empire.

Immediately after the fusion the Nationalists doggedly launched the attack on their two arch-enemies: capitalism and imperialism. Leadership was in the hands of what one could call members of the lower middle class: lawyers, teachers and lower civil servants whose culture and career were jeopardized by the English language and standards, and by the policy of the United Party. This lower middle class was politically isolated, especially in Transvaal where the wealthy farmers supported the United Party. Thus for them only the white working class remained as an ally. Yet they feared that the fusion would force the Afrikaner working class to organize themselves on a class basis and would thus become denationalized.

In order to understand the Nationalists well, the atmosphere of the 1930s has to be taken into consideration. The disruption as a result of the extensive urbanization of the previous three decades, had caused a deeply rooted feeling of insecurity. The Afrikaner townspeople did not only belong to the poorest population groups, but were moreover considered to be culturally backward and uneducated. For Afrikaners with a countryside background the city was a foreign place full of humiliation. It was the trauma of the 1930s that caused people to feel attracted to the 'solution' that apartheid offered as a radical re-ordering of society (elsewhere in the world radical social ideals also caught on in those days!).

Both Hertzog and Malan courted the Afrikaner electorate. Hertzog tried to establish a middle-class party and spoke of a 'nuwe Afrikanerdom' (new Afrika), to which Afrikaans and English speaking whites could belong as 'gelyke Afrikaners' (Afrikaner nation) on the condition that they approved of the principles of 'Suid-Afrika eerste' (South Africa first) and equality of the two white subgroups. Malan, on the other hand, aimed at nothing else than uniting all Afrikaners in his party.

Ethnic mobilization was thus his prime goal; to Malan an Afrikaner was a person whose language was Afrikaans; his religious or socio-political views did not really matter. What did, was recognition of the Afrikaner's right to acquire his own place in his South Africa. Not a fusion, only the restoration of the republic would end the injustice against the Afrikaners; national unity could only be achieved on that principle. One condition for this was that the English-speaking Afrikaners had to exchange their loyalty towards England for fidelity towards a South African Republic, governed by Afrikaners on the basis of their right of primogeniture. Malan did not only propagate ethnic mobilization in politics and culture, but also economically. He wished to improve the Afrikaners' socio-economical position by means of group mobilization. 'Ekonomische volkskongresse' stimulated an economical 'Afrikaner red jou self' (self help) movement (1939); Volkskas, Federale Volksbeleggings, Uniewinkels supplemented the activities of Santam, Sanlam, Kaapse Wynverkopers Vereniging and Nasionale Pers (all of them founded as early as 1918). However, apart from the economic growth of the 1940s and afterwards, the position of the 'armblanken' has improved more due to protective legislation than to the 'volkskapitalisme' which was propagated by Nationalists to replace capitalism and socialism.

With all these attempts of Malan and his followers to mobilize the Afrikaner people in the political, social and economical fields, the Afrikaner's own identity was constantly emphasized. Religion and history were of good service here. Maintaining the Afrikaans national identity was a task imposed by God. History proved that the Afrikaner people was a chosen people with a mission: Slagtersnek, Blood River, the Anglo-Boer Wars, even the suffering in the

▼ Dr D.F. Malan (1874-1959).

▲ *This panel shows how the Boers defeat a superior force of Zulu warriors. The Blood River Monument is one of the many places where the history of the Afrikaners is emphasized.*

concentration camps were significant signs of God's concern for the Afrikaners. A large number of ordinary Afrikaners considered themselves as members of a chosen people and saw the National Party as its political expression.

In September 1939 Hertzog's long-standing ideal of a union between the English and the Afrikaner elements into a new South African nation, was shattered by the issue of South Africa's participation in the Second World War. A parliamentary majority of the Verenigde Partij (United Party) headed by Smuts, in co-operation with some English parties, caused South Africa to become an active member of the alliance. Hertzog was compelled to resign, Smuts became Prime Minister. He deployed South Africa's forces and natural resources in the battle against Hitler and national-socialism. At home he was confronted with a revival of anti-English sentiments and a decreasing support among the Afrikaners. Hertzog, who had not wanted to sacrifice the unity of South Africa to entering the war, soon withdrew from politics. Co-operation with the Nationalists seemed impossible to him.

Yet Malan did not want to go as far as some extremist Nationalists in the north. To him the Afrikaners were indeed the only indigenous white population group in South Africa, but the rights and language of the English-speaking group had to be preserved. This saddled him with a conflict with the Ossewa Brandwag. The Ossewa Brandwag was an organisation, numbering at least 200,000 members in its heyday, believing in authoritarian leadership and using fascist symbols. The Ossewa Brandwag stated that there was only room for one people within a nation and that the nation ought to be the personification of the people. According to them the Afrikaners had the right of primogeniture in South Africa. The English speaking people, according to this undemocratic recipe, had to give up their existence as a group, merge into the Afrikaner people or emigrate. Malan detested a number of elements in this ideology and considered an organisation that competed with the Nationale Partij as a threat to the process of ethnic mobilization. Owing to Malan's actions the influence of the Ossewa Brandwag and other organisations among Afrikaners could be pushed back. That is how the Nationale Partij became more and more the only home for the Afrikanerdom. At the elections of May 1948 the NP gained a majority in the Volksraad of 79 seats to 74.

The view that the Nationalist election victory of 1948 was the triumph of the apartheid ideology, and the result of an insolent exploitation of racist sentiments and opinions among the Afrikaners, is wrong. Of course the racial issue played a role in 1948. In the preceding decades the number of urban

blacks had doubled. Around the cities of South Africa *plakkerskampen* (squatters' quarters) had mushroomed up. In the rural regions the costs of black labour increased, in the mines, factories and cities it provided more and more competition for the whites. Many Afrikaners considered this no longer acceptable and blamed the liberal view of the Verenigde Partij on this issue. They wanted action, apartheid. This term was more or less new in 1948, its meaning – segregation and protection of 'civilized labour' – was not and the call for it had also resounded at earlier elections. Therefore no mature apartheid ideology existed or a complete concept based on it for a system of regulations. During the election campaign the Nationalists had often proposed not to let the racial issue grow into a political conflict between the parties. Only then, in their view, did South Africa have a chance to find a solution for its racial problems.

The election victory of the Nationale Partij in 1948 was in fact the victory of the Afrikaner volkseenheid. The apartheid slogan did form an additional reason for some to vote for the NP, but this party's programme points concerning the position of the Afrikaners as an ethnical group were just as important: it promised national independence and promoting the cultural and economic interests of the Afrikaners. The Nationale Partij presented an alternative solution for the problems of the rural farmers, the urban labourers, the middle class groups as well as everybody concerned about racial problems. However, the significance of 1948 for these Afrikaners, and also for the businessmen, the teachers and the civil servants among them, was above all to 'weer ons land terug te kry' (get back our country) and to 'weer eens tuis te voel in ons land' (feel at home again in our country).

Unity and Apartheid, 1948-1966

Being one's own master in one's own country; the ideal seemed to have been accomplished in 1948. But the Nationalist leaders knew how instable the basis of their position of power was. A majority of five seats only, thanks to the constituency voting system: less than half of the voters had put their trust in the NP. They envisaged two tasks: solidifying their position of power by increasing the ethnic unity, and restructuring South African society by developing the apartheid policy. These tasks were mutually closely connected: apartheid was not an aim in itself. The Nationale Partij was emphasized as a people's party, it represented 'the people in action'. A network of Afrikaner cultural organisations consolidated and strengthened the Afrikaner unity. Conflicts were solved by the elite behind closed doors, public criticism or deviating opinions were not tolerated. Whoever sinned against this, was thrust out of the *'kraal'* like a national traitor.

Not only the centralized leadership, but also a number of concrete political actions had to consolidate the Afrikaner unity and position of power. Thus the number of adherents of the NP in the Volksraad was increased by granting the right to vote to the white inhabitants of South West Africa (1950) and by removing the Coloureds from the joint voters' list in the Cape Province (1956). The NP's preponderance in the Volksraad in this way increased to more than a two-thirds majority of 105 in 1961. Yet is was not until 1966, when no fewer than 126 seats were gained, that the NP election percentage comfortably exceeded 50 percent due to the influx of English speaking voters. The Verenigde Partij lost political significance correspondingly. This party was divided and was led by a traditional anti-Afrikaner group of liberal-conservative signature, especially after some eleven VP members of parliament had dissented in 1959 and had formed the Progressive Party. Although they lost all their seats but one, due to the constituency voting system of the time (which considerably favoured the rural regions), the

Progressives had an eye-catching representative in Helen Suzman.

The Nationale Partij did not believe in a self-evident victory of the white man and his culture. That had to be achieved and maintained by means of persevering efforts. The Afrikaner leaders of the 1950s mistrusted their own 'armblanke' fellow Afrikaners as much as the English-speaking people and the non-whites. The 'armblanken' had to be educated to learn how to preserve their white identity. Therefore legislation was deemed necessary to allot fixed places for whites and non-whites in society and to limit the social intercourse between them as much as possible.

A series of laws implemented these views. The Mixed Marriages Act (1949) and the Immorality Act (1950) prohibited sexual contact across the colour bar. The Population Registration Act (1950) obliged everyone to possess an identification card (denoting the race one belonged to). The Group Areas Act of 1950 prescribed separated residential areas and the Separate Amenities Act dating from 1953 prescribed segregation in trains, buses, post-offices, hospitals etcetera.

Legislation and its implementation developed their own logic. They were autocratic in character, especially under the leadership of Hendrik Verwoerd who, as minister of Naturellen Affairs and since 1958 as Prime Minister, set his stamp on the apartheid policy. Verwoerd made apartheid an all-embracing system and provided it with a philosophical foundation, making everything compulsory and inevitable. Verwoerd's starting-point was also the traditional Afrikaner nationalism, his aim its complete realization and thus the safeguarding of the Afrikaner future. That is why he gave new life to the old republican idea and implemented it in 1961: he withdrew from the English Commonwealth and managed to gain a bare majority vote in favour of breaking the final constitutional ties with England and the proclamation of the Republic. Maintaining the Afrikaner dominance also formed the background of Verwoerd's involvement with the so-called Bantustans or black 'homelands' and with education for blacks.

In 1950 a committee had been appointed to advise on ways of halting the urbanization of the black population and therefore the 'blackening' of the white regions, and, if possible, on ways of reverting it. On the basis of a thorough investigation the Tomlinson Committee concluded that in the long-term the black regions might be able to take care of their own population growth. A condition was that a development action to stimulate the economic and social potential of the 'homelands', costing hundreds of millions, would be immediately set up. Verwoerd did not want to know anything about the Tomlinson Report, refused to publish it, except for a short survey, and did not make the necessary funds available. Whereas Tomlinson had advised industrial development, Verwoerd categorically refused the investment of white money in the 'homeland' industries. His alternatives were the 'border industries', costly drawing-board projects, without any economic viability. For his defence Verwoerd pointed to the danger of foreign capitalistic dominance of the black regions and to the necessity of developing themselves in their own way and in accordance with their own initiatives. Assimilation would bring the blacks subordination and loss of their own character and culture, Verwoerd lectured; a guardianship, allowing space for maintenance and development of their own culture would be better. These lines of thought also formed the main background of the enforcement of separate black education, even up to university level. But simultaneously that same education had to prepare the pupil and the student for a place in a society dominated by the white Afrikaner tribe. That explains the attention given to useful knowledge for that purpose, for example the Afrikaans language.

During Verwoerd's reign, covering the first half of the 1960s,

▲ Until recently a large number of laws limited the freedom of mobility of the coloured and black population. However, the white economy was so dependent on black labour, that the 'homeland' policy was doomed to fail.

shifts in apartheid policy and its realization can therefore be noted. The Afrikaners now had firm political power, even proclaiming the Republic had succeeded. The colour bar was legally anchored and implemented in several fields. In the socio-economical and cultural areas this began to yield rewards. Partly owing to a substantial economical growth, the 'armblanke' problem was in fact solved, fitting in the Afrikaner in the urban pattern of life was reasonably successful and the economic backlog of the Afrikaners was for the greater part made up. The price of all this was the aversion the apartheid policy invoked worldwide. Decolonization, in those years fully in process in Africa, the removal of guardianship and the emancipation of the coloured peoples isolated South Africa further and further. Verwoerd in particular was fully conscious of that foreign rejection of apartheid and white 'baasskap'. It was also clearly pointed out to the whole of South Africa in the Winds of Change speech delivered by the British Prime Minister Harold MacMillan to the parliament in Cape Town in February 1960, and even louder and clearer in reaction to the Sharpeville bloodshed, the subsequent 21st of March.

The shifts in apartheid policy affected in the first place the position of the Afrikaner people. Their exclusive identity was no longer emphasized, more and more often the unity and solidarity of the white South African nation, of which the Afrikaners formed the kernel, was preached. Now that South Africa was a republic, loyalty towards England could no longer divide the English-speaking people and the Afrikaners, at stake was now the defence of common civilized values. In 1961 Verwoerd introduced two English-speaking ministers into his cabinet.

Another shift was the replacement of the term apartheid by separate development. Since racism was condemned worldwide, Nationalists underlined the black peoples right to develop their own cultures and characters, separate but equal. They stressed the fact that the South African blacks are numbered under

◄ Premier H.F. Verwoerd and chief Leabua Jonathan, Prime Minister of the kingdom of Lesotho, during a meeting in September 1966.

several race groups and ethnic minorities. Just like the Afrikaners they had the right to be recognized and to experience their own identity. Self-government in 'homelands' was part of this. The Xhosa in Transkei were the first group to get such a self-governing Bantustan in 1963. In a subsequent development phase complete independence could be acquired, of which Transkei (1976), Bophuthatswana (1979), Venda (1979) and Ciskei (1981) made use: decolonization that was recognized nowhere outside South Africa. Mesmerized by Verwoerd's dream numerous Afrikaners, however, believed for some years that now, after all, the time of a righteous apartheid had come: distinction but no discrimination, owing to a reform-policy warranting progress, prosperity and freedom for all in a peaceful co-existence.

Reality, however, proved different. The gap between white and black seemed to be getting wider and deeper in all respects. Afrikaner nationalism and black consciousness were irreconcilably opposed. In 1960 the protests in Sharpeville caused a crisis in the relations; violence and counter-violence evolved step by step from then on.

The take-over of 1948 by the Nationale Partij and the subsequent apartheid legislation stimulated black protest. It was the ANC in particular that tried to lead this process. The organisation had been revitalized in reaction to the suppression of protest actions and strikes by the Smuts government during and immediately after the Second World War. An ANC youth-league, founded in 1944, under the leadership of among others Walter Sisulu, Oliver Tambo and Nelson Mandela steered the ANC in the direction of mass movement, militant action and black nationalism. Around 1950 the ANC was the main black protest movement.

This was apparent from the size of the demonstrations and strikes, taking place in that same year. There was co-operation with other organisations, such as the South African Communist Party (SACP), founded in 1921. Just like the ANC, the SACP was open to sympathizers from all races; in 1950 the latter party was declared illegal by the government and went underground. In 1952 the Defiance Campaign took place. Disciplined black activists wantonly broke the apartheid laws, such as the pass laws, which led to mass arrests and punishments but also to worldwide publicity. In places serious conflicts arose. Tightening of legislation against public unrest and imprisonment of several leaders was the result. This caused a strengthening of solidarity and an increased interest in the ANC. In 1955 the movement organized a Congress of the People at Kliptown near Johannesburg, where the Freedom Charter was accepted. This manifest demands equal rights for all population groups, a democratic state and socialization of mines, banks and industries. The Strydom government considered the congress a state-subversive activity and imprisoned several leaders. However, despite lengthy trials, none of them were sentenced. It did however bring the leaders of the anti-apartheid resistance from black, Indian, Coloured and white circles closer together.

That co-operation, as was laid down in the Freedom Charter, was exactly what was unacceptable for some freedom fighters. The gap within the ANC between the Africanists or the nationalists (in the 1970s advocates of black consciousness) and those people who were in favour of the official line of a colour-blind democracy, became clearer and clearer. The Africanists wanted a free Africa for the Africans,

▼ *Many men have moved to the industrial centres, leaving women and children behind in the 'homelands'.* ▼

rejected all co-operation with the whites (even anti-apartheid inclined whites), especially with the communists. In 1958 there was a split and in 1959 the Africanists founded the Pan Africanist Congress (PAC), of which Robert Sobukwe became chairman. Born out of a conflict with the ANC and its ideology, PAC and ANC remained sworn enemies. Within a year the PAC proved to have sensed the growing impatience and radicalism among blacks very well. Even more than the ANC it led the protest actions against the pass laws in 1960, which have become history due to the violent incident of Sharpeville. Even more significant evidence than the shooting at Sharpeville (where nervous white policemen opened fire at an unarmed crowd which resulted in 69 dead) was the day of mourning one week later, when nearly half a million black labourers stayed at home. All this did not form a real threat to the government, but it did give rise to a prohibition of the ANC and the PAC, who went underground and radicalized. In June 1961, shortly after and in reaction to the foundation of the Republic, Umkhonto we Sizwe, the Spear of the Nation, was founded. Under the leadership of Nelson Mandela a final attempt was to be made by means of sabotage and violence (not against persons, but against objects) to overthrow the apartheid regime. Two years later and several sabotage deeds further, on 11 July 1963, the South African police rounded up the headquarters at a *plaas* in Rivonia (near Johannesburg). The police seized the plans for Operation Mayibuye, an armed coup, and a list of names of the full national Command of Umkhonto we Sizwe. During the Rivonia Trial the leaders were sentenced to life-imprisonment: Sisulu, Govan Mbeki, Ahmed Kathrada, Bram Fischer, Nelson Mandela, Dennis Goldberg and others. It was to take years before a new generation of resistance leaders would come to the fore.

▲ *Nelson Mandela was one of the leaders of the Defiance Campaign, a non-violent organization fighting for the rights of the black South Africans. After the bloodshed in Sharpeville Mandela became one of the founders of the militant wing of the ANC. In 1964 he was arrested and sentenced to life-imprisonment. After an imprisonment of more than 27 years, of which he spent the main part on Robben Island, he was released in 1990.*

Identity, Pragmatism and Crisis, 1966-1983

The inflexible apartheid ideologist Verwoerd was killed in 1966 by a mentally disturbed usher of the South African parliament. His successor was B.J. Vorster, at one time interned by Smuts during the Second World War for his activities in the Ossewa Brandwag, more recently known for his rough suppression of the black anti-apartheid movement (among other things by means of the notorious 90-days imprisonment without trial). Despite all 'kragdadigheid' (vigour) Vorster proved to be a pragmatic leader, a realistic anti-ideologist. Their sizeable material progress as a group

enabled the Afrikaners in the 1970s to view themselves as a political class of rulers, with vested interests which were mainly due to the control of state power.

The rhetoric of the 1960s and the belief that apartheid would bring social harmony through 'separate liberties', had disappeared. It had become all too apparent that apartheid signified power, wealth and privileges to the whites. Inequality was not any longer defended in ideological but in economic terms: a rapid closing of the income gap between whites and blacks was declared economically or politically unattainable. Racist enunciations were only rarely stated in public, no more than Verwoerd's idea that black progress was delayed by their cultural traditions. Yet Vorster declared that the black 'homelands' possessed the right to demand their independence at any time they chose (as was noted, some of them put this right to use). He emphasized that the differences (as, for instance, laid down in laws) between white and black did not denote inferiority: group demands were now legitimated on a pragmatic-historic basis. In the mid-1970s it became obvious that the apartheid ideology and the policy of separate development started to lose their attraction for the Afrikaners. In the authoritative Afrikaans daily paper Die Burger it was stated as early as 1972 that human plans are not unassailable and that elevation of them to the status of undisputed statements with eternal value could signify a national disaster. The economic developments thwarted an unaltered continuation of the policy and also dashed to the ground the expectation that a justifiable distribution would be reached.

It could no longer be obscured that the urban blacks had come to stay; continuation of the control of black residential areas by white governmental bodies was therefore no longer defendable. The riots of 1976 in Soweto and elsewhere, for that matter, showed how widespread the black resistance against the apartheid regime was. Then it also became apparent that no co-operation in the administration of the black suburbs, or in controlling the influx of people to them from the impoverished 'homelands', was to be expected. Let alone for re-settlement of movement projects.

In the early 1970s protection of white labour by the colour bar was still considered to be a corner stone of the government policy. The whites formed a labour aristocracy, the blacks a non- or semi-skilled rightless proletariat. Their unions were not recognized, they received no education and they were not allowed to take the place of white labourers, the so-called job reservation. However, the crisis of 1976 clarified that this situation, already disputable on economic grounds, could not go on existing any longer. Immigration decreased, the natural population growth of the whites had never been large, and therefore too few whites entered the labour market. From 41,000 in 1976 this number dropped to 25,000 in 1978 and that is how the blacks got the jobs for which no whites were available. For many realized that economic growth was more important than maintaining an impossible apartheid. The influx of skilled blacks on the labour market of course meant that the 'job reservation' had to be abolished, the right to strike for blacks had to be recognized (1973) and the black unions had to be permitted (again). In 1979 the labour legislation was completely revised.

And that is how a process of gradual undermining and abolition of apartheid started, a silent social revolution. More and more blacks carried out skilled labour and received higher wages. The salary gap between white and black gradually began to close from around the year 1975. Black spending power increased and a black middle-class evolved. The small apartheid was mitigated, abolished. Black pupils were allowed to enter private white schools and universities. White and black sports clubs held inter-club matches. Hardly anybody recognized the importance of this silent social revolution. For it was overshadowed by more striking matters, such as the fall of the Portuguese colonial empire in 1974, followed by the failed South African invasion in Angola (1975) and the permanent involvement with the civil war in that country. And there were the developments in Rhodesia and Moçambique. As well as the battle against Swapo who tried to bring about the liberation of Namibia by armed struggle. The Nationalist leaders started to talk about a 'total attack' directed towards South Africa which had to be averted. This explains the involvement in the surrounding countries (destabilization policy).

The developments elsewhere in Africa provided a stimulus for anti-apartheid movements. The years of discrimination and suppression strengthened the unrest and resistance. Especially among the young there existed a powerful and flourishing black consciousness. The South African Students Organisation headed by Steve Biko gave direction to it. Inspired by the Black Power movement from the United States this organisation preached Black Consciousness: blacks were to liberate themselves on the basis of their regained self-confidence (Black is beautiful). This of course also required a different kind of education than the one offered by the state schools. But the mass protest action of youths and pupils which started on 16 June 1976 in Soweto and which led to an open confrontation with the police and the white state power, acquired a wider objective. It became in fact nothing less than an attempt to overthrow the apartheid state by means of mass action and acts of violence. Despite strikes, consumer boycotts, demonstrations, much violence and hundreds of victims the goal was not attained. Many youths fled the country and joined the ANC in exile, who accepted the violent struggle as a means to overthrow the apartheid regime. The world reacted extremely negatively to the riots and their suppression and called for boycotts and sanctions. That call became a loud one when Steve Biko died in 1977 as the result of maltreatment during interrogations in prison. South Africa, pariah among the nations, became internationally isolated.

Pragmatic Afrikaner leaders who assessed the results at the end of the 1970s, realized that cosmetic changes alone no longer sufficed. The Afrikaners formed an ethnic minority group who could only survive in co-operation with others. They were part of a bourgeoisie that could only maintain a civilized pattern of life and a reasonable standard of living through economic growth and in co-operation with others in a similar position and with similar interests. Afrikaner exclusivism had become impossible; the costs of apartheid – economically, politically, financially, morally – had risen too high.

In 1979 Prime Minister P.W. Botha, since a year the successor to Vorster who had been brought down due to the Muldergate Info scandal, declared that there was no other way for South Africa than to adapt or die. He announced changes in the apartheid legislation and s sharing of power. That declaration in itself led to a breach in the Afrikaner ranks: in 1982 the Konservatieve Partij led by dr A.P. Treurnicht was founded. The following year a new constitution was introduced. This instituted a three-chamber parliament, with separate chambers for whites, Coloureds and Indians.

A New Beginning, 1983 - 1990 - ?

The constitution of 1983 indeed introduced a sharing of power in theory, albeit with a strong white preponderance and with the exclusion of the largest population group. The three-chamber parliament received little support. Hundreds of black organisations formed the United Democratic Front (UDF), that showed affinity with the ANC, or the National Forum, which was more oriented to the PAC. These movements again used the method of mobilizing the masses, which led to demonstrations, conflicts with the police and violence – and also to mutual black violence. In 1985 the government declared a state of emergency, dissolved the

UDF and numerous other black anti-apartheid organisations and imprisoned its leaders. It seemed to take no notice of the worldwide protests, or the flow of boycott and sanction measures. The abolition of the influx control (pass laws) in 1986, withdrawal of the Immorality Acts, the return of citizenship to the inhabitants of the independent 'homelands' and creation of the possibility of land ownership for blacks in white regions (all of them measures within the framework of the above-mentioned power sharing process) could not improve the national and international atmosphere. The reform process came to a halt, Botha did not cross the Rubicon. South Africa seemed on its way to a violent crisis. On 2 February 1990 State President F.W. de Klerk, Botha's successor since six months, announced the release of Nelson Mandela and other political prisoners, the legalisation of all prohibited anti-apartheid organisations, including ANC, PAC and the Communist Party, the withdrawal of the last apartheid laws as well as his readiness to negotiate about a new constitution for a democratic South Africa. When, nine days later, in front of a worldwide T.V.-audience, Nelson Mandela left his prison as a free man after 27 years, a new era commenced in South African history.

Meanwhile it has become clear that the new South Africa is not taking shape without difficulty. The economic position and the living conditions of the mass of the population have not changed; the political contrasts have acquired a different form due to the legalisation of the formerly prohibited and exiled anti-apartheid movements, but are no less vehement or fundamental in character. And violence has in fact increased and demands more victims than ever. In order to gain insight into this topical situation it is necessary to have another glance at the preceding history. What actually happened in February 1990 and what had caused it? Structural and fundamental social changes had demanded rapid dismantlement of the lasts traces of apartheid. The demographical curve revealed a continuously decreasing share of the whites in the total population (from 21,4 percent in 1911 to 14,4 percent in 1990 and an estimated 10 percent around the year 2,000). The population explosion (with 2,7 percent annual growth the number of South African inhabitants has risen to a total of 38,1 million people in 1990) daily causes a continuing urbanization, with all its consequences: immense problems as regards housing, education, health care and employment. The growth of the South African economy kept lagging behind with the needs. The huge costs of clinging to apartheid (double government structures, maintaining order and safety) were raised even more with the effects of boycotts, sanctions and disinvestments. Especially the attitude of the international bankers/money-lenders, who as a reaction to the on-going riots in 1985 had stopped the flow of credit, had a negative effect on the economy. Moreover, for a number of years that economy had been suffering from the consequences of a worldwide depression aggravated by its one-sided character: the South African economy was too much focused on the export of minerals and raw materials, technically insufficiently advanced, revealed too low a productivity per capita of the population and an unbalanced production structure with too few middle-sized and small companies. Although it was mainly the non-white population groups who, due to the social structure, suffered from the negative effects, these effects also afflicted the whites and demanded from them change and improvement for socio-political reasons.

A part of the deadlock was also that none of the parties involved in the South African conflict was strong enough to win. For various reasons the international community was not capable of forcing a solution. The liberation movements were unable to bring about a revolution. They were divided, did not have enough grip on the realities of South Africa and could not raise the armed battle to something of real importance or create a massive people's revolt. White South

▲ *Steve Biko, the leader of the South African Students Organization who lost his life in 1977 during his time of imprisonment as the result of torture.*

Africa was not on the verge of breaking down, its fall under internal and foreign pressure could not be expected. But at the same time it was obvious that it could not stop black resistance, nor realize a break-through to win internal allies, and was threatened to be permanently confronted with the moral and material consequences of the continuing struggle and isolation.

The realization of the deadlock and of the necessity to find a solution for the South African conflict in another way, led to a careful exploration of the possibilities to achieve this from around 1975 onwards. Tentative talks were held, at first in secret, later more openly. There were trial processes, such as in South West Africa/Namibia, where initially, as an alternative for Swapo, an internal process of gaining independence was activated, including the abolition of apartheid and political co-operation across the colour bar. Real chances and a clear acceleration were achieved for all of this when communism collapsed in Eastern Europe and the power of the Soviet Union behind the liberation movements fell away. This made a solution for the Cuban presence in Angola and an agreement with Swapo over Namibia possible. And also to a certain extent an agreement between Pretoria and the ANC.

As was mentioned, president De Klerk took the initiative in February 1990 and overcame the deadlock. He declared to be willing to negotiate about a new South Africa on the basis of sharing of power. He offered no surrender, no transference of power to the ANC. This is how the negotiation process in Codesa (Convention for a democratic South Africa) was initiated, after the last and fundamental apartheid laws had been abolished in 1991: the Population Registration Act and the Group Areas Act. The negotiation process has to produce a new constitution for a unitary and democratic South Africa, where general suffrage and constitutionally recorded basic rights will hold equally good for everyone. In view of previous history this process is subject to all kinds of limitations. Conservative whites objected severely against it. However, a referendum (17 March 1991) indicated the real power relations within the white population group: more than two-thirds of the whites backed president De Klerk and his striving to achieve a

peaceful creation of a multi-racial democracy. This has not solved the mutual distrust and opposed perceptions of the possibilities and realities of South Africa. Neither has it solved a fundamental difference in the basic philosophy: the National Party bases its thinking on a past of ethnicity and sharing power, the ANC on the tradition of transference of power and democratic centralism. The ideas about economic and social ordering are also far apart. Another limitation is formed by the different power bases of the parties involved, the discord in black circles and the ethnical contrasts – not the only one, but still an important background to the increased, rather than decreased, amount of violence after February 1990. A final limitation is the socio-economic situation: the contrast between the small, wealthy top layer and the poor masses, the difference in education and development, in living and housing conditions, the economic stagnation and the rapid population growth, the unemployment, the violence, the criminality. It is notably this latter limitation which can not be undone by political decree or compromise and which, due to its influence on all the other difficult aspects, is making the process of transition from the old to the new South Africa a laborious one. Thus the past is also a visible part of the present in these transitional years in South Africa.

◄ ANC-leader Nelson Mandela and president De Klerk during the historical peace deliberation on 14 September 1991.

29

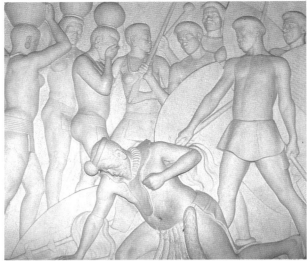

▲ The Swazi against the Zulu... A panel in the Voortrekkers' Monument shows how king Dingaan is murdered by the Swazi in 1840.

The history of South Africa is characterized by an age-long battle between the different groups. Below Utimuni, Shaka's nephew; in the background Zulu warriors exercising with the traditional large
▼ shield. Colour lithograph by George French Angas. From: 'The Kafirs illustrated' (1849).

▲ The Zulu against the Boers... Picture of a laager; made after a sketch of an Afrikaner who had participated in a fight against the Zulu in the first years of the history of Natal. From: 'Illustrated London News'.

▲ The English against the Boers... The British occupation of Spioenkop during the Anglo-Boer War. From: 'Illustrated London News'.

The Zulu against the English... Relief of the British garrison at ▶
Rorke's Drift. Right the burned-down hospital, left missionary
Witt's house behind a defence wall consisting of bags of 'mielies' (maize) and cans of biscuits.

To a new South Africa

In the following part of this chapter the history of the country, as described before, will be approached from a sociological point of view. South Africa is saturated with history. While in most other countries the political and economic discussions take place in the present tense and are directed towards the future, South Africans tend to mobilize the past. They refer to historical achievements and to acquired rights from olden times; they remember old grievances and long-past conflicts.

The consciousness of the Afrikaners is imbued with historical notions. The struggle against the black tribes in the previous century and the wars against the British were such traumatic experiences that they have rooted in the collective memory. They are remembered in annually returning commemorations, they are expressed in numerous monuments and in the names of cities, city-districts and streets.

The British colonists on the other hand have put their stamp on notably Natal and the south-eastern regions. More recent is the historic awakening of the black population, in which old kingdoms and leaders are recollected and rehabilitated. The Inkatha movement of Chief Buthelezi has proclaimed Zulu King Shaka to its patron and has placed a memorial stone in honour of king Dingaan, who is the pre-eminent example of black unreliability in the history books of the Afrikaners.

The divergent and even conflicting interpretations of the past reflect a split national consciousness. Undoubtedly the country knows a solid polity, but South Africa is not a nation state in the actual sense of the word; it has not a single nation carrying the state, but a conglomerate of population groups. However much South Africans, of any origin, are attached to their country, they miss a common frame of reference. Each group claims to have a special place, constantly compares itself to other groups and preferably appeals to its own contribution to the mutual cause. Naturally the apartheid policy has confirmed and strengthened this dissension, but it has not created it. The exceptionally strained relationship between the white minority and the black population stems from previous centuries, when the struggle for economic sources and political power was fought with great vehemence. The toned down, but not completely disappeared, controversy between African and English-speaking whites, also a result of historical conflicts, has nothing to do with apartheid. Contrasts within the black camp, such as between Zulu and Xhosa, have certainly been strengthened by the 'homelands' policy of the government, but would also have existed without apartheid; the many inter-ethnical conflicts in tropical Africa bear witness to this.

The recent abolition of the apartheid laws therefore does not at all signify the disappearance of social segregation. To a certain degree there is even a revival of group nationalism. The uncertain future the white minority is facing has in places led to an extremely nationalist radicalism. The Inkatha movement which has appointed itself to be a mouth-piece of the Zulu people, more than ever before demonstrates a militant ethnocentrism. 'Black languages' have recently been involved in competition to obtain the status of 'official' means of communication. In the religious field, although not as strong, something similar can be discerned; the South African Muslim population, for example, has become more conscious of its identity and of its ties with the Islamic world. Yet the two protagonists in the current political field, the white National Party and the black African National Congress, are not unsuccessful in their attempts to gain followers outside their own population group. Still the ANC, although basically non-racial, appears to have greater difficulty with broadening its basis than the National Party, which was until recently exclusively white. A part of the so-

▲ *The Voortrekkers leave the Republic of Natalia after the British occupation in 1843. This panel in the Voortrekkers' Monument shows how they cross the Drakensberg Mountains with their ox-carts once again.*

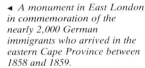

◄ *A monument in East London in commemoration of the nearly 2,000 German immigrants who arrived in the eastern Cape Province between 1858 and 1859.*

◄ *This bronze statue of an immigrant couple is can be found opposite the 'Settlers National Monument' in Grahamstown.*

called coloured population seems to prefer the NP to their own political organisations and president De Klerk enjoys a certain popularity among the educated blacks. The ANC probably suffers under the current close relations with the Communist Party, in a predominantly Christian country like South Africa a formidable obstacle.

Apartheid has, certainly in its intention, been considerably more than a system of political dominance and economic exploitation. It was also an all-embracing social experiment, meant to dissolve the racially mixed society into homogeneous communities and 'national' states – the 'homelands' – under the ultimate leadership of the strongest: the Afrikaner state. In this manner it was to have been achieved that the composite parts of the plural system would experience a process of 'separate development'.

Apartheid thinking mainly rested on two pillars. One was formed by the world view of the Afrikaners, religiously legitimated, in which there was only place for racially and culturally completely homogeneous communities. In the way they demanded a similar community for themselves, secured by the state, they prescribed a separate state-existence for the black peoples, in which forced moving of blacks who lived elsewhere was executed on a mass scale.

The other pillar of apartheid formed the striving of the white minority to safeguard themselves against black domination. The only method to prevent this was the consistent geographical deconcentration of the various black population groups. Suffrage per 'homeland' might prevent that via a national democratic system the white minority could be voted out.

The advocates of this 'grand strategy' compromised themselves, however, by regularly attributing everything to themselves as regards land ownership, settlement areas, economic activities, educational provisions and political rights. Moreover by no means did they reckon sufficiently with the economic development of the country: a system which had a chance to succeed in a predominantly agrarian system with a semi-autonomous, regionally spread population, was doomed to fail in the industrialized and urbanized society arising in South Africa. The black population that was to be dispersed over the 'homelands', concentrated itself more and more in the big industrial and mining centres. The more the economy developed, the more it alienated itself from politics. A contrast that drove the white community into two camps: on the one hand the Afrikaners who dominated the state, on the other the English-speaking group who steered business. The controversy sharpened when in the late seventies and the eighties international sanctions, notably concerning capital investments, caused serious economic damage. It was in those years that the multinationals began strongly and more openly to become opposed to the apartheid policy.

Yet international pressure has probably not been the main reason why the government decided to phase out apartheid and finally end it completely. It had appeared earlier that the 'homeland' policy was no success, and that the regulation of labour mobility together with the settlement of black labourers was impossible to maintain. Under the eye of the government the population groups, who should formally have remained separated, inter-mingled.

At the same time a differential population growth will have played a part, causing the economy to become more and more interested in skilled and motivated black labourers. This crumbling demographical pyramid must have aroused the consciousness that the tide was turning: that a defensive policy would only get increasingly difficult and that waiting longer to reform would become more and more risky. That explains the choice for 'a flight forwards' in 1990.

Political Reconstruction

The social and political reconstruction that has been implemented these recent years, can be characterized as a 'revolution from the top'. Critics of the regime speak of 'a miracle'; they had expected cosmetic changes, but now have to admit that the government has drawn up a daring reform programme, in resolute steps that quickly succeeded each other.

The National Party, which has dominated the political scene in South Africa for more than 40 years, has supported the new direction from the very beginning. Although on the right wing a considerable amount of votes were lost to the Conservative Party, the main force managed to keep the ranks closed. This fact is of decisive importance: no other political formation except the NP would have been capable to lead and achieve the risky transition to a new system. It was an exceptionally fortunate move that the ruling NP took the ANC – its strongest rival – as its main ally on the journey to 'a new South Africa'. For it involves the mass of the black population directly and indirectly with the reform process and it obliges them to comply with the result of the negotiations.

The central issue everything is pivoting around at this moment is the choice of the future constitutional system. There is agreement between parties as regards the introduction of a parliamentary democracy with general suffrage. Discord arises at closer inspection of the political consequences flowing from such a general suffrage. Given the composition of the South African population general suffrage would result in an almost unassailable power position of the black majority, which makes every oppositional movement chanceless in advance. For the white population this is the great spectre. Although this group shows willingness to share power with other population groups, it refuses to agree on a complete transfer of power. The white population justifies this attitude by referring to views also held outside South Africa. According to them in a plural society special, in any case, additional demands should be set to the democracy in order to correct the mere numerically based power structures.

It is this issue that determined the subject and the course of the current negotiations. What matters is that a stable and effective democratic system is designed, which expresses the black majority position without making the other population groups completely dependent on that majority. Forms of co-operation are sought, within and without the parliamentary system, which can mitigate the 'winner takes all' effect. Besides the provisions of the parliamentary system, counterbalances can be created by taking protective provisions that also exist elsewhere: constitutionally guaranteed individual freedoms, recognition of cultural and religious group interests, an independent judiciary and an impartial body of civil servants. Within the parliamentary democracy a plural presidency is now contemplated, with a rotating chairmanship, a ministers council in which all major parties are represented, a House of Commons with equal membership for all parties of a certain size, and a far-reaching decentralized administration that gives due to the specific composition of the population in the various regional and local communities.

That there is black opposition to a limitation of the numerical preponderance of the black voters, is obvious. Not only is the comfortable position of the black majority afflicted, but it is also feared that such regulations will protect the privileged position of the whites. They will benefit the 'haves' and harm the 'have-nots'.

The argument diverts the attention from the political to the economical field. Rightly so, because however important constitutional reforms may be, the true test for 'the new South Africa' is of an economical nature. The achievements of the future political class of South Africa will eventually be judged on the basis of the question to what extent it will succeed in having a growing welfare and passing the fruits of the welfare on to the different population groups.

Old and New Expectations

The white population of South Africa has always been a minority. For a long time the extent of the colonist population was negligible: some tens of thousands. Even when immigration, in the final quarter of the nineteenth century, had become stronger, the white group did not grow to more than a million, being one fifth of the entire population of the country. As a comparison: the United States numbered four million whites as early as 1800, a number which had grown to 67 million in 1900.

Given these numerical relationships the whites in South Africa have always felt themselves extremely vulnerable. In order to maintain their position, they continuously braced themselves: military, politically and culturally. Their precarious position forms the main explanation of Afrikaner nationalism, which strongly opposed both the black majority and the British intervention. The fact that, despite their numerical weakness they managed to hold their own against the internal end eventually also the foreign enemy, caused the Afrikaners to come to consider their presence in South Africa as a miracle, their country as the Promised Land, their history as a holy history: the pilgrimage of a small people, chosen by God and capable of great works owing to his blessing.

When out of the traditional Boer society a modern, urbanized industrial state arose, this national myth had to lose its force. From a historical point of view, apartheid was the final sizeable effort to save what could be saved through forced segregation. Started in 1948, it was already obvious in the seventies that the apartheid project could not succeed. It appeared incompatible with the demands of modern economy and met with increasingly heavy resistance internally and internationally.

As a reaction to the exclusive white view of reality a competing black ideology arose in those years, characterized by completely opposing future expectations. As violent resistance increased, notably in the mid-eighties, 'a march for Pretoria' according to some appeared to belong to the possibilities. South African writers such as J.M. Coetzee and Nadine Gordimer represented the oncoming fall of white supremacy in almost apocalyptical novels: 'Life and Times of Michael K.' and 'July's People'. However the expectation did not become reality. As was demonstrated before there was no question of a real revolution, merely of a lengthy perseverance of violent resistance. Moreover the violence was mainly limited to the black residential areas; the majority of the whites, although seriously worried, did not feel themselves directly threatened. The idea that South Africa would fall as the final domino stone after the decolonization of the entire black continent, misjudged the power of the South African state, sustained by a white population of millions. South Africa appeared to be the exception to the rule that the white presence in Africa and Asia was coming to an end after the last World War.

The strange, not to say unique, point about South Africa lies in the combination of two colonization forms: a settlement colony and an exploitation colony. Just like the United States, Canada and New Zealand South Africa was of old a settlement region for white colonists from overseas. As the whites formed a minority, they were at the same time constantly confronted with strong black tribes who could only be incorporated with difficulty into the white political and economical system. Just as in the British, French and Dutch colonies in Asia and Africa, the ruling white group recognized the traditional authority of the tribal chiefs; just as in other colonies the non-white population was enlisted on a large scale as labour forces in white-run business.

The story of Barney Barnato's life

One of the founders of Johannesburg, as well as one of the richest men in the world, was Barney Barnato. As a young man he arrived in South Africa with the proverbial penny in his pocket and opened a saloon near the diamond mine in Kimberley. He himself performed there as a boxer, a billiard-player and a conjurer. Due to his unbridled energy and commercial insight he finally, after a period as a diamond trader in London, gained control over an important part of the Kimberley mine. The following year a merger between his Barnato Brothers Company and Cecil Rhodes' De Beers Company was arranged. The latter was to become prime-minister of the Cape colony in 1890. Ten years later Barnato's seemingly indestructible constitution appeared to be affected by his stressful way of life to such an extent, that he left for England to obtain the best possible medical help there. Just before the island of Madeira he ended his life by jumping overboard.

This photograph of Barney Barnato comes from a reprint of the daily paper 'The Star' (1897).

Union Building. The ▶
sandstone building, designed by
Sir Herbert Baker, seats the
government and houses the
national archive. Here the
constitutional basis of the new
South Africa has to be laid.

The double character of a settlement and exploitation colony can explain why the decolonization of Africa stopped on the border of South Africa. Nowhere else was white power mighty enough to turn the black tide. Even the French 'colons' in Algeria and the British 'settlers' in Kenya had, albeit after heavy resistance, to yield to the majority; in as far as they did not return to their mother country they became a small powerless minority among a non-white people. Only in South Africa the number of whites was too large and the white state too solidly founded to be really threatened by the black majority. The fact that most white South Africans have no mother country to fall back on in time of need, naturally strengthened the resoluteness with which they offered resistance.

Nevertheless their opposition had to end in a stalemate. Quite different from the white population in countries like America and Australia – in no way threatened by the original inhabitants – the whites of South Africa saw themselves confronted with a large and growing majority of non-whites who, supported by the international community, demanded an equal position.

The future South Africa, now in the scaffoldings, will therefore require far-reaching compromises from both white and black. The black majority will have to recognize the rightful presence of the whites and to safeguard the protection of their fundamental interests. On the other hand the white population will not be able to deny the black South Africans the rights they acquired elsewhere in Africa, or in any case aspire to: the position of fully-fledged citizens and the opportunity to develop in freedom. Put otherwise: whether they want it or not, white and black are condemned to one another.

What are the prospects for the future? At least three scenarios are doing the rounds. The most optimistic image of the future takes example from the Swiss and believes in a formula in which the many-coloured and multi-racial society takes shape in federal structures and tolerant relations. Those who believe in this perspective, point to the wealth of raw materials and human capital and to the existence of a highly-developed economy; between Johannesburg and Milan, it has been noted, exists no comparable industrial centre. Despite all the differences, it is this economy that will keep the various population groups together, like a giant labour machine.

The second scenario compares the future of South Africa with recent experiences in North and South America, where despite economic dynamics and progressive emancipation of the poor masses, a sizeable impoverished under-class still exists. Given the massive poverty and unemployment among the South African blacks and the huge backlog in training and education, it is hardly presumable that the economy will be capable to carry the necessary provisions; neither will it be possible to create sufficient employment. Most likely is the emergence of a dualistic economy, in which alongside modern business there will be a large informal sector; this will contain massive chronic poverty besides a prosperous white and black middle-class.

The third scenario is downright pessimistic. In the best case a certain 'Africanisation' of society and economy will occur, a gradual decrease of welfare for the white population and a diminishing of the competitive power of the economy. In the worst case it may appear that the envisaged multi-cultural South Africa is not viable. The tensions between the various population groups will again and again express themselves in violent conflicts. According to this view there could even be 'Lebanonization', in which the separation of a part of the whites in a Boer state of their own is not excluded. Which prospect is the most likely, is not to be said. Comparable developments elsewhere, from which something could be learned, are lacking; the oncoming South African adventure knows no historical predecessors. Nowhere in the world has a white population dared to invite a non-white population, who used to be excluded from power, to share the power; neither has it up till now occurred that a non-white population, dominated and exploited by whites for centuries, revealed the readiness to offer yesterday's rulers a place in tomorrow's society.

If this experiment succeeds, South Africa – in a world of increasing inter-ethnic violence – will have achieved something really exceptional.

◄ Shepherd in East Transvaal. The results of the political innovations will eventually be judged on the basis of the question whether or not it will be possible to increase the welfare and to pass the fruits of that welfare on to the various population groups.

TRADITIONS IN TRANSITION

Fossils from palaeontological sites in South Africa have greatly furthered the quest for knowledge on human origins. By means of an archaeological exploration of the past, this chapter outlines the evidence for human evolution in the African subcontinent from the earliest times to the present.

For many thousands of years before the European settlement of southern Africa the subcontinent had been inhabited by nomadic hunters and gatherers. Archaeological evidence reveals that by 25,000 years ago hunter-gatherers were not only using a wide range of stone tools but were wearing ornaments made of bone or shell and using ochre and other pigments to represent their world-view in paintings on the rock-faces of caves. These 'Stone Age' hunter-gatherers were the ancestors of the present-day San people, popularly known as the 'Bushmen'. As to the terminology there is little consensus; both San and Bushmen are regarded by some people as being derogatory. The remains of domestic sheep, dated to the first century AD, provide evidence of the fact that the San people were early pastoralists, forebears of Khoikhoi herders. Also by that time agriculturalists using metal tools had moved into the subtropical coastal regions of south-eastern Africa. These early farmers were antecedents of the Bantu-speaking people of southern Africa. This chapter outlines the evidence for human evolution in the subcontinent, and provides an introduction to the cultural traditions of the indigenous inhabitants of southern Africa.

The sections on human origins and Khoisan people were written by Professor Hendrik P. Steyn. Dr Patricia Davison presents a contribution on the cultural heritage of black South Africans.

◄ *Rock painting of the San people, the original inhabitants of South Africa. Such representations provide information regarding rituals and animal species from prehistoric times.*

South Africa and human origins

Africa is now widely regarded as the most likely place where mankind evolved from earlier *hominids*. The 'dark continent', however, was reluctant at first to provide the proof of human evolution and antiquity. This changed dramatically in 1924 when the limestone quarries at Taung, to the north of Kimberley, yielded a vital clue in the form of the ancient but well-preserved skull of a child. Professor Raymond Dart, an anatomist of the University of the Witwatersrand who first studied the find, named it Australopithecus africanus ('Southern ape of Africa'). Though ape-like in some features, the skull also suggested features that strikingly contrasted with the apes, namely virtually upright posture and small canine teeth. This discovery was followed by the unearthing, in 1936, of an adult Australopithecus africanus specimen at

◄ *One of the seven earthenware heads, excavated near Lydenburg, Transvaal (dated to about 500 A.D.). The Lydenburg heads were probably used on ritual occasions, such as initiation ceremonies. These heads are the earliest expressions of three-dimensional art on the African subcontinent.*

Sterkfontein, near Krugersdorp, by Dr Robert Broom. Soon after, in 1938, the near-by Kromdraai caves yielded a new *hominid*, originally named Paranthropus robustus, but now generally known as Australopithecus robustus, representing a more robust creature than its gracile relative, Australopithecus africanus. Subsequently robust Australopithecus remains were also found at Swartkrans, close to Kromdraai, while Makapansgat, near Potgietersrus, produced further Australopithecus africanus fossils.

That these *hominids* had a much wider distribution in Africa was demonstrated by a number of Australopithecus finds in Kenya, Tanzania and Ethiopia since the 1950s. These fossils also represent gracile and robust forms, all of which have smallish brain-cases (with an average volume of less than 500 cc), relatively small canine teeth and a height of about 1,5 metres. Both *hominid* species were bipedal, which represents a major evolutionary step, as upright walking freed the hands for

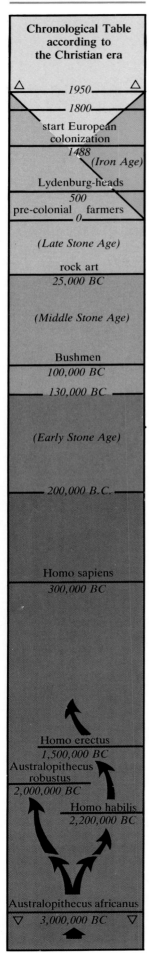

Chronological Table according to the Christian era

△ —— 1950 —— △
—— 1800 ——
start European colonization
1488
(Iron Age)
Lydenburg-heads
500
pre-colonial   farmers
0
(Late Stone Age)
rock art
25,000 BC
(Middle Stone Age)
Bushmen
100,000 BC
130,000 BC
(Early Stone Age)
200,000 B.C.
Homo sapiens
300,000 BC
Homo erectus
1,500,000 BC
Australopithecus robustus
2,000,000 BC
Homo habilis
2,200,000 BC
Australopithecus africanus
▽   3,000,000 BC   ▽

tool-use and for creative activities. The great age of this ability of human predecessors was confirmed by the discovery of *hominid* footprints dating back some 3,5 million years at Laetoli in Tanzania. While the gracile Australopithecus africanus had an estimated body weight of 20-40 kilograms, the sturdy australopithecines had larger bodies and a body weight of some 35-60 kilograms. The latter also had a more robust, crested brain case and a massive lower jaw with large molar teeth, a feature that is probably related to a vegetarian diet. Though tool-using by the australopithecines is a possibility, Professor Raymond Dart's early postulate of an 'osteodontokeratic culture' based, as the name suggests, on the use of bones, teeth and horns, has not as yet been confirmed by subsequent research.

The oldest East African Australopithecus fossils date back more than 3,5 million years, while the oldest South African fossils (found at Makapansgat) date back three million years. The youngest australopithecines in South and East Africa are about a million years old. The gracile Australopithecus africanus, now widely regarded as a likely direct ancestor of humans, became extinct some two million years ago. Competition with its better equipped, fully human successor, Homo habilis, probably contributed to its demise. Homo habilis ('able man') appeared on the scene some 2,2 million years ago and, as in the case of the australopithecines, fossil remains of these earliest of humans were found in East Africa. Homo habilis had a much larger brain capacity than the australopithecines (+ 640 cc), and was probably a hunter of small animals as well as a scavenger. These early humans shaped and used the earliest formal stone tools, known as Oldowan tools (from Olduvai Gorge in Tanzania where they were first found), consisting of choppers and smaller flake tools.

When the robust australopithecine became extinct about a million years ago, its early human contemporary, Homo habilis, had already been replaced by an even more successful *hominid*, Homo erectus, whose presence in East Africa dates back some 1,5 million years. Possible Homo erectus remains were also found in South Africa (at Swartkrans), indicating its presence in the Transvaal at least a million years ago. Homo erectus had a body size that approached that of modern people, and a brain of about 1,000 cc, housed in a thick, heavy-browed skull. They used a variety of stone tools, probably used fire, and had a diet based on meat and plant foods.

As fossil remains of Australopithecus and early *hominids* have up to now been found only in Africa, present data strongly support the view that Africa was the cradle of archaic humans. Archaeological excavations in cave sites such as Klasies River Mouth on the southern Cape coast and Border Cave in KwaZulu, have confirmed the presence of anatomically modern people in southern Africa prior to 100,000 years ago. This predates anatomically modern humans elsewhere in the world by thousands of years and suggests that not only archaic man, but also anatomically modern people originated in Africa, probably between 300,000 and 120,000 years ago. At both the above-mentioned sites the remains of early man are associated with Middle Stone Age stone tools, characterized by the absence of handaxes and cleavers (typical of the Early Stone Age) and the presence of blades and flake tools. The 70,000 year old Howieson Poort type toolkit is of special significance as its flake blades may have been hafted and used as projectiles or other composite tools, which would make them the earliest examples of such tools.

Though the human bone remains from Border Cave and Klasies River Mouth have ostensibly modern features, it is more difficult to demonstrate a concomitant modernity in behaviour patterns. The extent of the mental and

cultural abilities of these Middle Stone Age populations is still debated, but there are grounds for believing that they were in fact 'modern' in the sense that they were knowledgeable about environmental resources and efficient in utilizing them. There is evidence for systematic exploitation of marine mammals, shellfish and birds such as penguins, while a variety of ungulates, particularly the more vulnerable old and young animals, seem to have been selectively hunted and the carcasses brought to caves or base camps. They also collected delicacies such as tortoises and ostrich eggs, and used fire extensively. They possibly even stimulated the growth of plant foods by means of alternating forms of cultivation.

The early anatomically modern people may well have been the ancestors of the present-day Bushmen. Bushman-like people seem to have been present in southern Africa more than 100,000 years ago, and the Bushmen are widely regarded as the product of lengthy isolation and local evolution. This is supported by archaeological evidence, as stylistic elements of the Middle Stone Age technology, and particularly the so-called Howieson Poort industry, are congruent with an apparent regional isolation of the area south of the Zambezi River that continued through Later Stone Age times, as is reflected in artefact assemblages and elements of rock art.

This does not, however, divorce the Bushmen from their African genetic past. Despite their apparent physical differences, Bushmen have the same basic genetic profile as sub-Saharan black populations. In the light of this, the marked differences in outward physical appearance must be sought in a lengthy separation and divergent evolution, possibly dating back to the beginning of the Late Pleistocene (some 125,000 years before the present), during which the later Khoisan (Khoikhoi and Bushmen) developed characteristics such as a lighter skin and a gracile body, whereas to the north, development favoured a darker skin and a larger body size.

There may be some doubt as to the behavioural modernity of their Middle Stone Age predecessors. However, the southern African hunter-gatherers of the Late Stone Age,

San hunter in the Kalahari desert. The San are considered to be the descendants of the people who populated southern Africa more than ▼ *100,000 years ago.*

especially during the last 20,000 years of that period, had both the technology and the knowledge to adapt to a variety of local environments and to exploit the full range of food resources available to them. Not only did they become very competent hunters, eventually also using bows and arrows, but they utilized a variety of plant foods, as well as marine mammals, birds and fish. Shellfish were exploited to such an extent, especially in Holocene times (the last 10,000 years), that a large number of shell middens can still be found along the southern African coast. There is also evidence for seasonal migration and exploitation of coastal and inland food resources by the same groups of people.

The material possessions of Late Stone Age people included a variety of small stone scrapers and blades, bows and arrows, leather bags and garments, bone needles and awls, ostrich eggshell beads, seashell pendants and bored stone weights for digging sticks. They also practised formal burial of their dead, while rock art and painted burial stones demonstrate a close connection between art and ritual.

In archaeological deposits, dated to within the last 2,000 years, clay pottery appears which was rapidly introduced into large areas of southern Africa. Also at that time evidence of domestic stock becomes apparent, thus adding the element of pastoralism to the existing hunter-gatherer mode of subsistence. The adoption of pastoralism by local populations broadly forms the basis of distinction between Khoikhoi herder-hunter-gatherers and the Bushmen, who represent those populations that did not integrate herding into their economy. This broad socio-economic division of Bushmen hunter-gatherers and Khoikhoi pastoralists was what the first European travellers found, after first setting foot on South African shores in 1488.

Contact, colonization and change

When the two small ships under the command of Bartolomé Dias in 1488 approached land near the present Mossel Bay, they saw Khoikhoi herdsmen with so many cattle that they named the bay Angra dos Vaqueiros. The terrified herdsmen fled inland with their cattle, but their isolation from outside influence had been broken and the scene was set for a process of change that would ultimately destroy their way of life. The pattern of the next few decades of contact between the Khoikhoi and Europeans was set by the subsequent visit to South African shores by Vasco da Gama. He went ashore twice and had totally different experiences with the Khoikhoi, being attacked and wounded with a spear at the west coast, whereas at Mossel Bay he and his men were met by friendly Khoikhoi and entertained each other by playing on flutes and trumpets.

In 1503, when Antonio de Saldanha visited Table Bay, he was also involved in a skirmish, and was wounded in the arm. Viceroy Francisco d'Almeida, who went ashore in Table Bay in 1510, was less fortunate. He and his party were attacked and the Viceroy, together with more than 50 of his men, was killed in an incident where the Khoikhoi used their spears and trained oxen with devastating effect. The Portuguese, who were at least partly to blame for the skirmish, henceforth avoided South African shores, and few ships stopped over until more than 80 years later when English ships started trading with the Khoikhoi again.

The success of this trade, one ship in 1601 bartering 42 oxen and more than a thousand sheep for pieces of iron, created renewed interest in Cape shores. The trading boom, however, was short-lived. The Khoikhoi soon satisfied their need for iron, used for spearheads, and after 1610 preferred copper and brass, which they used

▲ *Print by Samuel Daniell dating from 1804/1805: 'Bosjesmans frying Locusts'. From: African scenery and animals. Collection Africana Museum Johannesburg.*
▼ *San hunter in the southern Kalahari desert. The San still use bow and arrows while hunting.*

Engraving by Abraham Bogaert dating from 1711: Cabo de Goede Hoop (Cape of Good Hope). The
▼ *seafarers who moored at the Table Bay found Khoikhoi shepherds with large herds of cattle there.*

▲ *The Drommedaris, Jan van Riebeeck's V.O.C.-ship, sails into Table Bay. Panel in the Cultural Historical Museum Cape Town.*

▲ *Engraving by Sir Thomas Herbert dating from 1658: Europeans trading with the Hottentots. From: 'A relation of some yeares travaile, begunne 1626. Into Afrique…'.*

for ornaments. By 1620 the cattle trade became unpredictable and subject to the specific needs and circumstances of Khoikhoi groups. The immense herds that the Europeans thought the Khoikhoi possessed were largely based on myth. As the herds had to satisfy a variety of economic, social and ritual needs of their owners, for most families a marketable surplus was probably the exception rather than the rule.

After some 150 years of intermittent and usually brief visits by European ships' crews the Cape Khoikhoi had no reason to believe that the Europeans were interested in settling at the Cape. They were wrong. Favourable comments on the climate and agricultural potential of the Cape have been made by British and Dutch visitors over decades but they were not acted upon. However, after the Dutch ship Haarlem in 1647 stranded in Table Bay and crewmen remained there for a year, Janszen and Proot wrote a highly favourable report to the Dutch East India Company (V.O.C., Vereenigde Oost-Indische Compagnie), highlighting the agricultural potential, abundance of fish and other animals, and painting a positive picture of the local inhabitants. The Lords Seventeen were convinced, and as a result Jan van Riebeeck and his party of some 90 people landed at Table Bay on 6 April 1652. Though the Dutch East India Company at that stage only saw it as a refreshment station and as a means to facilitate trade with the East Indies, the process of colonization of the sub-continent had in fact begun.

In the period between 1488 and Van Riebeeck's landing at the Cape, reports of European visitors mention only two indigenous population groups, namely the pastoral Khoikhoi, and the so-called 'Watermans' or 'Strandlopers', who had a coastal hunter-gatherer mode of subsistence. We know that groups of people who became known as 'Bushmen' from time to time also utilized coastal and marine food resources. However, the Table Bay Strandlopers seem to have been impoverished, cattleless Khoikhoi. Their strained relations with pastoral Khoikhoi and their dealings with European visitors often put them at odds with both parties. Numbering only some 50 people, the Strandlopers gained historical importance through the clever manipulations of their leader, commonly known as Harry. He had the advantage of a knowledge of English (gained on board an English ship to Java in the 1630s) and Dutch, which he subsequently learned, and thus often acted as a local interpreter, a position also given to him when the Dutch under Van Riebeeck settled at the Cape. Harry, to the dismay of Van Riebeeck, often did not facilitate trade with the Khoikhoi, but rather manipulated the situation to this own advantage. In 1658 his dealings caught up with him, and he, together with two of his men, were 'imprisoned' on Robben Island, which in more recent times gained notoriety as a place where political prisoners were held. This, however, was not to be the end of Harry, as he escaped from the island in 1659.

◄ *The Arms of the Dutch East India Company. The slate panel originated from Robben Island and depicts the monogram and the Dutch lion. The stone coat of arms was found on Schapen Island in the Saldanha Bay in 1975 by A.C. Koch, who donated it to the South African Cultural Historical Museum in Cape Town.*

Economic and cultural importance of livestock

The Strandlopers, despite their proximity to the fledgling Dutch settlement at the Cape, were never a central concern of the Dutch. Their primary aim, beyond the production of fruit and vegetables, was to barter as many cattle and sheep from the Khoikhoi as possible. This proved to be a major source of frustration to the Dutch and an objective that was never reached, mainly because they never understood Khoikhoi society and culture in general and, in particular, also the role of cattle that they so desperately sought.

The dealings of the Dutch East India Company not only brought it into contact with Khoikhoi groups in the vicinity of the Cape, but also led to expeditions into the interior to establish trade with distant Khoikhoi in attempts to meet the demand for more cattle. Apart from the Strandlopers, two separate pastoral Khoikhoi communities, the Goringhaiqua and the Gorachouqua lived in the Peninsula area itself. A fourth population group, the Cochoqua, seasonally moved down to the Cape from Saldanha Bay and other west coast areas. To their north lived the Guriqua and Namaqua, while the Chainouqua and Hessequa lived to the east of the Hottentots Holland Mountains. Tribes such as the Inqua, Outeniqua, and Attaqua lived even further to the east. These groups not only had their own territories, but formed separate political communities under the authority of a chief, whose position was based on seniority within a *patrilineal* descent system.

Within each territory, tribesmen moved freely with their herds of humped cattle and fat-tailed sheep, camping together whenever environmental conditions permitted or social and political reasons compelled them to.

Together with their herds they formed a close community. Khoikhoi had excellent control over their animals, which responded to a variety of whistles and calls; trained cattle even took part in military activities, trampling the enemy and acting as a defensive wall from behind which they could throw their spears.

Milk was the staple, supplemented by a variety of wild plant foods. Though fond of meat, the Khoikhoi were not keen to slaughter their animals and preferred to hunt wild animals. When near the coast, the shepherds also utilized marine foods such as shellfish and seals, and speared fish in the shallow waters.

As the Khoikhoi were nomadic pastoralists, they did not have fixed settlements but mat-covered huts which could easily be broken down, packed onto oxen and re-erected at a new site. Old people and children were often also transported on oxen, as were the other possessions of the Khoikhoi, including their characteristic earthenware pots with pointed bases and lugs, by means of which the pots were fastened to the pack-oxen.

Though Khoikhoi ritual was never properly described by

▲ *Coloured lithograph by George French Angas dating from 1849: Cape Town, from the Camps Bay Road. From: The Kaffirs illustrated...*

early observers, their beliefs about two animals have survived to this day as part of general South African mythology. The one concerns the praying mantis, also known locally as the 'Hottentotsgod', which was regarded as an omen of good fortune. In contrast, the meat of hares had to be avoided by men as it was considered harmful, based on the myth where the moon sent the hare to earth with a message about man's immortality which, unfortunately for man, was distorted to his detriment.

Within 20 years after Van Riebeeck's landing at the Cape, Khoikhoi society was well on its way of change and disintegration. European settlement was now established, 'freemen' started farming on Khoikhoi land, chiefs started selling land to the Dutch East India Company and many impoverished Khoikhoi settled on the farms of colonists as labourers. The final blow to their independence came in the form of several smallpox epidemics that raged through the Cape colony since 1713, virtually wiping out the southern Khoikhoi.

Before Van Riebeeck's time no visitor to South Africa had mentioned the Bushmen (or San as they were called by the Khoikhoi). Their existence was confirmed in 1655 by Jan Wintervogel who reconnoitred areas of the western Cape at the instruction of Van Riebeeck and found a small group of people clad only in skins, without any huts or cattle. These people, usually small groups of close kin, who lived in caves or small huts covered with mats or grass, were nomadic hunter-gatherers. They moved often, owned few possessions, and had a subsistence cycle based on the seasonal availability of

Coloured aquatint after a drawing by William J. Burchell dating from 1822/1824: View of a Bushmen kraal. From: Travels in the interior of ▼ *Southern Africa.*

▲ *Coloured aquatint by William J. Burchell dating from 1811: A Hottentot Kraal on the banks of the Gariep. From: Travels in the interior of Southern Africa.*
Bushman from the Cape Province. Small groups of Bushmen continue their traditional way of life in
▼ *the Kalahari semi-desert.*

wild plant foods such as various species of bulbs, berries and fruits. They hunted animals such as rock hyraxes, small and large antelopes, and collected delicacies such as tortoises, ostrich eggs, locusts, termites and wild honey, whenever it could be found. In drier inland areas, water-bearing plants such as the tsama melon, gemsbok cucumber and some underground bulbs made possible the utilization of other food resources and were often crucial for survival.

Although the bulk of the diet of Cape Bushmen may have been provided by gathering plant foods, at least seasonally, they are perhaps best known as hunters, using bows and poison-tipped arrows. Snake venom or the juices of poisonous plants were used for this purpose. Larger, more dangerous game, including elephants as well as plains game that gathered in large herds, were driven into game pits. Small animals and birds were trapped by means of snares, while dogs and fire were used to good effect, particularly in hunting burrowing animals. After the hunt, Bushman ethic required the hunters to share meat with others, thus continuously strengthening social bonds within camps.

The relations between the Bushmen and the white colonists who increasingly moved into the interior during the years around 1700 rapidly deteriorated into armed conflict. Ultimately, as was the case elsewhere in the world with hunter-gatherers, the Bushmen with their small groups and inferior weapons could not stem the tide of white expansion into the interior. Similarly, in the Drakensberg area of Natal, one of the last historical Bushman strongholds, the Bushmen were ultimately caught between white settlement in the lowlands and black expansion into the Lesotho highlands. By the end of the nineteenth century, the only Bushman communities in southern African that had an 'independent' lifestyle were those confined to the southern Kalahari desert. Today even they have largely lost their old culture, though some individual families have survived. Loss of cultural identity indeed seems to be the fate of all living San peoples. Though Bushmen in Botswana and Namibia number more than 60,000 their traditional lifestyle has been severely disrupted and is rapidly disintegrating.

Rock art

South Africa is probably the richest rock art region in the world, and areas such as the Drakensberg Mountains, Orange Free State, Eastern Cape and Sederberg Mountains contain thousands of rock art sites. Though Khoikhoi communities may also have painted on the rocks, this extensive body of art is attributed to the Bushmen, who were the inhabitants of large parts of southern Africa in prehistoric and historic times.

Two types of rock art are found: paintings, usually in rock shelters and overhangs in the mountainous areas; and engravings, usually on rocks and boulders in the open veld of the South African interior. While the engravings mostly depict animals, animal tracks and geometric patterns, the paintings depict animals, people, hunting scenes, conflict between people, group life, domestic scenes and material possessions. One also finds hand prints, finger dots, mysterious *therianthropes* (figures that combine animal and human features), and 'rain animals'. Though many painted scenes at first glance simply seem to portray what these early hunter-gatherers saw and experienced, the interpretation of rock art in terms of belief systems has added much to our understanding of the ideology behind some of the paintings. Studies of modern-day Kalahari Bushmen and reports on historical Karoo Bushmen tell us that some Bushman art could best be explained by seeing it in the context of ritual,

◄ *The rock paintings found throughout southern Africa provide an indication of the former wide dispersion of hunter-gatherers. In the Drakensberg Mountains the eland is the most frequently depicted animal. Recent ethnographic research has revealed that the eland was a symbol of power in San cosmology.*

specifically trance cure dancing, and the concomitant altered states of consciousness.

Rock art scenes often depict actions that resemble the trance cure dances of present-day Kalahari Bushmen. Typically it involves men who dance in tight circles to the rhythmic clapping of hands and singing of women. The dances can go on for hours and the combination of the rhythm, physical exertion, concentration and auto-suggestion induces a state of trance. In this condition men may sweat profusely, their bodies tremble and as they may stagger, they are sometimes assisted by others. The trancers are believed to have special powers of curing, due to a supernatural potency that is activated by trance dancing.

This altered state of consciousness also provides clues to rock art, as many rock art scenes are thought to depict the hallucinatory experiences, actions and visions of trancers, often presented in a symbolic manner. Men are often shown in typical trance dancing situations, bent forward, sweating, and even bleeding at the nose, formerly a common occurrence in Cape Bushman dancing. In this hallucinatory condition, some men are thought to be potent healers through their own curing powers, but they are also able to manipulate the potency of other animals and things, such as the eland, lion, and rain. Trancers also have vision into the normally invisible world of the supernatural, and may even become part-animal, as is depicted by the therianthropes.

As at least half of the adult men in present-day Kalahari Bushman communities may be trance performers, Bushman rock artists were probably often trancers themselves, depicting their own ritual healing experiences through mutually intelligible symbols.

Though rock paintings in open sites can as yet not be accurately dated, there is no doubt that the art tradition as such is an old one and in southern Africa covers a period of more than 25,000 years. The youngest of the paintings may date back only some 200 years, as they depict historical phenomena, such as ships, people on horseback, and people with rifles.

Rock paintings of the Khoisan often show trance dances, ► *hallucinations and visions.*

▲ *From rock paintings by the Bushmen it can be deduced that elands, hartebeests, black and white rhinos were present on a large scale in southern Africa in prehistoric times.*

▲ *Both in prehistoric times and these present days the animal world forms a source of inspiration. Top: a rock painting in which Bushmen have depicted a hunting scene;*
▼ *bottom: a painting by Sakkie Eloff in the Nelspruit Art gallery.*

Despite the antiquity of the rock art, it is a very vulnerable part of South Africa's cultural heritage and much of it has already been lost through natural processes or the actions of people. Though some paintings show remarkable preservation, others have faded beyond recognition. Exposure to the sun, rain and other chemical processes are partly to blame, but in some instances the paint itself is not particularly durable. White, in particular, probably made from white clay or gypsum, tends to fade away first. Fortunately, the frequently used reddish brown and yellow, for which earth pigments such as red and yellow ochres were used, proved to be more durable. These pigments were probably mixed with substances such as animal fat, bone marrow, blood, egg, or plant juices and applied with the fingers, birds' feathers or sticks.

Though much of Bushman rock art may primarily have been functional to the artists in terms of ritual or other considerations, the paintings as well as the engravings are also extremely pleasing from an aesthetic point of view. Some, in fact, are excellent works of art in their own right, and show that the artists were acute observers and had superb qualities of creativity and expression. The art in the South African veld is also testimony to a people physically and spiritually in harmony with nature and their fellow-men. It is a colourful but silent record of the evolution and demise of an ancient African culture.

The cultural heritage of black South Africans

Up to the 1960s, many writers assumed that there was no southern African history prior to the records of literate travellers and colonizers. Oral history was not taken into account, nor was the material evidence of early settlement. Over the past two decades this Eurocentric perspective has been proved wrong by an impressive body of archaeological research, revealing not only the time depth of African occupation of southern Africa but a wide range of technological innovations. The new view affirms the pre-colonial existence of complex, stratified African communities, who made a lasting impact on the landscape. During the apartheid era in South Africa, however, the long history of African settlement in the subcontinent was not officially acknowledged.

Over the past forty years, ethnic differences have been unduly accentuated for political reasons and formed the basis of the policy of 'separate development'. There is still a pervasive tendency in the official media to emphasize tribalism and ethnicity. Although it is misleading to overstress adherence to traditional practices and values, it would also be wrong to claim that cultural differences do not play a significant role in contemporary South Africa.

Traditions in action

The term 'traditional' is often incorrectly taken to mean a passive adherence to custom. In practice, however, traditions are never static but are continually reshaped in relation to changing circumstances. Time-honoured traditions may be given current significance as a means of claiming group affiliation or coping with social conflict. In contemporary South Africa this process is exemplified by the use of ancient cultural symbols in the iconography of political parties. At another level, traditional African design motifs have been readily incorporated into the material culture of South Africans whose cultural roots are European - modern clothing design and contemporary architecture provide good examples of this cultural synthesis. The African traditions discussed further

*Coloured aquatint by Samuel Daniell dating from 1805: Scene in ▶
Sitsikamma; romantic impression of the hunting area of the hunter-
gatherers on the south coast. Collection Africana Museum.*

on are best regarded as dynamic resources used actively by
people in the varied contexts of everyday life.

Exploring the archaeological past

Evidence of the ways of life of the early inhabitants of
southern Africa is found in the archaeological remains
of their food and material possessions. Information is also
derived from the impact of their occupation on the
landscape. The archaeological record is uneven in that
only certain materials, such as stone,pottery, shells and
beads, survive over long periods of time. Preservation is
also affected by environmental factors. Carbonized food
remains and charcoal are particularly important forms of
archaeological evidence as they can be used to date the
site by means of *radiocarbon dating*.
Archaeological remains of the semi-permanent
settlements of early African farmers include sun-baked
mud floors of dwellings, hearths, grinding-stones, pottery
and the residues of metal-working technology. Relatively
settled village life, the cultivation of grain crops and a
knowledge of metal-working, which provided the most
effective tools for clearing and tilling the fields, were
essential features of what archaeologists refer to as the
Southern African Iron Age. [Note that the South African
archaeological chronology does not run parallel to that
of Europe]
The life of Iron Age farmers differed from that of hunters
and gatherers in a number of ways: the former group
cultivated crops and kept domestic livestock, lived in
semi-permanent villages, melted and forged iron and
produced pottery of characteristic ware. Khoikhoi
herders also had domestic animals and pottery but they
did not cultivate crops or produce metal tools.
Although it is impossible to know for certain what
language was spoken by the inhabitants of early farming
settlements, it is generally accepted that they were Bantu-
speakers on the basis of continuity in the archaeological
record from the earliest sites to the more recent,
historically documented past.

Migration and settlement
before AD 1000

Around AD 200 early farming communities, using iron
tools, had moved south of the Limpopo River into areas
previously inhabited only by hunter-gatherers and
herders. By AD 500 the early farmers were well-
established in what is now the eastern Transvaal and
coastal Natal. They spread southwards fairly rapidly until
they reached drier areas unsuited to their means of
existence, which was particularly well-adapted to the
savanna, summer rainfall regions. It seems that there was
a selective preference for river-valleys with rich, deep
soil or areas near the coast where initial clearing of forest
would have provided humus-rich agricultural soil.
The size of villages was initially relatively small (two to
three ha.) but by AD 600 settlements had grown to about
eight ha. and might have been occupied by 100 or more
people, for a few years at a time. Each village was
probably fairly self-contained and could produce its own
pottery and metal tools but there are indications of trade
in particular items, such as sea-shells, salt, soapstone and
pigments such as ochre and graphite.
The most important crops were various kinds of sorghum
(Panicum miliaceum), bullrush millet (Sorghum

*Zulu woman in the Msinga region (KwaZulu).
The combination of western dress together with more traditional attire reflects a
▼ society in transition.*

vulgare),legumes, such as ground-nuts, and cucurbits. Maize, the current staple grain, was only introduced to southern Africa in the sixteenth century. Agriculture meant not only that communities could feed themselves but that they had to invest labour and time in clearing land, hoeing, sowing, weeding, harvesting and threshing. Farming communities had to be well-organized in order to reap returns over a number of agricultural cycles. Growing crops, however, did not signify that farmers depended only on their produce for food. They also hunted game, fished and gathered plant foods. From at least AD 400 there is evidence of domestic cattle, and cattle-keeping eventually became of great cultural and symbolic importance to the Bantu-speaking people of southern Africa.

Little is known about the social and religious life of people in the early Iron Age but inferences can be made from archaeological remains. Of great significance are the Lydenburg heads which come from a site, dated by the radiocarbon method to AD 500, near the present town of Lydenburg in the Transvaal. Seven ceramic heads, in form rather like inverted, elongated vessels, were found eroding out of a gulley. The heads had been deliberately broken and were buried in a pit. Although the meaning of the heads must remain speculative, it is very probable that they had ritual significance. As objects of aesthetic expression they are among the earliest records of African art in the subcontinent.

After AD 1000

As time passed, very large settlements emerged in certain places, usually on hill tops or other elevated sites. During the period AD 950-1050 important capitals were established near the confluence of the Limpopo and Shashi rivers. These were trading centres controlled by powerful rulers. The sites reveal increased numbers of cattle, a growth of wealth and political stratification. Between AD 1050-1200 at Mapungubwe on the Limpopo river, there is evidence of extensive trade in ivory and tortoise-shell for glass beads, cloth and Chinese porcelain. Trade networks reached as far as the Indian Ocean coast and indirectly to Arabia and the Orient. The site of Mapungubwe is divided into an elite hill-top

area and a surrounding village settlement believed to have been occupied by commoners. The rich graves on the hill-top containing precious gold objects affirm the status of the rulers. As a centralized state, controlling a far-reaching trade network, Mapungubwe can be regarded as the forerunner of Great Zimbabwe to the north.

Most Iron Age settlements were, however, more modest and an indication of how ordinary people lived at the time of European contact can be gained from written accounts of early travellers and the survivors of shipwrecks. The written records present more detailed information, which allows a picture of the past to be drawn with greater clarity.

African traditions: from past to present

As the name implies, Bantu-speaking people have been classified into groups on the basis of language. They form part of the large Bantu-speaking family, comprising over 100 million people, living in the area stretching southwards from the Great Lakes in equatorial Africa. About 300 different languages classified as 'Bantu' share certain linguistic features and have a core vocabulary in common, although as a result of sound shifts, which have occurred over a long time, similarities are not always immediately recognized.

Indigenous languages

Languages in South Africa are as diverse as the customs and cultures of the South African population. The two official languages, English and Afrikaans, are the mother tongues of 94 percent of the white population as well as a large number of Asian and coloured people. The dominant Bantu languages are Zulu and Xhosa, spoken by more than half of the black population, followed by Tswana, Northern and Southern Sotho, Tsonga, Venda, Ndebele and Swazi. The other languages consist of a variety of European and Indian languages and the remnants of the San and Khoikhoi languages. The bar charts show the individual components of the language of South Africa and also include Transkei, Venda, Ciskei and Bophuthatswana.
In 1991 the 'African' population of South Africa, including the four 'Homelands', numbered 29 million people, that is to say 75.6 percent of the entire population.

Whites		Coloureds	
language	percent	language	percent
Afrikaans and English	1	Other	0,2
Other	5	Afrikaans and English	0,8
English	37.	English	11
Afrikaans	57	Afrikaans	88

Blacks		Asians	
language	percent	language	percent
Venda	3	Afrikaans	1,5
Tsonga-Shangaan	4	Other	11,5
Southern-Sotho	9	Telegu-Gujarati	12
Northern-Sotho	11	Hindi	19
Tswana	12	Tamil	24
Ndebele	3	English	32
Swasi	3		
Xhosa	27		
Zulu	28		

The figures are estimates from the 1980 census.

Mapungubwe ('Hill of the Jackals') is a flat-topped hill west of Messina in the northern Transvaal. Archaeological finds from the twelfth century included ceramics, iron tools, copper wire, glass beads and the renowned gold-plated ▼ rhinoceros.

It should be remembered that linguistic classification is an arbitrary way of dividing people and that speakers of any one Bantu language do not necessarily live in the same geographical area, nor do they conform to a common physical type or culture. It should also be noted that there is no predictable correlation between culture and race. This is very simply explained by the fact that culture is acquired through learning and socialization, whereas race is genetically determined.

Today many black people live permanently in urban areas and rural South Africa is influenced by western economic systems and industrialization. Labour migration to the cities is an essential factor in the rural economy, and new cultural practices have arisen in response to the resultant changes in family life. Although it could be argued that former cultural traditions have long since been overtaken by history, certain practices have proved remarkably resilient and adaptable. New ways have not entirely displaced the old but instead there has been a blending of old and new to create a dynamic synthesis that continues to be modified in the varied situations of daily life. This intermeshing of values is manifested, for example, in urbanized youths aspiring to be initiated in the customary manner and in the strength of ancestor beliefs among people who have also embraced Christianity. Thus the cultural heritage of the past remains a vital part of the present. That heritage will be described in more detail below.

Environment, settlement and economy

Before industrialization had a marked impact on the Bantu-speaking people, they lived as subsistence farmers practising a varied mix of agriculture, livestock husbandry, foraging and hunting. Differences in environment and social organization, however, resulted in local variations within a general pattern. Both livestock husbandry and agriculture were limited by environmental factors. The south-eastern areas had far better grazing potential than the areas to the north and west, which had sourveld pasturage, were more subject to drought and plagued by tsetse-fly. Hoe-cultivation was also restricted by environmental conditions, particularly by rainfall during the months of sowing and germination. Both subsistence and settlement pattern were influenced by climate, soil types and vegetation.

Two major environmental regions - the south-east of the subcontinent, stretching from the sea to the Drakensberg range and, secondly, the hinterland west of the Drakensberg Mountains, encompassing the plateaux of the Highveld and beyond - provided the geographical setting for contrasting forms of settlement. In the south-eastern region a pattern of dispersed homesteads tended to prevail and in the west more concentrated villages occurred. Although in practice the situation on the ground was more complex and variations within these areas existed, a pattern of dispersed settlement was generally characteristic of the Nguni-speaking people, while more concentrated villages were typical of Sotho-speaking people on the Highveld and in Botswana. In both regions cattle were of great importance beyond the economic realm. Indeed, the value of cattle as bride-wealth and their ritual significance as a means of approaching the ancestral spirits were common elements among all Bantu-speaking people in southern Africa.

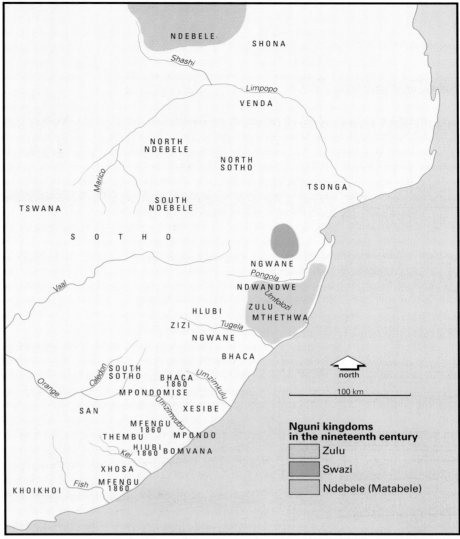

Nguni kingdoms in the nineteenth century
- Zulu
- Swazi
- Ndebele (Matabele)

Zulu homestead in the Melmoth district (KwaZulu). The circular layout of houses around the central cattle enclosure exemplifies the typical settlement pattern in the region between the Drakensberg Mountains and the sea. The central location of the fence indicates the significance and the value of ▼ cattle among the Nguni speaking population.

▲ *Coloured lithograph by George French Angas dating from 1849: Kraal on the Umgani Zulu cattle and sheep. From: The Kafirs illustrated…*
▼ *Young shepherd in Lesotho.*

Settlement pattern in the South-East

Xhosa- and Zulu-speaking people tended to live in *patriarchal* homesteads comprising an extended family. This family consisted of a man, his wives (*polygyny* will be discussed in a later section), unmarried children, married sons, daughters-in-law and their children, and any unrelated people who had attached themselves to the residential group. A cluster of dwellings, *izindlu*, usually numbering between ten and twenty, were arranged in a semi-circle around a central cattle enclosure. Chiefs' homesteads tended to be larger than those of commoners and the large Zulu military settlements of the early nineteenth century had to accommodate thousands of people. This, however, was exceptional. The more common pattern was of relatively small, family-based homesteads dispersed across the landscape, each having access to water, adequate grazing, arable land and other natural resources. The environment of the south-eastern region facilitated this pattern of land-use and settlement. Homesteads were often sited on ridges and oriented eastwards, to face the rising sun. Within the homestead each married woman had her own 'house', comprising sleeping, cooking and storage units. The houses were ranked to the right and left of the central 'great house', which faced the gate of the cattle-byre and was occupied by the headman's mother. The *inkundla*, the area between the great house and the byre, was a meeting place for men. Out of respect for the senior men of the family, young women of the household had to avoid this area and the cattle-byre, as well as the areas within houses that were set aside for men. Excluding wives from the cattle-byre had an important economic implication in that this denied them access to the grain-pits that were located there.

The oldest type of dwelling was a circular, domed, grass-thatched shelter, roughly 3,5 metres in diameter, with a very low doorway and a central hearth. This kind of beehive shelter was similar in shape to the mat-houses of nomadic Khoikhoi herders, but was constructed differently. In the early nineteenth century the beehive shelters started to be replaced by houses with conical thatched roofs and up-right walls. Initially they were made of wattle and daub, and later from sods of turf or mud-bricks. By the end of the century this kind of house known as 'irontawuli' (from *rondawel* in Afrikaans) predominated and more modern rectangular houses had also come into use, especially in areas near mission stations.

Homesteads photographed from the 1950s onwards show a tendency to decorate outer-walls with white-wash, especially around the doorway and as a frieze near the top of the wall. Mural decoration in the south-east of the country did not become elaborated in the way that it did in the Ndebele branch of Nguni-speakers in the Transvaal. This can be explained largely in terms of the particular history of the Ndebele people, who developed their characteristic form of mural painting as a way of expressing their identity at a time of social dislocation. It serves to remind us that seemingly timeless traditions may have relatively recent origins.

Importance of cattle

The central focus of Xhosa and Zulu homesteads was the *isibaya* or cattle enclosure. It was associated not only with cattle but with the authority of the patrilineage, past and present, and the handling of cattle was restricted to men of the lineage. The *isibaya* was the most important spiritual centre in the homestead and, together with the great house, provided the arena for the enactment of all

Mural art

Mural decoration is found throughout the country but Ndebele wall painting has become famous for its vibrancy and colour. During the late nineteenth century the Ndebele people were defeated by the forces of the Transvaal Republic and dispersed to live as labourers on white-owned farms. In these alien surroundings they developed ways of expressing their identity visually. At first only earth colours were used, but as coloured paints became commercially available women started to use these to decorate the facades of their homesteads. The result was both creative and dynamic. Design elements included in mural paintings were drawn from the most prosaic of sources, such as razor-blades, telegraph-poles and light-shades, but they were transformed into remarkable aesthetic compositions that have been justly celebrated by art connoisseurs.

◀ *The Ntwane people of the Transvaal Highveld decorated their villages in a characteristic way, using primarily earth pigments. Although coloured paints have been available for many years, the Ntwane have retained their traditional mural designs and colours. Stones for grinding sorghum and other grains are set into the floor of the verandah, which provides shadow as well during activities.*

◀ *A Ndzundza-Ndebele homestead in Transvaal, showing newly painted exterior walls. The predominantly grey and white colours are characteristic of the Goedgedacht region. The married woman on the left is wearing traditional ornaments: brass rings (idzila), a beaded hoop around her neck and beaded anklets.*

◀ *Mural and doorway in KwaNdebele (Transvaal). From the late 1930s there was a remarkable flowering of Ndebele mural design. Where formerly earth colours had been used to decorate walls, purchased paints and pigments added vibrancy to the colours used by Ndebele mural artists. Far from having its roots in the distant past, modern Ndebele mural design was a response to a situation of dispersal in which their cultural identity was threatened.*

▲ Among the Venda of the northern Transvaal traditional granaries for millet were constructed in such a way that they resembled small huts. Large stones kept the store-houses free from the ground.

Storehouse at a Mpondo homestead in East Transkei. The maize cobs hanging from the rafters are dried and serve as sowing-seed the following year. Dried bundles of sedge will be used for making ▼ baskets.

The capital of Chief Modjadji in the Transvaal Lowveld is a concentrated settlement accommodating some 400 people. Each married woman has her own courtyard defined by low, plastered walls. ▼ Ledges for storage of pots, calabashes and utensils may be built into these walls.

important ancestor rituals. The cattle-byre constituted a direct link with the spirits of former headmen who had been buried there, and it was the place were the ancestors were offered food when an animal had been sacrificed. Cattle used as bride-wealth provided men with the means of extending the family. They were also a means of gaining clientage, they had exchange value and could be used to settle debts or pay fines. In addition, milk constituted a major component of the diet, and oxen were used as draught animals.

Although cattle loomed large in the minds of men, agriculture was the primary source of food, and grain was the essential staple in the diet. In general, women carried most of the agrarian work-load, although since the introduction of the ox-drawn plough in the nineteenth century men have played a greater role in agriculture. Each family had a number of fields, often some distance from the homestead. For heavy tasks such as weeding, harvesting and threshing, work-parties among neighbourhood groups would be arranged, with beer and meat being offered in return for labour. In former times the harvested crops were stored in underground pits situated in the cattle-byre or the *inkundla* but more recently storage huts or purchased grain tanks have been used.

Since the nineteenth century economic self-sufficiency has been jeopardized from a variety of factors. The main threats were the imposition of taxation and a money economy that forced men into the migrant labour system and so removed their labour from the rural economy. Today all households depend on earning money to purchase grain. From the 1950s onwards, government-imposed resettlement schemes have changed the pattern of settlement completely in many parts of the country. However, in response to the threat of resettlement some communities have shown active resistance by adhering to their customary practices and traditional forms of settlement.

Settlement on the Highland Plateaux

Sotho-speaking people of the northern Cape, Transvaal and Botswana tended to live in concentrated villages rather than dispersed individual family homesteads. An early nineteenth century expedition to the Tswana settlement of Dithakong in the northern Cape found some 10,000 to 15,000 people living in over 3,000 houses. At other Tswana centres populations of between 2,000 and 20,000 were recorded. These veritable towns contrast markedly with the dispersed homesteads of Nguni-speakers, and are also considerably larger than Sotho villages in other parts of the country. The size of Tswana settlements has never been fully explained. During the sieges of the nineteenth century, defence would have been a major motivating factor, but trade may also have been the impetus to concentrated settlement. Essential environmental resources were not as evenly distributed as in the south-east, and this too would have encouraged the concentration of habitation near adequate water sources.

Large settlements were composed of numerous family groups. The basic household consisted of a married man with his wives, children and dependants. The living area of each household had a number of dwelling units opening onto a domestic courtyard, which was walled and divided by a lower wall into a front *lapa* and a more private back section. Sotho houses usually had conical thatched roofs and walls constructed using upright poles, lashed together and plastered with mud. The roof often extended beyond the walls to form a verandah around the house. Grain was stored in very large basket-work containers, pottery vessels or in pole and daga granaries

◄ A Ndebele homestead in the Middelburg district (Transvaal). The walls are painted by the women of the household as an expression of their cultural identity. These painted facades are visible from the road and passers-by can easily recognise that Ndebele people are living here.

◄ Ndebele homestead in resettlement area, KwaNdebele (Transvaal). Even in situations of extreme deprivation, Ndebele strive te create a sense order and cultural identity. This house, made from scrap materials, retains traditional elements. The domestic space is clearly defined by a low, painted wall.

◄ Farm labourers in Orange Free State often built their own homes on land allocated to them by their employers. This Sotho homestead shows the simple elegance of an adobe structure in the highveld landscape.

▲ *Chief Sekwati's village on the Transvaal Highveld is a good example of Pedi settlement pattern in which the courtyards of each family are demarcated by high plastered walls. It is interesting to note that unlike Ndebele mural painting that faces outward to the onlooker, Pedi mural patterning faces inwards. The designs are of introspective symbolic significance and relate to the cycle of life.*

▲ *Early morning landscape in Mpondoland (Transkei). The maize crop has been harvested and a span of oxen transports the harvest from the fields to the homestead.*
Xhosa women in Transkei, wearing traditional red-ochred clothing and elegant turbans. Their long tobacco pipes indicate that they have acquired the status of respected married women. The baby is
▼ *probably a grandchild.*

raised off the ground on a small platform. In some cases cattle enclosures were situated within the complex but in larger settlements the herds were kept at outlying cattle-posts. The meeting-place for men, known as the *kgotla*, was the main centre of the village and the court. Each family had an area of arable land, often situated some distance from the settlement.

Centralized authority and concentrated settlement tended to go together. As was the case throughout the country, the settlements of Sotho-speaking people grew from a nucleus of kinsmen. The Tswana groups and their tribal chiefs, however, knew a strict ranking from the rulers downwards through related lineages to recent immigrants, at the lowest level. A system of clientship developed in which men without cattle could tend the herds of a wealthy patron in return for milk and a share in the progeny of the herd. Chiefs controlled access to both arable land and grazing. With the Nguni-speakers this control was localized, while among Sotho-speakers it was more centralized.

Agriculture was of immense economic importance to all Bantu-speaking people but it was of greater cultural significance to those Sotho-speakers living in parts of the country unsuited to cattle-raising. The increased significance of agriculture was reflected in a greater dependence on grain for subsistence needs, in the participation of men in crop-cultivation, in the ritual importance of beer brewed from grain, and in the stress on rain-making and fertility of the land.

Nowhere was the economic domain set apart from the spiritual domain. It was widely believed that the well-being of people, the fertility of the soil, the vigour of the herds and the balance of the seasons were controlled by the ancestral spirits through the chiefs, the closest living links to the ancestors.

Power, kinship and the ancestors

Political hierarchy was inseparable from kinship and, similarly, the ancestor cult was rooted in kin-based relationships. Chiefs were chiefs by descent - the office was kept within the ruling lineage. There were, however, checks on a ruler in the form of his counsellors and in the possibility that dissident subjects might break away. Political power was always reinforced by ritual practices. Moreover, a chief was believed to mediate between the secular and the spiritual realms. The pervasive belief in the power of the ancestors was in itself a symbolic reflection of the kinship structure. Among Nguni-speakers *patrilineal* kin were given particular emphasis, while among Sotho-speakers both *patrilineal* and *matrilateral* kin were given equal status in ancestor rituals.

Marriage patterns

Kinship was expressed through descent or through marriage. The social recognition of these ties provided people with rules of conduct that governed their daily lives, their choice of marriage partners, their residence pattern and their inheritance. Among Nguni-speakers wives were always taken from an unrelated clan, whereas Sotho-speakers preferred marriages between cross-cousins.

Among all Bantu-speakers marriage was legitimized by the transference of cattle from the family of the groom to that of the bride. Marriage was essentially a linking of two families and gifts passed between both groups in recognition of this bond. On marriage a woman moved to live with her husband but she continued to maintain ties with her parental family. By transferring *lobola* (bride-wealth) a man gained legal rights to the children born by his wife. If this did not happen, the woman's

◄ A married Ndebele woman in the Nebo district in Transvaal. She is wearing a traditional, striped blanket edged with beadwork in the colours favoured by he Mahlangu clan in the 1970s. Just visible below the blanket is her beaded apron (ijogolo). She is also wearing the typical Ndebele brass neckrings and beaded hoop.

▲ *Small boy with a toy made of wire in KwaZulu. Throughout rural southern Africa teenage boys make toy vehicles from wire and other scrap materials. A group of friends may work together to accumulate the necessary parts. These ingenious 'wireworks' are usually fitted with a drive shaft and*
▼ *may be seen in action on rough gravel roads.*

father or brother would have these rights. Bride-wealth was not necessarily all paid at one time but a commitment to full payment was made. In the case of cross-cousin marriage the cattle and concomitant rights remained within the kinship group, while in marrying outside the clan, cattle were transferred to an unrelated group. Small stock and iron hoes were also used as bride-wealth, particularly in areas unsuited to cattle-keeping. In addition to giving cattle to his bride's family, a Sotho groom usually had to undertake a period of work for them. In more recent times, money and modern commodities have formed a significant part of marriage contracts.

Polygyny (ie marrying more than one wife) was considered desirable, and having a number of wives was indication of wealth. Chiefs usually had many more wives than commoners, who seldom had more than two or three wives. Women were important in the domestic economy and children increased the size of the group and its potential productivity. Strength in numbers was an important factor in a subsistence economy dependent on domestic labour. *Polygyny* also facilitated the contracting of political marriages with immigrant groups and the building up of loyalties within a chiefdom.

Childhood and initiation into adulthood

The birth of a child consolidated a marriage, and if a woman was unable to bear children the husband could reclaim part of the bride-wealth. Wives were incorporated into their husbands' family to a greater extent after having children. Traditionally children were indulged and they grew up in a secure and caring environment. From an early age children made their own toys and played games that imitated the roles of their parents. Play house-keeping was both recreational and a method of socialization. Young boys hunted birds and small game, and made miniature clay oxen in imitation of the cattle that preoccupied their fathers. In recent decades, vehicles made from wire and other scrap materials have become favourite play-things. Puberty marked the end of childhood and the beginning of adolescence During this time young men and women entered initiation school.

The details of Nguni and Sotho initiation schools varied, but in principle they performed a similar social function, that of a 'rite of passage' marking the transition from adolescence to adulthood. This was much more than a physical change, it was a change in social status. Girls' initiation was often explicitly linked to fertility, and the initiates were given instruction on appropriate sexual behaviour through the medium of songs, riddles and miming. Initiation prepared young women for the social responsibilities of adulthood and, in particular, for marriage.

Boys' initiation rites generally had three stages - separation, transition and reintegration. The first stage involved secluding the initiate from the rest of society and symbolically stripping away his former status. At this stage, Xhosa initiates were circumcised and smeared with white clay, which symbolized their separation from normal life. For the following months, they lived in an isolated lodge controlled by elders who taught them the rules of adult conduct. During this period elaborate costumes were worn for the well-known *abakhwetha* dances which were performed before large audiences in the surrounding districts. A phase that followed by reintegration into society. At the end of the school, the lodge and costumes were set alight. Not looking back at the flames, the *abakhwetha* ran to the river and washed the white clay from their bodies. Thereafter, they were dressed in new blankets and led back to their villages as

men. Since the last century, the Zulu have not practised circumcision but the transition into adulthood was always marked by rituals of separation and reincorporation. Going away to work on the mines has also come to be regarded as a rite of transition to adulthood. Other Nguni-speaking groups who do not circumcise are the Mpondo, Bhaca and Xesibe. Most Sotho-speaking groups maintain the custom, as do the Venda and Tsonga. Even in urban situations the transition to social adulthood is marked by ritual observances. Among those who still practise circumcision, initiation schools remain important although their outward form and timing is usually modified to fit in with an urban environment.
As in many societies throughout the world, Bantu-speaking people mark the important phases in the life cycle - birth, puberty, marriage, parenthood and eventually death - with ritual practices that are directed at affirming and perpetuating the conventional values of society as well as effecting the transition from one phase to another. At such times, when people are considered particularly vulnerable to adverse influences or impurity, spiritual beliefs come to the fore.

▲ *Shepherd boys in Natal. Although the Zulu no longer apply circumcision, the transition from childhood to adulthood is still indicated. When the young men leave their villages to go and work in*
▼ *the cities, this is also considered as a 'rite de passage'.*

A young unmarried Ndebele woman from the Nebo region. She is wearing multiple leg-rings with beads (isigolwane), representing her status. These rings of beads and grass are wrapped around the leg.
▼ *The rings can only be removed by cutting them to pieces.*

▲ *Witchdoctors, fortune-tellers and healers still play an important role in the daily lives of the black*
▼ *African population groups.*

Beliefs and values

A supreme being, or creator, was acknowledged by all Bantu-speakers. This creator figure, however, was regarded as being remote from the concerns of everyday life, and did not form an important focus of religious life. Far more important was the faith in the power of the ancestors to influence the lives of their descendants. The ancestral shades were believed to have a close and immediate involvement with the daily lives of the living - it was in their power to cause misfortune or to prevent it. Thus it was necessary to please the ancestors by making offerings to them, and by observing customary practices in the time-honoured manner. Should the ancestors become displeased it was necessary to appease them with ceremonial offerings.

The displeasure of the shades could be manifested in many different kinds of affliction and misfortune. Most people rejected the idea of chance or impersonal causation of adversity. Bad luck required a further explanation. It was asked, who sent the ill fate, why did it happen, what had been done, or not done, to deserve the affliction. The correct observance of customs and the offering of sacrifices to the ancestors served both to prevent possible misfortune and to restore harmony when there was discord. The ancestors, however, were not the only potential source of adversity, far more malign were witches and sorcerers. In order to counter their interference, it was necessary to consult a diviner or witchdoctor (this term literally means 'to doctor against witches', but is often misused).

Diviners and healers

Certain individuals were believed to have had a special calling by the ancestors to become diviners and healers. Herbalists were specialists who knew how to prepare medicines and cures for specific ailments but a diviner was relied on to diagnose the nature of the disorder. To become proficient in divining techniques, required a long apprenticeship, and divination practices took many forms, among which the throwing of 'bones' is possibly the best known. Once the cause of the disorder was known, suitable corrective measures could be taken. If the evil powers of witchcraft or sorcery had been at work, these malevolent forces had to be neutralized by counter-magic and protective medicines.

Treating a state of disorder was conceptualized as 'cooling' the forces that had caused 'heat' or impurity. Among the Lobedu (Northern Sotho) people 'heat' is believed to affect the fertility of the land, to make protective charms ineffective and to anger the ancestors. In all cases were 'heat' has been generated, the antidote is the application of 'cooling' medicines. For example, should the ancestral spirits be aroused by the 'heat' generated from an abnormal birth or miscarriage, their graves would be sprinkled with 'cooling', purifying medicines.

Among the Transvaal Sotho and Tsonga, a cult of spirit possession known as *malopo* became prevalent in the early twentieth century. It was probably introduced by immigrants from Mozambique and it was mostly adhered to by women. The possessing spirits were not ancestral shades but foreign spirits. By dancing, accompanied by drumming and singing, and wearing red and white cloth to attract the spirits, the possessing agent was appeased. This cult has been likened to a protest movement which gave women considerably more freedom and mobility than they were usually allowed.

Totemism

A way in which Sotho culture differs from that of Nguni-speakers is in the presence of totemism. This is, however, a relatively weak form of totemic association, confined primarily to bearing a praise name, such kwena (crocodile), ndou (elephant) or kolobe (wild-pig). People respect their totem animal but those sharing a totemic name never come together as a group for ritual or any other activities. Totemic association does come into play in the interpretation of divining bones, as certain pieces represent totem animals. It is possible that totemism may have been stronger at some time in the past but that only remnants remain.

◄ *The attributes of a witchdoctor: bones, shells and fetishes.*

Tsonga beliefs

In the nineteenth century Tsonga people (preferred to as Shangaan-Tsonga in the case of those who were subjugated by the Zulu warrior Shoshangane) moved into the eastern Transvaal as refugees from wars and famine in the area later known as Mozambique. Tsonga immigrants eventually settled among Sotho and Venda people and over the years a degree of cultural assimilation took place. Their system of beliefs emphasized the power of the ancestral spirits to influence the lives of their descendants. A distinctively Tsonga custom was to make a shrine to the ancestors in the form of a forked stake near the entrance of a settlement at which the offerings of beer, grain or meat were placed.

Sacred spirits among the Venda

Venda people had a highly developed belief in the spirits that were thought to dwell in sacred places, such as the groves where chiefs were buried or pools that had mythical associations with the origins of life. Foremost among these sanctuaries was Lake Fundudzi which still commands great respect today. Ancestral shrines among the Venda were usually small unobtrusive mounds situated in the domestic courtyard of the sister of the chief. Objects, such as metal spear-heads or glass beads, that had once belonged to the ancestors were used in rituals of propitiation.

Independent African churches

From their beginnings in the early twentieth century, independent African churches have increased in number to over 3,000 separate churches, with a membership of millions. It has been estimated that almost a quarter of the total black population belong to African-controlled independent churches, which fall into two main groups, Ethiopian and Zionist. The Ethiopian churches follow closely the pattern of the mission churches from which they broke away, while the Zionist churches have a revivalist nature and are noted for their healing services, their music and dancing, as well as the colourful apparel of their followers. These churches provide immense support for their congregations, drawing on the universal Christian message but combining it with African values and beliefs.

▲ *Modern 'witchdoctor' in Shakaland (Natal). The borderline between tradition and tourist entertainment is exceptionally vague here.*
▼ *Methodists in their formal, Sunday clothing in the surroundings of Hermanus.*

▲ *All over the world musicians are searching for the roots of their music.*

Traditions in transition

The common thread that has run through this chapter is that traditions are always in transition. From the distant Iron Age past to the present, cultural practices in southern Africa have been continuing and changing in relation to historical circumstances. The past forty years in South Africa have been particularly repressive and destructive but, as we have tried to show, cultural traditions are both resilient and adaptable. Music provides a clear example of this process. In the last decade, the African music of the subcontinent has been embraced by an international fraternity of music-makers, but this influence has been integrated with the essential characteristics of the local sound. Conversely, Western guitars are restrung by local musicians to transform them into African guitars, capable of producing music made to suit an African context. In a similar way, traditions and ideas are reshaped to meet changing aspirations.

The diversity of cultural origins and affiliations in the population of present-day South Africa defies easy generalization. Not only are there different cultural groupings among the descendants of the indigenous inhabitants of the country, but there is also cultural variety among the descendants of the colonial population. This diversity is the product of a long history of social interaction. In the wake of 'apartheid', the growing openness of South African society should make it possible for people to reclaim their traditional cultural affiliations without the former taint of political opportunism, but it is also giving black people greater freedom of choice to pursue an urban way of life.

At risk of having presented an oversimplified picture of African traditions in southern Africa, we conclude with a reminder that experience can never be expressed fully in words and images. It is all too easy to romanticize or exoticize the idea of Africa and in so doing create a myth that prevents deeper understanding. Readers are encouraged to visit South Africa and experience its complexity for themselves.

▼ *Street musician in Johannesburg.*

The art of beadwork

For centuries glass beads have been desired trade items and beads have been worked into a wide range of personal adornments. In recent years Ndebele beadwork has attracted much attention, but beadwork traditions are far more extensive, including regional variations among all the sub-groups of Nguni-speakers, Tsonga-speakers and, to a lesser extent, among Sotho-speakers. Much has been written about the 'language of beads' among Zulu and related groups but, while there is no doubt that beadwork was a form of visual communication, there is uncertainty about precisely what was being expressed. This is because non-verbal communication cannot be simply decoded; it depends on social context, and often communicates at a level that is not expressible in words.

Artistic traditions

In former times a wide range of domestic utensils, tools and other material requirements was produced by local craft-workers. Baskets were made so finely that they could be used as beer-containers; milk-pails and headrests were carved in wood and, where clay was available, pottery flourished. Clothing was made from the hides of domestic livestock and game, while bone, horn and ivory was fashioned into accessories and ornaments. Metal-working, the most necessary technological skill for the provision of tools, was the earliest specialized craft to be displaced by commercial products. Artistry is implicit in many African household objects. It is perhaps most overt in ornaments and other personal objects such as pipes, snuff-boxes, knives, staffs and headrests. Art, in the western sense of making objects solely for contemplation, was not a separate sphere of creative activity, but aesthetic awareness was incorporated in the forms of functional objects, in clothing and ornament, in house-decoration, as well as in dance and ceremonial performances.

▲ Tswana pottery is distinguished by its characteristic profile and its spout that is turned inside out. Skilled craftsmen often produce pottery for sale, such as this potter in West Transvaal.

The women of the Venda population are renowned for their skill in pottery. This woman is painting a beer pitcher with red ochre and graphite before it is baked. The foot of the pitcher, resting on a glazed bowl, is decorated the last. When the paint is dry, the pot is put ▼ in a shallow hole, covered with a layer of wood and then baked.

Zulu baskets. Two plaited mats (izithebe) and a beer basket of rope (iqoma). Traditional baskets of this type are nowadays especially made for sale in order to stimulate the ▼ local economy.

Since olden times the Venda men have produced striking slender baskets (mufharo). The material consisted of thin strips of acacia-wood. Such baskets were used by a married woman as a kind of ▼ tray, in which she offered her husband his meal.

4 THE FASCINATING NORTH

A safari through various enchanting nature reserves, the treasure-houses among the wildlife parks of the world. One imagines oneself to be an explorer while wandering through the canyon the river Blyde has cut in the northern Drakensberg Mountains. Gold-diggers sought, found and lost fortunes. Transvaal and Swaziland, immeasurable regions without coastlines.

Transvaal and the Venda territories in the extreme north, Bophuthatswana in the west and the kingdom of Swaziland along the eastern border, are the main focus points in this chapter. Innumerable animal species still live an unthreatened life in the Kruger National Park and the adjoining reserves in East Transvaal. A journey by old-fashioned steam-train from Pretoria to Graskop is followed by a car-journey through Venda, the 'delightful country'.
Then the route continues through North Transvaal and the eastern region of the Highveld, where from God's Window one has a view across the infinite Lowveld. Via Nelspruit and along deserted gold-fields the kingdom of Swaziland, once the cradle of blacksmiths from prehistoric times, is reached.
South and West Transvaal are traversed and subsequently the Pilanesberg National Park in Bophuthatswana. The surroundings of Lichtenburg, once the site of the largest rush of fortune-hunters for diamonds, are also explored.
The tourist sights of Pretoria, the capital which acquires an ethereal blue hue in spring due to the thousands of blossoming jacaranda trees, and a visit to Johannesburg, the commercial centre of South Africa, conclude this chapter.

Wildlife parks in East Transvaal

The various nature reserves are highlights in the tourist kaleidoscope of South Africa. In East Transvaal the Kruger National Park and the surrounding wildlife parks are captivating destinations.
The first warden of the Kruger National Park, James Stevenson-Hamilton, implemented the decisions which had, among others, been taken by the pater patriae of the Afrikaners: Paul Kruger. In 1898 he signed the proclamation for the foundation of the reserve 'Gouvernement Wildtuin', which was heavily opposed by many farmers and hunters. The reserve comprised the entire region between the rivers Sabie and Crocodile in the Transvaal Lowveld. It was a desolate area, where the tsetse fly (Glossina morsitans) and the malaria mosquito (Anopheles maculipennis) could still roam freely. Especially during the Anglo-Boer War around the turn of the century the Boer, Briton and African hunters shot game as much as they liked. As a result of this neither elephant nor eland lived any more in the north of the Krugerpark at the end of the previous century.
Possibly the greatest threat for wildlife arose in 1896, when the whole of South Africa was smitten with a terrible epidemic of

rinderpest. As early as 1889 the disease had been brought to North Africa by contaminated animals from Asia Minor. From the north the pest epidemic spread at the speed of an ox (at the time a commonly-used draught animal) further south, causing the plague to reach the then-called country of Rhodesia after seven years. During the spring of 1896 the pest afflicted the region of the Sabie Game Reserve, with disastrous results: nearly all kudus, elands and buffaloes died and whole populations of reed bucks, ibexes, divers, water bucks and wart-hogs suffered severe losses too. Strangely enough numerous gnus (wildebeests) and impalas were spared, as if they were immune to this fatal disease. Another striking thing was that there seemed to be a relation between the existence of the tsetse fly and the rinderpest. For when the pest had left the Lowveld, it appeared that the tsetse flies had also completely vanished! Fortunately the adjoining region of Moçambique, at the time a Portuguese colony, was full of game as it was sparsely populated. Still it took until 1905 before the first elephant and eland were spotted by Harry Wolhuter, the ranger of the reserve, near the river Elephant.
A second cousin of Paul Kruger, the Minister of territorial affairs, Piet Grobler, brought definite relief regarding the permanent protection of animal life in the 'wild-garden'. He became convinced of the fact that private cattle-owners in the region had to exchange their territories for plots of land offered to them outside the reserve. Grobler, a voluble orator, made a fiery speech in parliament. He called on his audience, once Paul Kruger's biggest ideals had been realized, to fulfil his wish to establish a national park as well. Thereafter the opposition leader at the time, general Smuts, made an animated plea to protect the miraculous animal and plant-life of South Africa. The foundation of the almost two million hectares large Kruger National Park became a fact. In the course of the years the Krugerpark developed into what is probably the best protected nature reserve in the world, owing to the support of the government and many individual persons.

◄ *Leopards are more treacherous and shrewd than their big cousins, the lions. They sometimes leap upon their prey from a tree and often devour their victim while sitting on a branch, out of the reach of scavengers.*

◄ *The three founders of Kruger National Park. From left to right: Piet Grobler, Paul Kruger and James Stevenson-Hamilton.*

The first game warden

▲ *Harry Wolhuter, the first ranger in Kruger National Park. From: 'Memories of a game-ranger' by Harry C. Wolhuter.*

When, immediately after the end of the Anglo-Boer War, Stevenson-Hamilton was appointed as the first warden of the Sabie Game Reserve, he was looking for a reliable naturalist and game specialist who could assist him as a ranger. He chose the 25-year-old Harry Wolhuter. This man was respected both by the Boer hunters and, because of his knowledge of the language, by the black population groups who lived in and around the game-reserve. Wolhuter was a man who combined a strong character with the desire to lead an adventurous life. He was offered ample chances for this in the first years of the reserve. Involving a lot of risks, actions had to be undertaken against the numerous poachers and animals of prey that threatened to dominate the wildlife park.

Thus he was on patrol near the river Elephant in the late afternoon of one dry day in August 1903 together with some black guards on horseback. Wolhuter and his party wanted to spend the night on the edge of a water-hole, which, however, appeared to have dried up. Thereupon Wolhuter decided to go on to a small river twenty kilometres further on. His companions, hampered in marching pace by a few pack-donkeys, stayed behind. Accompanied by his dog Bull who was trained for lion hunting, he proceeded on his own. While dusk fell, Harry Wolhuter rode through a region that was scorched but where the fire had spared the high grass in some places. Suddenly he heard the sound of leaping animals and two lions jumped at him. As quick as lightning Wolhuter reacted by giving his horse the spurs, but it was already too late. One of the lions jumped upon the horse that pranced and threw off its rider. While the gun slipped out of his hand, the ranger almost fell on top of the second lion, right in front of the horse. Hardly had the ranger hit the ground when the lion brutally seized him by the right shoulder and started dragging him along in the direction of the nearby river.

In contrast to Livingstone, who reported an attack by a lion in his book 'Missionary travels' (1857) but claimed to have

felt nothing when the sharp teeth of the predator perforated his shoulder tissue, Harry Wolhuter suffered unbearable pain. However, he kept his nerve to such an extent, that he remembered carrying a knife on the right side of his belt. With great difficulty he managed to grasp this knife behind his back. While his head was pressed against the manes of the lion, he succeeded in bringing the knife in front of his breast with his left hand. In a desperate backhand movement he then thrust twice with all his might in the region of the lion's heart. The lion roared furiously and then the ranger also thrust into its throat. He hit the artery and felt a stream of blood flowing over him. At that moment the lion released its grip and groaning heavily retreated into the long grass where it soon died. The hide of the lion killed by Wolhuter, with the three holes caused by the thrusts of the knife, and the knife with its fifteen centimetres' long blade now hang in the museum of the visitors' camp Skukuza.

A trip to the Lowveld of East Transvaal

The journey to East Transvaal can be made from Pretoria or Johannesburg by coach, (rented) car or train. However, a train-journey with the Victorian 'Pride of Africa' provides a unique way to travel from the Highveld in Central Transvaal to the Lowveld in the east. In this region, that in former days boasted gold-fields along or in the vicinity of the canyons of the rivers Sabie and Blyde, lie the most splendid wildlife parks of South Africa.

Some years ago the steam-train enthusiast Rohan Vos decided to found the Rovos-Rail company. He invested his capital in four locomotives, dating from the years before the last World War, and in a number of old carriages that he furnished in Victorian style. Today the 'Pride of Africa' travels from Pretoria to Graskop on the river Blyde every Saturday. At the rear of the train are a dining-carriage and an observation-carriage with large panoramic windows offering a view on the constantly changing Transvaal landscape. This steam-train safari forms a climax for train romantics, nature lovers and travellers appreciating comfort. The journey starts around lunchtime and leads past the coal city of Witbank, where about 45 percent of South African coal is dug. After 50 kilometres the train passes Middelburg, a city owing its name to the fact that it lies exactly halfway between Pretoria and Lydenburg, and then Belfast, a station located at a height of 2,025 metres. Further to the east the Transvaal Highveld abruptly ends at Waterval-Boven and subsequently the descent to Nelspruit is set in during the night. This station, which was built on the territory of the Nel family, lies on the bank of a river, denoted in Afrikaans as *spruit*. In the early Sunday morning the train steams on from Nelspruit through a beautiful landscape, while the land is gradually rising. Via Sabie on the river of the same name, flowing up to the very heart of the Krugerpark, the 'Pride of Africa' journeys on to Graskop. The river Sabie owes its name to the Shangaan word 'ulusaba', which means 'the abominable'. Rapacious crocodiles still inhabit the lower course and the same floods occur that have also given the river its dreaded name. During the course of the morning the train arrives at Graskop, named after the farm that once belonged to the famous pioneer Abel Erasmus. The pass of the same name in the north provides access to the fascinating canyons of the river Blyde. In Graskop the travellers alight the 'Pride of Africa' and have the opportunity to pay a visit by bus to a private wildlife reserve. In the afternoon and evening safaris are held with special landrovers, and elephants, lions, giraffes, rhinoceroses, hippopotamuses and antelopes can be observed. The night is spent in a Game Lodge. The following morning another journey through the wilderness is made, after which the guests are taken by bus to the historical gold-town of Pilgrim's Rest. Here Alec Peterson, better known as 'wheelbarrow Alec' because he always transported all his possessions on a wheelbarrow,

▲ *David Livingstone being attacked by a lion (Panthera leo). From: 'Missionary Travels' by David Livingstone.*

Livingstone and the lion

The hopeless situation of ranger Harry Wolhuter was exactly the same as that of explorer David Livingstone in 1843. He shot at a lion that had become a torment for the village population in the extreme north of the present-day Cape Province. Livingstone seriously injured the lion, but was, while reloading his gun, attacked by the predator which grabbed him by the shoulder and shook him to and fro. When Livingstone's black assistant, the teacher Mebalwe, wanted in his turn to aim at the lion, his gun refused twice. Thereupon the beast rushed to Mebalwe and bit his thigh. A second black helper came running and tried to stab the lion with a spear, which also failed as the predator grabbed him by the shoulder. Meanwhile the injuries afflicted to the lion by Livingstone's bullet had become fatal for the animal, because immediately after the attack of the spear-bearer the animal let go and dropped dead.

◄ *Scenery in East Transvaal*

found gold for the first time in 1873. The town, which had become an ants' nest of activity around 1875, derives its name Pilgrim's Rest from the gold-digger William Trafford. After he had discovered gold of a good alloy, he was convinced he had found his El Dorado and with it his so-called pilgrim's rest.

On Monday afternoon the travellers depart again with the 'Pride of Africa' in the direction of Pretoria, where they arrive the following morning. During the train-journey through East Transvaal, overlooking the constantly changing scenery, it is almost possible to follow, in thought, the footsteps of writers like Rudyard Kipling, Rider Haggard and Sir Percy Fitz-Patrick. The latter described the adventures of his loyal bull-terrier Jock in his famous book 'Jock of the Bushveld' that has also been filmed. The travellers experience the kind of landscapes the transport-riders at the end of the nineteenth century had to transverse as well. With wagons drawn by twelve or more oxen they brought goods from Komatipoort in the east, the connection with the old Delagoa Bay on the Indian Ocean, to the gold-diggers in the interior. One can imagine the pioneer Louis Trichardt and his men. One hundred and fifty years ago they managed to travel with their ox-wagons from the interior to Maputo Bay, harassed by malaria which according to them was caused by the spooky 'fever trees'. When the 'Pride of

▲ *The Victorian furnishings of the panorama carriage of the Pride of Africa.*

Africa' climbs the region and makes a sharp turn now and then, heavy black plumes of smoke rise up from the shining Tiffany-locomotive and disperse over the pine trees and eucalyptuses. The atmosphere of the nineteenth century appears to have descended on the travellers.

◄ *The 'Pride of Africa', steaming through East Transvaal, en route from Pretoria to Graskop.*

▲ The spiral horns of the large kudu can reach a length of more than one-and-a-half metres. The females have no horns.

▲ The ibex (Raphicerus campestris) belongs to the family of the dwarf antelopes (Neotraginae) and only reaches a height of 50 centimetres. At danger ibexes often flee into the burrows of earthhogs (Orycteropus afer).
Leopards usually hunt at night. A leopard has a short jaw and strongly developed incisors enabling him to kill his prey in one grasp. A tree-branch forms a safe storing place where the
▼ prey can be devoured in peace and quiet.

On safari

Very early in the morning we climb the elevated back-seats of the landrover together with six other tourists for a safari through Londolozi. Hardly outside the entrance of the camp, two giant kudus (Tragelaphus strepsiceros), adorned with spiral horns, cross the path. Their impressive bodies, on very long legs, have vertical stripes. It is especially these stripes that seem to provide good camouflage against predators. Without any effort kudus can jump over two metres' high fences. While the kudus disappear as shadows between the thorn bushes, the spry figures of a family of wart-hogs loom up. The mother walks in front, her bare tail with a tuft on the end almost straight into the air, serving as a guiding stick for her offspring, following in a long row behind her. The short tripping legs of the pig's body are out of proportion to the enormous snout, from which curved, dangerously long tusks protrude on both sides. Approaching us, the mother suddenly goes back into cover, followed by her comical offspring. In a pool three hippopotamuses (Hippopotamus amphibus) show their round little ears, snorting nostrils and inquiring eyes. A water buck (Kobus defassa) stands on the edge of the small lake, but our attention is drawn to the lonely figure of an old buffalo (Syncerus caffer), standing stock-still with its head down against the alleged cover of a group of thorn trees. The strings of waterplants on his tremendous horns prove that he has been standing in the water. The ranger tells us that the buffalo was attacked by five lionesses the previous evening. 'The buffalo is hurt in its flanks, if you watch carefully you can see the animal has a deep wound on its right side surrounded by traces of a lion's claws. The buffalo has probably saved his life by fleeing into the lake. There is a big chance that he will be attacked by the same group of lionesses again tonight'.

Deeper into the thornbush wilderness, two elephant bulls (Loxodonta africana) are occupied with tearing down heavy branches from big trees. Somewhat later, with joint forces, they even push over a complete tree. A secretary-bird (Sagittarius serpentarius) strides in front of the car on its long legs. Only when we are very close, the more than one-metre-high bird rises on its wide wings. These curious birds walk through the field the entire day and cover distances of about 30 kilometres. Secretary-birds are protected in the whole of South Africa, not in the least because they are excellent snake-repellers.

Yellow termite hills rise all over the savanna landscape. Sometimes these hills have pointed towers of up to one or two metres in height; propped up against trees they can reach a height of four metres. Here and there in the area lies a bleached skeleton or a part of it, one among these the bright white skull of a buffalo. In a shallow dried-up riverbed, a donga, stands a lonely waterbuck, behind it some dozen impalas (Aepycerus mepampus) scatter. They are the beauty queens and kings of the Lowveld: the bucks with their lyre-shaped horns that end in dangerous long daggers, the females with graciously slender heads and their unlikely big outstanding ears. A small ibex (Raphicerus campestris) stands as a statue on the edge of the bumpy path. They are the favourite prey of leopards. For some time the landrover follows a leopard (Panthera pardus) that has not managed to catch a prey for two days on end. In the course of the years the animal-world has grown so accustomed to the landrovers driving about, that they hardly pay any heed to them.

The snow-white skull of a buffalo. Hyenas, jackals, vultures, flesh flies (Sarcophaga haemorrhoidalis) and carrion beetles
▼ (Thanatophilus micans) make sure that little remains of carrion.

▲ *The anti-toothache tree (knobthorn). The bark of this thorn tree is covered with blunt knobs. The Shangaan use these protrusions to cure toothache.*

◄ *In the Londolozi Game Reserve emphasis lies on top quality and comfort for the visitors, as is shown by these fully-laden dinner-tables in the boma of the Tree Camp.*

The Londolozi Game Reserve

The privately owned Londolozi Game Reserve was founded in 1921 by two hunters and naturalists and has, ever since, been managed by the same family, that of Dave and John Varty.

Londolozi, which means 'the guard of everything that lives', belongs to a group of privately owned parks, also including Sabi-Sabi. The guests' quarters in these reserves are luxurious chalets or rustic *rondavels*. In Londolozi these quarters are divided over three camps. The guests have lunch and breakfast on a broad balcony, which seems to hang in the giant ebony trees (Diospyros ebenum). The view across the river Sand, a regular drinking-place for game, is magnificent. Dinner is served in a *boma*, a space surrounded by high thorny branches. The two other camps, Bush Camp and Tree Camp, provide equally comfortable lodgings. Early in the morning the safari-goers are driven around in open landrovers, which can seat eight persons, for more than three hours. They are accompanied by a ranger, who is also the driver and by a tracker. The latter, evocatively referred to as *spoorsnyer* in Afrikaans, has a special seat on the front bumper and usually spots the game first. Just as Sabi-Sabi, Londolozi borders on the Krugerpark. The game is free to roam from the privately owned parks to the Krugerpark and vice versa. Later in the morning the guests can join a walking party in the company of a well-trained and armed Shangaan guide. After lunch and a short rest the last safari starts at four o'clock in the afternoon. With the help of strong search-lights it is sometimes possible to discern several wildlife species from a close distance when darkness falls.

A nightly raid

Shortly after the evening safari has left through the Londolozi Game Reserve, the ranger receives the message via his radiotelephone that the five lionesses, which made a failed attempt to attack the old buffalo the previous night, had gathered on the landing-strip of the nearby airfield. The buffalo has in the meantime also been spotted again, a few kilometres further on in a dry river-bed, close to the pool in which it had managed to save its life the night before. 'The injured buffalo stands in between two other healthy buffaloes. Still we think the lionesses will make another attempt to attack the old one', the ranger says. The landrover gives the lionesses a wide berth and drives to the same spot. The three buffaloes are grazing among the acacia trees. For a moment the search-light illuminates the three colossal bodies that do not pay any attention to the sound of the car and the light.

Meanwhile darkness is almost complete. Now and then the buffaloes move in the bushes at a distance of some twenty metres. And suddenly there is an enormous pandemonium! A fierce cracking in the bushes and an even more furious roaring rings through the night. While the tracker aims his search-lights, the two healthy buffaloes each go in one direction. The old buffalo remains standing in a bowed posture. On its broad black back hangs one of the lionesses that has struck her claws into the flanks of the buffalo and is doggedly working her way forwards. Meanwhile three other yellow shadows swirl around the old buffalo, a fourth one throws itself with all its might against the right shoulder of the buffalo in an attempt to reach the broad neck. The attackers make no sound, but the buffalo roars with an awesomely deep bass sound, while he makes a quick dash with his right hook-shaped horn to the attacker beside him. His heavy body completely revolves in dealing out that severe blow and due to that the yellow devil on its broad back falls to the ground. With incredible speed the buffalo then rumbles past the landrover. Pursued by the lionesses his race comes to an end at about twenty metres behind the car. There the animal is again leapt upon by two of the five lionesses. Again his heavy roaring stiffens the spectators in the open car. The landrover starts moving in order to keep at a distance of the kill, which will probably occur at close range. But it never comes to this! With its head bent down deep the old buffalo storms in the direction of his attackers, which immediately scatter. Then the buffalo breaks through a couple of bushes, en route to the pool that also served as a shelter for him the previous night. There he is, in the water up to his shoulders, while four of his waylayers wait on the bank. The fifth lioness, possibly injured by the buffalo horn, keeps more distance from the gleaming black beast. There it stands stock-still in the beam of the search-light, the unyielding die-hard, for at least twenty minutes, until its starts to move, straight in the direction of his attackers! With his head bent, swaying his pointed horns from left to right, he walks towards the lionesses, which then leave the field and disappear behind a couple of hills.

▲ *The gnu or wildebeest is a much coveted prey for lions and leopards. The leader of the herd keeps watch at a considerable distance from his females.*

▲ *The leopard's prize often hangs in the fork of a tree. Scavengers like white-backed vultures (Gyps africanus), marabous (Leptopilos crumeniferus) and white-necked ravens (Cornus albicollis) will devour the rest of the cadaver.*

The Game Reserve Sabi-Sabi

During a safari in the adjoining Game Reserve Sabi-Sabi it is also possible to observe a number of special animals, such as gnus (Connochaetes taurinus), wart-hogs (Phacochoerus aethiopicus) and lions. Male lions generally become independent after two years and then try to gain the position of leader of a group of lionesses and their cubs. The cubs in the group are always the leader's offspring. As soon as a lion, coming from outside the group, has chased or killed the up to then dominant male, he immediately bites all the cubs present to death. He only accepts his own blood in the cubs living in his territory.

Just like cheetahs, lions are in fact the only animals among predators that sometimes reveal signs of cannibalism. A male lion will, however, never devour a female, but only – often after a fight for domination – a male rival. This was stated by the great naturalist Stevenson-Hamilton in his book 'The low-veld' from 1929, after he had studied the behaviour of lions in the Krugerpark for 27 years. During the first years it proved quite often that, when a hunter had left a shot male lion during the night, this lion had been completely or partially devoured by morning. From tracks it could then be deduced that other male lions had to be considered as the offenders. Lionesses hardly ever eat an animal of the same sex; very rarely they consume a severely injured or already dead lion.

Besides the fascinating fauna a variegated flora can also be enjoyed during the journey through the Sabi-Sabi Game Reserve. Orchids hang down from the forks of several trees; in the humid summer season they bear beautiful large blue and yellow flowers. Sometimes a half-eaten carcass of an impala, left behind by a leopard, can be seen through the branches of a low ebony tree. At a watering place buffaloes often lie at rest. It is advisable not to approach the animals, weighing 700 to 800 kilogrammes, too close because they can become aggressive. Buffaloes are the really dangerous animals in the region, much more dangerous than lions or even elephants. These latter animals do not like a close proximity of curious persons either, especially if they are on foot. Buffaloes however, especially the solitary bulls, are even less to be trusted. 'Keep a distance is really the golden rule in our park', the ranger of Sabi-Sabi says.

▲ *With the African buffalo the horns are directed outwards and not, as with the Asian water-buffaloes, backwards. With the red buffalo (Syncerus caffer nanus) the skin has a light-red colour, the ear-rims* ▼ *have striking fringes.*

◄ *The impressive manes of a lion, which can reach a length of up to 40 centimetres, are in fact extended breast and neck hairs.*

◄ *Lion with slain zebra. Lions play an important role in maintaining the natural balance among the large herds of hoofed animals.*

◄ *Lioness with cub. A litter of lion cubs usually consists of two to three young which are born after a gestation period of more than 100 days. The nest-hair of the cub shows dark-brown patches on the yellowish fur.*

Meeting a giant

During a trip through Sabi-Sabi our landrover crawls up a slope. Around a bend in the sand-path a giraffe (Giraffa cameleopardis peralta) stretches itself to its full height in an attempt to pick the highest leaves of an acacia. Then the road descends and without any warning the landrover stops. The ranger has spotted three elephant bulls slowly coming in the direction of the car. The attention of all passengers is drawn by a large giant with tusks reaching to the ground. The ranger tells us that this elephant, called Mandleve, very rarely ventures outside the growth along the bank of the river. 'Mandleve is 55 years old and the elephant with the biggest tusks in the world. He misses a sizeable bit of his left ear, just like the legendary 'Hapoor' that used to live in Addo Elephant National Park in the Cape Province. Mandleve, 'Hapoor the second', used to be the strongest fighter in this region. Now, however, he is very old, which is very obvious from his sagging body-shape. He is always accompanied by two young males that act as his scouts and protectors', the ranger says. Both males also have sizeable tusks, but they shrink into comparison with the enormous tusks of Mandleve.

The trio seems to be much closer than at the 60 metres' distance where they really are, due to their girth. Suddenly Mandleve turns his mighty body around, stretches out both his ears and raises his trunk between his tusks. Now it seems as if his mighty figure is even a third bigger! One of the young bulls also turns around with wide outstanding ears and raised trunk in the direction of the landrover. Immediately the ranger increases the distance to the elephants and the trio disappears through an opening in the thick growth along the river.

The evening falls. The silhouettes of the acacias (Acacia detinens a.o.) and umbrella thorn trees (Acacia tortilla) stand out sharply against the violet sky. There is not a breath of wind. Stars begin to glitter. Through the radiotelephone the ranger speaks in a kind of secret language with the drivers of two other landrovers, who have spotted hyenas, lions, a leopard, kudus, innumerable antelopes and – in the distance – a herd of elephants in the neighbourhood. Until deep in the night the picture of Mandleve stayed with us. No wonder, we had seen one of the biggest living elephants of the continent.

▲ Hapoor the second. The African elephant distinguishes itself from
▼ its Asian relative by its huge ears.

▲ *The reception-area at the Skukuza visitors' camp in the Krugerpark.*

▲ *Impala buck.*

The Kruger National Park

The headquarters of the Kruger National Park are established in Skukuza. Just like most other camps Skukuza offers a variety of accommodation possibilities. There are modern huts with thatched roofs of various sizes with two to six beds; outside the huts are central washing and showering facilities and toilets. Furthermore some lodgings are equipped with private showers and toilets, a large room with sleeping-accommodation for two or three persons and a narrow veranda. Besides these there are family-cottages with two to six beds and a kitchenette. On the outskirts of the camp are detached bungalows (so-called guests-cottages). In the Krugerpark a well-considered 'population programme' is implemented. This means among other things that certain animal species are being kept to a maximum number in order not to disturb the natural balance. The gamekeepers see to it that there are many impalas (120,000), so that it is also possible for lions – who mainly kill impalas as prey – to live there. The number of elephants kept in the park is around 7500, which is considered a maximum, in order to limit the damage they cause. Within the boundaries of the Krugerpark a maximum of 27,000 buffaloes can graze and their numbers are also kept in check. Finally there is an annual immunization of certain animal species, such as eland-antelopes (Taurotragus oryx) and roan-antelopes (Hippotragus equinus). Only the number of elephants and buffaloes has to be kept within the set limit by means of shooting. The rhinoceros population of about 1,400 is kept in check by selling the superfluous specimens to other nature preservation areas and parks.

Such special circumstances are strengthened by educational officer Van der Merwe of the Krugerpark. The information and education of visitors is a very important task of the rangers. 'It is enough to drive one to desperation, when we see how some visitors – fortunately a minority – totally ignore the regulations. Some even get out of their cars or drive into the wilderness leaving the tracks and they approach dangerous game, such as lions and elephants, far too close. Some tourists even went as far as swimming in rivers that house crocodiles! What we do is informing people, as soon as they enter the park, if necessary we fine them and we expel serious violators'.

Impalas

Before the mating-season male impalas (Aepycerus melampus) often break away from the large herds in which they live together with the females. Severe and lengthy fights take place among the bucks in that period. Sometimes the confrontations are so fierce that many are weakened around the mating-season. During this season the most powerful bucks have their own territories, in conformity with the hierarchy as it has been determined in the fighting season. The strongest bucks occupy the areas with most of the water and the finest grass. The females visit the various territories and are of course attracted by those areas offering the most favourable conditions and, therefore, the strongest bucks. For this reason these bucks have most of the females around them. The weak bucks often do not have a chance to mate at all.

Impala female. ▼

69

The northern zone of the Krugerpark consists of areas of sand-ground and densely overgrown forests with
▼ *rivers. Large herds of buffaloes and elephants live in this region.*

◄ *Cheetah with slain springbok. In the open veld the cheetah can, for*
a short period of time, reach a speed of 120 kilometres per hour in
order to catch its prey.

An extensive organization

The annual shooting of elephants and buffaloes requires an
efficient organization. About four kilometres outside
Skukuza is a factory where the elephants that have been shot
are 'processed' by circa 300 staff members into numerous
products. In fact all parts of the animals (including hairs and
nails) can be processed. The meat of the animals goes to the
local population. In former days individual elephants,
preferably sick or old specimens, were chosen to be shot.
Nowadays every effort is made to shoot complete families in
order to avoid the arousal of lengthy sorrow, fear and
aggression with the remaining animals of a family. Three
helicopters take care of the annual shooting of 400 to 500
elephants. The helicopter flies over a herd, which falls apart
in family groups of about ten to fifteen specimens while
fleeing. On board of the helicopter is the ranger of one of
the 22 sections of the Krugerpark in which the elephants
concerned live. The ranger himself shoots the anaesthetic
arrows at the selected animals. As soon as the elephants are
unconscious on the ground, under the influence of the
anaesthetic scoline, the transport crew arrive. This group
consists of about 30 men, who were already standing by with
a large crane and transport trucks in the neighbourhood.
The numbed animals are subsequently killed with a bullet in
the brain and transported to the factory, where all further
activities take place. For the rangers the shooting is one of
their most difficult tasks, as they know the animals very
well. Only the very young elephants are spared and sold to
other nature reserves. Buffaloes, the number of which had
grown explosively to about 30,000, are also shot annually.
On a site with notably high grass, Van der Merwe explains
that the various animal species each consume a part of the
grass: the top layer is consumed by buffaloes, the less high
grass is cut by zebras (Equus quagga chapmani) with their
sharp teeth, the then following length is grazed by
wildebeests and finally impalas consume the lowest part of
the grasses. With trees it is the same story: the higher leaves
and the bark are stripped by giraffes and elephants, then
buffaloes and nyalas (Tragelaphus angasii) respectively get
their turn and impalas finally nibble at the very low parts.
During Van der Merwe's story a recently killed zebra was
torn to bits by two impressive lions on the left side of the
road, at a distance of about 60 metres. The bigger one now
and then uttered a deep growl, as a warning for the smaller
one not to come too close to the rear part of the zebra, which
he apparently considered as his private share of the booty.
It was clearly audible how the bones of the prey were being
broken into splinters.
The car had hardly driven off again when a cheetah
(Acinonyx jubatus) came within viewing distance. It sat erect
on a termites' mound and produced miaowing and plaintive
sounds. 'Its partner is probably walking further on', van der
Merwe said, 'cheetahs usually hunt in pairs and they are now
communicating. It is quite possible that, as soon as one of
them spots a prey, they will start to attack. At that moment
cheetahs develop a true explosion of power, during which
speeds of up to 120 kilometres per hour can be reached
across a short distance.'

The most hunted animal of Africa

Inadvertently the conversations of tourists with rangers and trackers constantly return to the subject of the captivating life of elephants. The elephant is the most profusely hunted animal on the black continent. A mere 100 years ago ten million elephants roamed through African nature. In 1979 this number had shrunk to about 1,3 million due to the ruthless pursuit for the possession of their tusks. Amply ten years later African poachers had already reduced this number to half a million. If the tempo of slaughtering had continued at the pace set, the African elephant would have become extinct in about 50 years. In Tanzania 130,000 specimens have been killed since 1980, in Zambia circa 115,000 and in Kenya 25,000. This does not merely jeopardize the existence of the elephant in these countries, but also tourism.

At the end of the nineteenth century there were hardly more than 100 elephants roaming about on the savannas of East Transvaal. By means of a conscious conservation policy this number increased from 500 in 1946 to 1,000 1960 and 2,500 in 1965. At that moment the management of the Krugerpark realized that the number of elephants had to be kept within viable limits through a good method of selection. Eventually a growth of up to 7,500 specimens was unimpeded. Until 1963 it remained questionable whether poachers from Moçambique would not strongly afflict the existing number of Kruger elephants. They were prepared to take enormous risks, because ivory had a value of hundreds of U.S. dollars per kilo on the world market. In that same year however, the heavy, also elephant-proof, fence along the border between the Krugerpark and Moçambique was finished. In combination with a well-trained and very alert organization of gamekeepers the poaching in the Krugerpark was almost halted. The past few years the number of elephants has been stable in only four countries, as in South Africa, or has even increased, notably in Zimbabwe, Botswana, Malawi and Namibia. An adult elephant consumes 250 to 350 kilogrammes of leaves and branches daily. Especially by tearing the bark of trees and by pushing over entire trees elephants destroy immeasurably more than would be necessary if they had a more selective diet. For that reason shooting elephants in the Krugerpark had to start in 1966. Together with the selling of tusks of elephants that had died in a natural way, the annual shooting was, up to recently, an important source of income. With this money a part of the nature conservation policy was financed. On the initiative of His Royal Highness Prince Bernhard of the Netherlands the C.I.T.E.S (Convention of International Trade in Endangered Species) decided on a world-wide ban of the ivory-trade. Since that time the price of ivory has decreased to a level that has made the costs and risks of poaching no longer rewarding.

It has proved an effective measure: the elephant population in the world has not gone down these past few years. In some regions, such as Botswana and Moçambique, the growth is even too strong, damaging the interests of local farmers. That is why, recently, there have been strong voices in favour of reducing the elephant herds in those regions. Fortunately there are well-advanced plans to combine the sparsely-populated neighbouring country Moçambique, where more than 50,000 elephants live, with 'Kruger' into one nature conservation area. For its maintenance co-operation will have to be set up between South Africa and Moçambique. One condition will be that the civil war in Moçambique soon has to come to an end. This could mean the realization of the largest nature reserve in the world. That the project is of world-importance also appears from the fact that the independent department of the World Wildlife Fund, the South African Nature Foundation, was involved in the creative process of this plan.

▲ With their agile trunks elephants can grasp fine twigs and young leaves very accurately. However, while foraging, elephants also
▼ cause a lot of unnecessary damage.

▲ *The razor-sharp teeth of a crocodile are firmly rooted in the jawbones. The teeth clasp together in such a way that, even if the snout is closed, the 'eye-tooth' of the lower half of the jaw remains visible.*

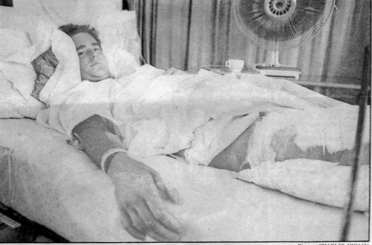

Survi[...] of bat[...] life wi[...]

KIM HELFRICH, Staff Reporter

MR GRAHAM TOSH, [...] had to fight for his life [...] being attacked by a crocodi[...] Lake Kariba, has taken his [...] tentative steps on the road [...] full recovery by attempting [...] put weight on to his badly [...] ten right leg in the H F V [...] woerd Hospital.

Today a hospital spokes[...] described his condition [...] "fair".

"He is expected to have [...] other small operation today [...] his condition is as good as [...] be expected," he said.

Mr Tosh (22) was attac[...] by a crocodile in Lake Kar[...] on the Zambian side last S[...] day while spearfishing and a[...] fighting the massive reptile [...] had to endure intense pain [...] discomfort in three Zamb[...] hospitals before he was airlif[...] to Pretoria.

Speaking from his hosp[...] bed on Saturday he said [...] most frightening moment [...]

Picture: CHARLES HYMAN

I'll make it: determination and fighting spirit have seen Mr Graham Tosh (22) through an ordeal with a crocodile and he is now looking forward to getting fit and back to work.

▲ *Victim of a crocodile. This photograph, printed with the article in the 'Pretoria News' of 14 October 1991 shows Graham Tosh in his hospital-bed, recuperating from the horrible wounds on his thigh.*

Crocodiles can reach an age of more than 100 years; due to over-hunting such old specimens hardly ▼ ever occur.

Treacherous crocodiles

Rangers and trackers walking through the parks must always be on their guard against crocodiles (Crocodylus niloticus). These animals generally lie in the water along the banks of rivers and lakes invisible for other animals and humans. Only their eyes and the top of their long snouts emerge above the surface of the water. Often they also inhabit dense reed-fields. Sometimes crocodiles traverse great distances across land to other regions. Although they usually feed on fish, they now and then try to catch monkeys, antelopes and even bigger mammals such as wildebeests and kudus. When the prey has approached the reptile closely enough, the attack of the crocodile often develops as follows: by a twisting movement of its tail, executed with enormous force, the animal thrusts its body forwards and grasps the prey near the head with its terrible jaws, preferably from a sideways direction. Sometimes the crocodile uses its bony snout as a hammer, to hit its victim against the ground or into the water. Then he pulls the prize under water as quickly as possible, where the victim usually sooner drowns than dies from its injuries. If the catch is too big to pull into the water in one go, the crocodile revolves several times around its own axis, holding its prey jammed into its jaws. There are but few animals and humans that have managed to live through an attack of an adult, or even half-mature crocodile. In the national parks staff members and visitors have also fallen prey to these monsters more than once. Only a number of years ago a ranger of the Krugerpark was attacked by a crocodile. Together with some fellow-rangers and their wives he was out fishing on a site where normally many tiger fishes (Hydracyon lineatus), a favourite sporting-fish, occur. (For that matter, fishing in the rivers of the Krugerpark is only a privilege for gamekeepers). The ranger took a few steps in shallow water along a reed-border when a large crocodile emerged from the water, grasped him by his thigh and immediately started to haul him in the direction of deeper water. One of the ranger's friends, a giant of a man, jumped directly into the water. He threw himself onto the crocodile and lifted it half out of the water in an attempt to pull the animal off his friend. A third man also went into the water and was in his turn grabbed by the crocodile, which had let go of his first victim. At that moment one of the women present jumped into the shallow water and handed the ranger, who was standing free, a long knife. He thrust the knife with force into one of the crocodile's eyes, whereupon the animal ceased its attack and quickly fled to deeper water.

People are still falling victim to crocodiles. Thus the Pretoria News reported on 14 October 1991 how a young man, Graham Tosh, was swimming in Lake Karibu on the border with Zambia. He was trying to shoot fish with a harpoon-gun when he was attacked by a crocodile. Fortunately he managed to escape alive. 'At first I thought', Graham Tosh told, 'that my thigh, which suddenly seemed to be stuck as if in a propeller, was caught by an obstacle under water. I realized a crocodile had got hold of me when it tried to pull me into deeper water. After the animal had felt my resistance, it started to roll up in the water. I lost my harpoon-gun, but managed to thrust the loose harpoon with great force into its neck. The brute then let go of me and I swam back ashore across a distance of six metres'. There friends came to his aid. However, in three different Zambian hospitals they could not treat Tosh, so that he was taken to the H.F.Verwoerd Hospital in Pretoria, where he underwent surgery.

▲ *Red bishops live in swampy regions. After the breeding season they migrate to warmer regions to hibernate.*

South Africa's avifauna

Due to its diversity of climate and vegetation zones South Africa has an unknown wealth of bird species. Bee-eaters (Meropidae) are splendidly coloured birds that love to live in sandy banks but also in open landscape. The scarlet red bee-eater (Merops nubicoidus) often breeds in enormous colonies in the savanna regions. The swallowtail bee-eater (Dicrocerus hirundineus) has a deeply forked tail, in contrast to its relatives that often have strongly elongated middle quills. The red-black grenadier weaver (Euplectes oryx) belongs to the subfamily of the wida-finches (Vinduinae) and can reach a length of more than thirteen centimetres. Some weaverbirds build their ingenious nests in acacia trees and thornbushes, others live among the reeds or low riverbank vegetation. The redbilled weavers (Quela quela) are especially numerous and form a true pest for farmers as they settle in large flocks on the crops in the fields.

Kingfishers (Alcedinidae) have a thick-set body, a short neck and a large head with a long pointed beak. Most of the 84 species have strikingly coloured feathers with bands, spots or dots. Kingfishers hunt, diving for fish and insects, from a fixed lookout along the water. Their nesting cavity is located in steep sandy banks of rivers and creeks. Malachite kingfishers (Corythornis cristata) can, in particular, be found in the swampy regions of Africa. The vegetation consisting of reed (Phragmites) and papyrus (Cyperus papyrus) forms the ideal biotope for this emerald-green bird. The hornbills (Bucerotidae) are striking appearances in the tropical forests and in the bushveld. With their heavy bodies they fly and jump in an agile way in the tree-tops. They usually forage on the ground.

The giant kingfisher (Ceryle maxima) lives along rivers,
▼ *brooks and lagoons.*

The scarlet bee-eaters can reach a length of 34 centimetres. They mainly hunt for insects, such
▼ *as bees, wasps and locusts.*

The beautifully coloured swift-tail bee-eaters nest at the end of tunnels
▼ *that they dig themselves in loam walls and steep sandy banks.*

The yellowbilled hornbill (Tockus flavizostris) belongs to the family of the rhinoceros birds
▼ *(Bucerotidae). The birds live in regions with thorn bushes and in the bushveld.*

▲ *Impalas quench their thirst in a pool. With these gracious antelopes only the buck has 50 to 60 centimetres' long lyre-shaped horns, which are strongly curved outwards.*

A ranger and a tracker ▶ searching for tracks in the game reserve.

▲ *The 'Nasionale Krugerwildtuin' attracts half a million visitors a year.*

A safari through the Kruger National Park

A trip from the south to the north through the 350 kilometres' long Kruger National Park resembles a journey through another world. A wonder-world, where the wilderness reveals a variety of creatures and their natural way of life, which the visitor will find both strange and known. During the journey only a fraction of the 147 species of mammals, 114 species of reptiles and almost 500 species of birds living in the park are seen.

The enormous wildlife park covers different vegetation zones. The southern zone comprises the dense bushveld around Berg-en-Dal and Crocodile Bridge and in the south-west around Pretoriuskop. The middle of the park, the region between Tshokwane and the river Elephant, forms the second zone. This is a somewhat more open savanna area with many marula- and thorn-trees (Parkinsonia africana) and rolling grassy plains. Spread over these plains live herds of gnus and zebras. That is why a strong concentration of lions is found in this zone. Satara Camp and Elephant Camp are the big well-accommodated visitors' camps here. North of Elephant Camp the scenery of the third zone is dominated by the mopane-trees (Colophospermum mopane) with their butterfly-shaped leaves, which close during the warm hours of the day in order to prevent a complete evaporation of the moisture in the leaves. Further to the north the capricious branches of the incredibly thick baobabs (Adansonia digitata) mark the landscape. It seems as if they stand upside down with their roots in the air. Large herds of elephants and buffaloes live in this northern zone, while rare roan-antelopes, sable-antelopes (Hippotragus niger) and eland-antelopes (Taurotragus derbanius) can also be found here.

▲ *Small herd of gnus at a drinking-place. These grass-eaters live in groups and huddle together when they are disturbed. A moving or fleeing herd forms a sensational spectacle.*

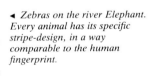

◄ *Zebras on the river Elephant. Every animal has its specific stripe-design, in a way comparable to the human fingerprint.*

◄ *On the 'Elephant Route', running straight through the Krugerpark, one can come across zebras and wildebeests.*

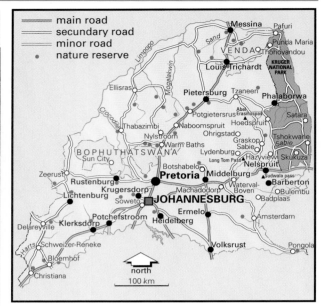

▲ *The inauguration feasts for the BaVenda girls often take several weeks. The python dance or 'domba'*
forms the climax of the initiation ritual.

Straight across Venda

Whoever drives out of the Kruger National Park in a
northerly direction, can leave the park at two places. In
order to drive to the south of Venda to the capital of
Thohoyandou, the R525 is followed at Punda Maria. From
the fossilized footsteps in rock masses at Kokwana it appears
that this region with its pleasant climate was already
inhabited by people in a distant past. Around 1700 the
ancestors of the BaVenda migrated from Zimbabwe across
the river Limpopo. They found their Venda, meaning
'enchanting country', in the region of the Soutpansberg. The
BaVenda have always been very artistic, which appears,
among other things, from remains of very old handmade
pottery. Similar pots are still produced in the same fashion
over grass-fires. Woodwork, wickerwork and woven
materials are also offered for sale in several parts of Venda,
but especially in the trade centre of Ditike near the capital
of Thohoyandou (Elephant's Head).
North of Thohoyandou lie the forests that are sacred for the
BaVenda and where in a distant past the chiefs were buried.
The triangular Lake Fundudzi, the habitat of the python,
symbol of fertility, is just as sacred and may only be visited
with the permission of the local chieftain. North of the sacred
forest lies Mwanedzi National Park, where good lodgings
can be found.
In numerous Venda villages ritual initiation parties are held
for boys and girls who have reached adulthood. For girls
they extend over a period of many months. During that time
they receive sexual education. Besides this they have to
learn the *domba* dance, also called the python-dance. Merely
clad in beautiful skirts made of strings of beads, in front of
which hang aprons woven in an intriguing pattern, and with
bracelets and anklets on their arms and legs the girls stand
in a long row. The big *domba* drums then start droning their
inflammatory rhythm. With their arms around each other's
shoulders the girls form a human row producing snake-like
movements.
In a separate hut, the so-called *murundu*, surrounded by a
wall, the boys experience the circumcision ceremony. After
this the youngsters have to crouch down for a long time
during six successive nights in a cold river, in order to 'rinse'
their childhood away symbolically and to relieve their pains.
The ceremonies end with climbing a long pole that has been
stuck into the ground; once they have reached the top the
young men give free vent to their joy about having reached
adulthood by uttering loud cries.
The second place along which the Krugerpark can be left in
the far north lies near Pafuri, near the river Limpopo that

▲ *Painted houses of the Ndebele in Venda.*
Venda women in special clothing. The artistry of the BaVenda is not only expressed in their weavings,
▼ *but also in their woodcarvings, painting and pottery.*

◄ *The clothes that these women are wearing are characteristic for the Ndebele in Venda.*

▲ *Tea-pickers in the vicinity of the Magoebaskloof. The road between Haenertsburg and Tzaneen meanders past vast plantations.*

▲ *A Tsonga potter in GazanKulu, North-east Transvaal, is surrounded by a group of interested spectators. In the foreground two grain baskets are visible that are characteristic for this region.*
▼ *Shangaan-Tsonga in the surroundings of Tzaneen.*

forms the border with Zimbabwe. The northern Venda region extends south of the river, boasting enormous concentrations of baobabs. The most splendid specimens of these miraculous trees can be found in the Messina Nature Reserve. The R525 forms the connection with Messina, the most northern town of Transvaal, at a distance of sixteen kilometres from Zimbabwe. In this region are very large copper mines.

North Transvaal

A broad motorway, the N1, leads from Messina southwards to Louis Trichardt and further via Pietersburg en Potgietersrus to Pretoria. In former times one took the route across Wyllie's Poort, the spectacular pass across the Soutpansberg, to the south. Today two long tunnels, the Verwoerd Tunnels, go through the mountains. The road, lying south of it, which is as straight as an arrow, takes the traveller to Pietersburg, the commercial centre of North Transvaal. The city owes its name to general Piet Joubert, who stormed the Majuba-hill during the Anglo-Boer War in 1881 and in that way forced a decision in this war. From Pietersburg the road goes on to the agricultural trade and mining centre of Potgietersrus, named after Piet Potgieter, the son of the first Pioneer Andries Hendrik Potgieter. Further to the south, just before the small town of Warmbaths, lies a river which the *Voortrekkers* called the Nile at the time. They thought they had come close to the source of this great river and gave the site the name 'Nylstroom'.

To the land of the rain queen

From Pietersburg the R71 leads the traveller to the most picturesque part of North-east Transvaal, the region around Tzaneen. Due to the subtropical climate this country behind the rough Magoebaskloof (Magoebas Gorge) is a delightful resort during the South African winter months. At the top of the pass lies the Magoebaskloof hotel, form where there is an unequalled view of the gorge and the landscape, covered with pine trees.
South of Tzaneen are vast plantations with all kinds of tropical fruit, such as papayas, mangos and breadfruit. The high eucalyptuses in New Agatha forest still stem from the time of the stage-coach. At the end of the nineteenth century the region was notorious for its mortality among horses, caused by the tsetse fly. That is why it was decided to have the coaches, which maintained the connection between Pietersburg and the gold-digger's town of Leydsdorp, drawn by zebras, as they were immune to the 'flies of death'.
North of Tzaneen lies the village of Duiwelskloof, by the gorge of the same name, in a heavily wooded landscape. Here the jacaranda (Jacaranda bignoniaceae) blooms in spring and in winter there is an abundance of bougainvillaea (Bougainvillaea spectabilis). Near the Duiwelskloof at World's View one has a splendid vista across the miraculous landscape of the rivers Little and Great Lethaba. The foothills of the Drakensberg Mountains here merge into the Strydpoortbergen. North-east of Tzaneen lies the country of the 'rain queens'. They succeeded the first queen, who once lived in Ga-Modjadji and was renowned for her capacity to arouse rainfall.
In the Hans Merensky Nature Reserve in the north-east (70 kilometres east of Tzaneen) the Tsonga Kraal Open-air Museum is located, where one can get acquainted with the way of life of the Tsonga in the nineteenth century. The entire north-eastern plain of Transvaal is called GazanKulu and forms the region where the Shangaan-Tsonga live. In villages that still cling to tradition, women are dressed in colourful attire. In the growing commercial centres people no longer live in huts but in modern houses.

Via the R528 the route continues along the river Great Lethaba to George Valley. During the journey an overwhelming explosion of colours can be enjoyed of the huge bougainvilleas and poinsettias, behind which numerous citrus, banana and mango plantations lie hidden. Gorges cut through the landscape around the large Ebenezer Dam, from where it is possible to return along the Magoebaskloof to Tzaneen.

Along the rivers Ohrigstad, Blyde and Treur

From Tzaneen the R36 leads to the magical Drakensberg Mountains in East Transvaal. From the Lowveld one drives via the J.G. Strydom Tunnel through the mountain range to the first high summits. They who stop before the tunnel and look back once more to the low countryside, can see a really vast outstretching landscape, taking in the meandering river Elephant. Behind the tunnel an almost even spectacular view unfolds across the sometimes 2,000 metres' high mountain region, in which the Abel Erasmus Pass is the highest point. From there one can look across the river Ohrigstad which lies hundreds of metres below. Travelling along the road to the south, following the river, it is clearly visible how the river has cut the mountainous landscape before and behind Ohrigstad. South of Ohrigstad lies Lydenburg (Town of Suffering), given that name by the *Voortrekkers* because they had suffered so many hardships before they arrived there. Sudden floods of the river Ohrigstad and the malaria mosquito in particular caused a lot of victims. The oldest church building of the Dutch Reformed Community in Transvaal is situated in Lydenburg. The local museum is devoted to important archaeological finds and the cultural variety of this region.

From Lydenburg the R37 leads across the famous Long Tom Pass to Sabie in the east. Before reaching that town the road takes a turn to the south in the direction of Nelspruit and then runs parallel with the railway most of the time.

An old Boer dream

Under the leadership of president Burgers the Transvaal Boers decided to make a long cherished dream come true in the 1870s. They wanted to establish a connection from East Transvaal with Lourenço Marques, the present-day Maputo on the Delagoa Bay in the south of Moçambique. With pick-axe and spade the road from Sabie to Lydenburg across the 2150 metres' high Mauchsberg was levelled to such an extent, that the first ox-drawn waggons were able to arrive from Delagoa Bay in 1874. An almost impassable obstacle was formed by that part of the route which was described by the 'transport drivers' as 'die duiwel se kneukels' (the devil's knuckles). This pass across 'the Hogepad', notorious among carriers, acquired a new name in the Anglo-Boer War: the Long Tom Pass.

The Boer trick with the Long Toms

Just before the start of the Anglo-Boer War the governmental leaders of both Boer republics decided to order four 155 millimetre cannons from the arms factory Le Creusot in France. Wen war broke out, 'die Fransmanne', as the Boer called their secret weapons, appeared to have a wider reach than the English cannons. To this they owed their first major victory – at Ladysmith in Natal. The English named their rivals' fearsome weapon 'Long Tom'. They were forced to send for naval guns. Even the heaviest 9.2 inch cannon from the fort at Cape Town's harbour was, installed on a waggon, carried into the interior of Transvaal.

The Britons thought the Boers would barricade themselves in Lydenburg. On arrival it appeared that the Boers, headed by the shrewd general Louis Botha, had in the meantime left the town. From the 2,000 metres' high Mauchsberg they opened fire – with two of their Long Toms – on the British supply column.

▲ *The impressive Abel Erasmus Pass with its height of 1224 metres connects the Lowveld with the plateau of the northern Drakensberg Mountains.*
▼ *With 'seekoeie', hippos are meant.*

▲ *The 'Long Toms' were the Boers' secret weapons in the Anglo-Boer War. These French cannons were also decisive in the battle for the Mauchsberg at Lydenburg in 1900.*

▲ *The reservoir lake at the Blyde River Dam, viewed from World's End.*
Klipspringer in the Drakensberg Mountains. Klipspringers are dwarf antelopes that demarcate their
▼ *territories with a yellow, aromatic fluid from a large eye-gland.*

On 10 September 1900 the Britons decided to set in a strong attack on the Boers in the neighbourhood of Lydenburg. The Boers evaded it by descending the Mauchsberg. 'Now is the moment' the British general thought and he ordered a wild cavalry-attack on the slowly moving ox-waggons and their cannons. The Britons made an outflanking movement over the top of the Mauchsberg in order to attack the Boers in the rear. Botha, however, had the Long Tom, which was riding at the head of the army-train, turned around, so that the long barrel of the cannon pointed over his men in the direction of the horsemen, who came galloping down in a long row from the hill. He waited until they had approached to a distance of 800 metres and only then gave the order to fire, with a disastrous effect on the attackers. Again a prolongation of 'the war that would never end' was achieved.

In 1953, at the opening of the modernised road, a memorial was erected with a replica of the famous cannon. In some places along the route the tracks of the wheels of the 'ossewa', which once literally had to slip down this frightful slope, are still visible. On the slope lies a resting-place called 'coffee height'; another place was called 'elephant's skeleton', after a macabre find from the past.

To the end of the world

Whoever descends the Abel Erasmus Pass from the north and turns left at the crossing with the river Ohrigstad to the R532, has chosen a route going past a number of magnificent view-points in the magical Drakensberg Mountains. It is a rough landscape, with deep canyons and unbridled wild water in places. At the Abel Erasmus Pass the Blyde River Canyon Nature Reserve is soon reached. The river Blyde flows along the southern slopes of the 2,284 metres' high Anderson Mountain north-west of Sabie. The deep canyon becomes more and more impressive as it approaches the cross-roads with the river Ohrigstad in the north. There the river changes into a large lake with long side-streams due to the Blyde River Canyon Dam. At the site, appropriately called World's End, the reservoir can be seen lying deep below. Above the foothills of the Drakensberg Mountains the clouds often form a second mountain ridge, even more impressive than the real mountains. In summer a bolt of lightning now and then flashes through this 'mountain world in the air'. Such views were again and again depicted by the South African painter Pierneef in his famous mountain landscapes.

After a steep descent an area along the river Blyde is reached, where, over a distance of 60 kilometres, a number of important sights are located. A table mountain, here and there partially cloven, rises in the highlands. Where the mountain ends, the rocky boulders, called the three Rondavels, form the transition to blue-tinged abysses. The Lowveld often offers panoramas bathed in sunlight, while above the mountains the sky can be as grey as lead. Almost ten kilometres further to the south the river Blyde joins the river Treur. After a short walk one of the most amazing natural scenes unfolds in front of the spectator, caused by a fundamental process of erosion. Due to the convergence of the two rivers deep pot-holes were cut in the quartzite stone and the river Blyde formed an immense, kilometres' long, gate-way in the rocks.

The riverbanks, rising perpendicularly on both sides, are red, orange and yellow in colour due to the many lichens growing against the walls and due to the iron oxide from the water. At the bottom of one of the potholes Thomas Bourke, a farmer whose land adjoined this site, discovered gold. From then on the site was therefore called Bourke's Luck. In the deep holes hundreds of large trout swim in the crystal-clear water. In the mountain wilderness around Blyde River Canyon baboons (Papio porcarius), leopards, forest swine (Hylochoerus meinertzhageni) and chamoises (Oreotragus oreotragus) live among the heather, ferns and breadfruit trees.

▲ *The Crocodile Valley in East Transvaal by J.H.Pierneef. Paintings by Pierneef often depict cloud masses as extraordinary castles in the sky over the remarkable Drakensberg Mountains. Collection Pierneef Museum, Pretoria.*

The three Rondavels, formed as a result of erosion of a mountain massif. ▼

Pot-holes in the river Blyde, where Thomas Bourke once discovered gold. The deep, cylindrical holes were ground away by the force of the swirling river-water. ▶

Monument in the surroundings of the river Blyde in commemoration
of the journey Andries Potgieter and his followers made from the
▼ Lowveld to the Delagoa Bay in 1844.

The huge 'gate' which the river Blyde has cut in the rocks of the Drakensberg Mountains, forms
an amazing natural phenomenon. The canyon is 26 kilometres long and, at some places, as deep
▼ as 700 metres.

The rivers of sadness and gladness

In 1844 Andries Hendrik Potgieter, together with some
companions, departed on horseback from a camp-site on a
tributary of the river Blyde in search of the Delagoa Bay in
the east. He left a large party of people, among whom many
women and children, at the river. An ultimate date was
agreed on which Potgieter and the other horsemen would
return to this site. However, the arranged date passed and
his followers assumed that their leader had died. They gave
the river along which they camped the name 'Treurrivier'
(River of Sadness) and started on their way back. However,
hardly had they covered some kilometres and reached the
river which the 'Treurrivier' flows into, when they heard
gunshots in the distance. Shortly afterwards Potgieter and
his men joined the *Voortrekkers* group. From that day
onwards the river where they were united again was called
'Blyderivier' (River of Happiness).
Further to the south the R532 leads to two waterfalls, the
Berlin and the Lisbon. A short detour via the R534 directs
the visitor to one of the South African natural wonders:
along the roadside a green inclining hill reaches far into the
sky. Between the grass the grey rocky soil is visible in places.
At the highest point of the slope, at a spot called Wonder
View, the world suddenly ends and caves in straight down.
A thousand metres below an immense woody area unfolds,
cut through by small roads and interchanged by fields in
colours that do not seem to be of this world. Somewhat
further on an even more fascinating panorama appears,
called 'God's Window'. One could imagine that the Creator
wanted to admire his own creation from this spot.
People who want to have a closer look at the forests in the
deep, can drive via Graskop to Hazyview, near the
Krugerpark, and then back to Sabie. Hazyview owes its name
to the curiously hazy views across GazanKulu and the
adjoining Krugerpark area. The next morning Casa del Sol,
with its splendid courtyard and gardens laid out in
mediterranean style, is a good starting point for a beautiful
journey to Sabie.
Just before Sabie the 1675 meters' high Spitskopberg rises
on the left. In 1870 gold was discovered here for the first
time in Transvaal. That year Henry Glynn, a big game
hunter, bought a small farm on the river Sabie. One day he
was target practising at a rock on his land. When he went to
inspect where his bullets had hit the rock, his eye was drawn
to a part of the rock that shone like gold. It appeared that
one of his bullets had scored a direct hit at a gold vein. This
vein on the land of the Grootfontein farm was excavated for
70 years, until it was exhausted.
Sabie itself used to be known as Saba, meaning 'fear' in the
Sotho language. During long-lasting wars between the Sotho
and the Swazi, fierce battles were fought along the river
Sabie. Later the region was feared by the population for the
spirits of the slain that were supposed to house there. The
great painter Thomas Bain, renowned for his romantic
paintings of South African landscapes, once camped on the
banks of the river Sabie and was inspired by this region.

The journey to Nelspruit and Barberton

As a guest of the Sabie Trout club one can spend a pleasant day along the river Sabie near the Lone Creek Waterfall. An unsurpassed stay is offered by the charming Country House, the Pink Tibouchina Lodge. Pink Tibouchina is the name of a giant tree bearing blossom that surpasses the purple-blue bellflowers of the jacaranda. The Lodge is a completely renovated former farm, 27 kilometres south of Graskop, with a strategic location between the old gold-diggers' town of Pilgrim's Rest, the Blyde River Canyon and the Krugerpark.

The road in the direction of Nelspruit leads across the Sudwala Pass to the Sudwala Caves. In prehistoric times human beings already found shelter in these stalactitic caves, where fossils of unicellular plants (Alga collunia) that lived two billion years ago were found. Not far from here lies the Dinosaur Park where life-size specimens of these giant lizards, which populated the earth in the period between the Trias and the Mesozoic, can be seen.

Nelspruit is known for its art gallery housing 70 works of famous South African painters, among which some of Sakkie Eloff. The city also has an impressive botanical garden. The cascades behind Nelspruit form a peculiar waterfall in the river Crocodile, of which the water rather glides from rock to rock than falls down.

The Valley of Death

Past Nelspruit the N4 leads eastwards to the Valley of Death. In former days the transporters and gold-diggers designated that name to the deep valley, just south-west of Kaapmuiden. The valley, now called Cape Valley, was notorious for the presence of malaria mosquitoes. The mosquitoes buzzed around the tents of the adventurers, who rotated their smooth gold pans in small rivers in the 1880s. Here and there in the valley still lies the red-rusted debris of old pans.

In 1883 Auguste Robert, who bore the nickname 'French Bob', was toiling at the bank of a river in a deep gorge, when he saw the promising glittering of gold-dust in his black pan. However, a gold-digger roaming in the vicinity disputed with him about the right to win gold at that spot. He appealed to rights that were supposed to have been granted to him by a queen of the Swazi. A fierce verbal contest between the men was the result, but French Bob kept calm and went to the upper course of the river to search for new luck. A high hill seemed to invite him to inspect the landscape lying behind. Just below the top he saw a glittering, resembling bright white quartz between the grass. It appeared to be the richest gold vein ever found in the world.

▲ *The Nelspruit Art Gallery houses several fascinating paintings by Sakkie Eloff.*
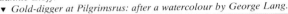
▼ *Gold-digger at Pilgrimsrus: after a watercolour by George Lang.*

The vein was only one metre in width, but extended over a distance of two kilometres. While climbing the hill, which used to be called 'Duivels Kantoor' (Devil's Office), one has a view across the valley. After French Bob's find thousands of gold-diggers from all over the world flocked to this spot, in search of their 'Promised Land'. Some did indeed find a treasure of gold, but for most of them the Valley of Death was merely a valley of sorrow. Later French Bob himself lost the bulk of his fortune too...

The land of 'Jock of the bushveld'

After a visit to the valley the R38 leads the traveller to Barberton, a town where Graham Barber discovered a gold vein in 1884. From the broad wooden verandah of Belhaven House there is a view across the deserted gold fields of bygone days. Barberton soon grew into a town where violence and sin reigned supreme. In 1885 Barberton was extremely popular among the gold-diggers because of the extremely frivolous bar-girl Cockney Liz, who danced on a billiard table every evening and sold her favours by means of a system of bidding to the raging gang of gold-diggers in the bar. After the Anglo-Boer War Barberton was burned down to its foundations. Meanwhile the town has been completely rebuilt and lies hidden beneath pear and jacaranda blossoms in spring. In the centre of the town, right in front of the town hall, stands a statue of the dog Jock, who often walked through the town with his boss Percy Fitzpatrick. The latter often traversed the route between Delagoa Bay and East Transvaal by ox-wagon as a transport-rider together with Jock. The numerous hunting and other kind of adventures that Jock and his boss, often accompanied by the Zulu Jim Makukel, experienced, were described by Fitzpatrick twenty years later. 'Jock of the bushveld' became one of the best read books in South Africa.

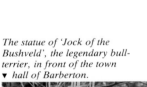
The statue of 'Jock of the Bushveld', the legendary bull-terrier, in front of the town hall of Barberton. ▼

Via Swaziland

The border of the kingdom of Swaziland, which was declared independent by the British government in 1968, lies near Barberton. It is a country full of rich traditions. The biggest ceremonial feast is the *Incwala*, which is celebrated every year at Lobamba during the first new moon. At the beginning of the feast the Swazi boys march 40 kilometres to Egundwini, where they pick branches of the lusekwane-tree. On the second day of the rituals a large *boma* is built with these branches. The next day a black ox is driven inside and slaughtered for the royal family. On the fourth day colourful dances are performed in the *boma*, in which the entire royal party participates. The fifth day is dedicated to meditation. On the sixth day there is a ritual burning of all the king's clothing and the remains of the ox. This marks the end of *Incwala* and heralds the new year.

Most of the organized tours through South Africa go from Pretoria to the Krugerpark, then straight across Swaziland, via the capital of Mbabane to the KwaZulu region in Natal, along the N2 to Durban and finally along the coast to Cape Town.

Barberton is a suitable starting point for an interesting car-journey through northern Swaziland. Via the R40 one first drives to the border at Bulembu. At the stalls on the side of the road, which leads from Piggs Peak along the eastern border of the Malolotja Nature Reserve, creditable stone and wooden carvings are sold. Past small farms of the Swazi and across the rivers Komati and Malante the mining area at Forbes Reef is reached, where the road soon bends in the direction of the capital of Mbabane.

Driving back on the R39 to Transvaal, it is possible to visit the traces of the oldest mine in the world near the border. This so-called Lions' Cave lies close to the modern Ngwenya

iron mine. Evidence has been found that mining activities were executed here as early as 10,000 years ago. Near the mine are a number of antique Sotho huts in the shape of beehives and woven from grass.

From the border post the road rises to the Naudés Plateau, from where one has a wonderful view across the surrounding woodlands. Finally one can drive back along the N40 through the Nelshoogte Forest and via Hilltop Pass to Nelspruit.

Along the river Crocodile

Journeying from Nelspruit parallel to the river Crocodile, a little further than the turning to the Sudwala Caves, one passes Montrose, one of the picturesque waterfalls in East Transvaal. In fact one can speak of a twin-waterfall, which forms a fascinating variation of colour against the decor of the heavily overgrown banks and the awe-inspiring river Crocodile itself. Along the broad current, which flows many kilometres along the right-hand side of the R539, the road leads to the Schoemanskloof and via Skaapwagterspas to the pass on the Chonse Plateau. At about two-thirds of the route between Pretoria and the Krugerpark lies a splendid Protea hotel, offering a beautiful vista across the highlands.

Back to Pretoria

Via the R36 the N4, leading to Pretoria, is reached again. It is in all respects worthwhile to take a left turning in order to visit the old 'Krugerhof', the hotel grounds in Waterval-Onder. Here Paul Kruger spent his last days in South Africa at the end of the Anglo-Boer War, before he left for Europe in desperate search of support for the Boer cause.

One hundred kilometres past Machadodorp the R35 bends in a northerly direction near Middelburg – where the so-

During the New Year's Eve festivities Swazi warriors are dressed most intriguingly. Ritual dances are then ▼ performed.

called Witkerk is a national sight – to a famous missionary station in the valley of the river Klein Olifant.

Botshabelo, which means 'place of protection', is a creation of the reverend Alexander Merensky, who served the Berlin Missionary Society. In 1865 he bought the *plaas* (farm) Boschhoek for the price of 500 Berlin Thalers and founded a missionary post. His house and the church are open to visitors, just as the museum that is devoted to the Ndebele culture. Behind the missionary post lies the Botshabelo Game Reserve, where a large herd of elands roams. The reserve is separated from the missionary post by the ruins of Fort Merensky. The fort was constructed at the time to protect the inhabitants of the missionary post against the warriors of the BaPedi chief Sekhukhuni.

The main point of interest at Botshabelo is, however, the Ndebele village, with striking paintings on the walls of the houses, applied by women. One of those Ndebele women, Ester Mahlangu, became internationally renowned. She depicts her interpretation of the colourful paintings on canvas and with exhibitions of her canvases she has fulfilled the function of ambassador for the Ndebele in South African society for years now.

▲ *Fort Merensky, constructed in 1865 to protect the Botshabele Mission Station against the warriors of BaPedi chief Sekhukhuni.*
▼ *The Elands river waterfall near Machadodorp plunges down into a sea-green valley.*

▲ Women in Botshabelo like to dress themselves in beautifully coloured woven cloth.

▲ The Ndebele are renowned for their remarkable paintings, which are applied by the women on ▼ the walls around their houses.

Through the south of Transvaal

Driving from Middelburg to the south, Ermelo is reached after about 90 kilometres. Here lie the important ruins of the so-called 'kliphutten' (klip = cliff), which were built by members of the extinct Leghoya-Tlokoa tribe. Journeying further southwards along the R36, the Majuba Hill behind Volksrust is reached. On this hill the British forces were beaten by the Boers in the first Anglo-Boer War. The English general lost his life in the battle, which is commemorated by a plaque on top of the mountain.

Via the R39 to Standerton one comes to Heidelberg, in the region baptized by the first *Voortrekkers* as 'Suikerbosrand' (Sugar bush ridge). During the first Anglo-Boer War Heidelberg was the temporary capital of the South African Republic. Here a curious church building was erected in 1890, the so-called Klip church of the Nederduitse Gereformeerde community. During the second Anglo-Boer War many children of Afrikaners had a backlog in education, as at the existing schools lessons were exclusively given in English. That is why in 1903 the reverend A.J. Louw founded a small school for war-orphans in the basement of the Klip church: the first school in Transvaal with Afrikaans as its official language.

Boekenhoutfontein, Paul Kruger's farm near
▼ *Rustenburg.*

▼ *Rough and cut diamonds. The value of the diamonds is determined by the colour, the purity and the weight.*

A car-journey through West Transvaal

Although the most important touristic sights are undoubtedly located in the east and north of Transvaal, West Transvaal also offers sights that are worthwhile visiting. Many of them lie close to Pretoria. Driving on the R27 to the west, the Magalies Mountains soon loom up. In the fertile valley of the river Magalies archaeologists can dig to their hearts' content near the village of Maanhaarrand. This name is derived from the steep slopes of the Magalies Mountains, which at this spot resemble the manes of a lion. In the vicinity of the village remnants of settlements dating from the Iron Age have been found. In a cave in the middle of the 'manes' in the rocks scratches were discovered, which were probably made by human hands during the Stone Age. In his younger years, Paul Kruger often used to go hunting in this neighbourhood. His most beloved hunting camp lay in the shadow of a giant baobab, in the northern part of the Rustenburg district on the bank of the river Crocodile. With a sense of devotion this tree was known over the years as 'oom Paul se boom' (meaning: uncle Paul's tree). Near Rustenburg lies Boekenhoutfontein, Paul Kruger's farm, which is open to visitors.

In the mountain region behind the valley several incidents took place between Boers and Britons during the Anglo-Boer War. After the Boers had climbed over the mountain ridge at Breedt's Nek during the night, they managed, headed by general Smuts, to defeat a British army on 13 December 1900.

Important parts of the region south-west of Rustenburg are characterized by immense maize and sunflower fields. For all that there are some interesting nature reserves in this area, such as the Barberspan, the largest resort for water-birds in Transvaal and the Lichtenburg Nature Reserve. In this reserve they have specialized in breeding rare and endangered animal species. Near the town of Lichtenburg itself lie the grounds that were once the scene of the largest rush for a diamond field in South Africa, after diamonds had been found in the dried up riverbed in 1926. Circa 100,000 fortune hunters burrowed simultaneously in the bottom of the old river and caused an almost impenetrable cloud of dust, which kept hanging there persistently. Today there are still dogged prospectors, who roam about on the spot in search for the much coveted glittering stones.

Potchefstroom, 119 kilometres south-west of Johannesburg, is the seat of the 'Potchefstroom Universiteit vir Christilike Hoër Onderwijs' (Potchefstroom University for Higher Christian Education). The many old buildings are reminiscent of the days when Potchefstroom was the first capital of the Transvaal Republic. The Ethnological Museum is a sight truly worth visiting, as is the old reformed church dating from 1866.

Potchefstroom

Around the white centre of Potchefstroom lies a small mosaic of non-white districts, each with its own administration and provisions. They are four separate small worlds as is obvious from the names of streets and roads, which refer to the origins of the population groups who live there. The 'actual' Potchefstroom is cut through by the inevitable Church Street and for the rest has numerous street-names derived from the iron stock of Afrikaner heroes and saints, such as Potgieter, Pretorius, Joubert, Botha, Kruger, Cilliers and of course Van Riebeeck. The coloured district of Promosa also has some really 'white' names, but they originate from a different source: Abram, Daniel and Samuel, Alabama, Willem Kloppers, MacDonald and also, appropriately: Kleurpoort (Colour Gate). In the Indian district of Mohadin the street-names are reminiscent of India: Omar, Gani, Khan, Hassim, Sooliman.

In the street-names of the black district of Ikageng, the M prevails: Mathambo, Makuku, Mahlubi, Mangope, Mgwe; but: Kgofa, Kgabo and Phuduhutswana, Sepotekele and Sebakwane also occur.

Bophuthatswana and Sun City

Rustenburg lies on the border of one of the six regions of
the so-called independent Bophuthatswana, which are
divided over Transvaal, Orange Free State and the Cape
Province. Since the fifteenth century the majority of the
Tswana population – one-and-a-half million people – have
lived here. Almost three quarters of a million Tswana still
live in Botswana. At one time another part of this population
group migrated to Lesotho and became known there as
Sotho. They speak a related language, however. In the
middle of Bophuthatswana lies Pilanesberg National Park.
When in a distant geological past a giant volcano exploded,
an immense *caldeira* arose in this place. In the funnel-shaped
crater a very successful experiment was executed in order to
re-introduce a quantity of game species within a fenced area.
This 'Operation Genesis' started in 1979. Today the region
houses black and white rhinoceroses (Diseros bicornis and
Ceratotherium simum) from Natal, giraffes and elands from
Namibia, elephants and buffaloes that were transported
from Addo Elephant National Park and finally a growing
number of impalas and springboks. The night can be spent
in several visitors' camps in the park.
Those people who would like to stay in the 'Las Vegas of
South Africa', can pay a visit to Sun City. This big building
complex of hotels, theatres and casinos has been built on the
edge of the Pilanesberg National Park. The proceeds of the
complex goes partially to the treasury of Bophuthatswana.
North of Bophuthatswana, above Thabazimbi, the ridges of
the Water Mountains seem almost to want to reach to the
clouds. They surpass those of the Drakensberg Mountains
in East Transvaal. Above the cliffs and gorges vultures
(Aegypiinae spec.) often circle around. Northwards, 90
kilometres north-west of Potgietersrus, lovers of the
wilderness can choose a sortie for exploratory trips into the
surroundings. From five bushcamps in the Lapalala
Wilderness Game Reserve all kinds of game can be spotted
along lonely tracks, such as white rhinoceroses, and the
horse-antelope (Hippotragus equinus) rare roan-antelopes.
Fast-running rivers also make the blood of sporting
fishermen run faster. Close to Potgietersrus lies the
Doorndraai Irrigation Dam, surrounded by a nature reserve
of 7,000 hectares. Roan- and sable- antelopes, kudus,
wildebeests, leopards, reed bucks and giraffes have found
an ideal biotope here. On the eastern side of the Water
Mountains are warm-water springs in the vicinity of
Naboomspruit. Bird-lovers can spot birds to their hearts'
content in the Nylsvley Nature Reserve, twenty kilometres
south of Naboomspruit, where more than 400 species of birds
have been counted. In fact the traveller has then already
left West Transvaal again and is on his way back to Pretoria.

▲ *Cape vultures (Gyps coprotherus) in the Water Mountains. This bird was common in former days,
but as a result of increasing land cultivation, use of pesticides and consequently a lack of carrion, they
are becoming more and more rare.*

*White rhinos in Pilanesberg National Park. The redbilled oxpecker (Buphagus erythrorhynchus) on the
▼ backs of the rhinos relieve the animals of ticks and insect-larvae.*

*Pretoria lives up to its name as 'garden city', especially in spring, when
the streets and parks are hidden beneath a lilac blanket of
▼ jacaranda blossoms.*

Pretoria

Just like South Africa can be characterized as a 'world in
one country', Pretoria can be characterized as the South
African 'world in one city'. The term 'South African' here
mainly applies to the world of the whites in South Africa.
A major part of the white history is rooted in this
administrative capital of the country, notably from the
moment when the first *Voortrekkers* crossed the river Apies.
The city owes its wide streets to the fact that during
construction it was taken into account that the waggons,
drawn by twelve or more oxen, had to be able to turn in the
streets without any problem. The first buildings arose in the
square in front of the church. Here the oldest building of
Pretoria, the 'Raadsaal' of the old South African Republic,
can be visited. This chamber replaced the first one, a small
grass-covered building with so-called pointed gables and a
lean-to roof. In 1890 the Transvaal Peoples' Council met in
the new establishment, that has a statue of a woman on top

▲ The Church Square in Pretoria. In the centre the statue of Paul Kruger, made by Anton van Wouw. Around the socle four Voortrekkers guard the 'Pater patriae'. In the background the Council Chamber ▼ of Pretoria.

of the bell-tower, as a symbol of freedom. Originally the head of the statue was uncovered. As president Kruger considered this improper, a helmet was placed on the head! On the balcony of this special building Kruger swore the oath as president in 1893, and again in 1898. On this spot the British flag was raised, after Pretoria had surrendered to the Britons in 1900. Subsequently the building became the seat of the British colonial government. After the proclamation of the Independent Union of South Africa in 1910, which was read out on the balcony, the parliament of Transvaal took possession of the chamber.

Also on Church Square stands the renovated Palace of Justice dating from 1898, which was in use as a military hospital during the Anglo-Boer War. In the middle of the square stands the impressive statue of Paul Kruger, designed by Anton van Wouw.

In Church Street one can visit the house of the former president. The ox-waggon, in which his family started out on the Great Trek, the state carriage and the railway waggon in which he made official journeys are on view in the garden. On the front veranda of this house the president received his guests, his tophat always planted straight on his sturdy head. Opposite the house is the reformed church that he visited regularly. Somewhat further on lies the 'Heldeakker', where Kruger was buried next to Andries Pretorius. In the Paul Kruger Street stands the historical town hall with its splendid bell-tower. In front of the building statues of Andries Pretorius and his son Marthinus Wessel, the first president of Transvaal (1857 – 1871) were erected.

In the Victorian Melrose House, with a view of the beautiful Burgerspark, the peace-treaty was signed at the end of the Anglo-Boer War. The stately building belonged to George Heys, a wealthy Transvaal entrepreneur, who endowed the house with the name of the old Melrose Abbey in Scotland. Pretoria boasts a number of interesting museums, such as the Natural History Museum of Transvaal and the Anton van Wouw house, where the sculptor himself lived up to 1945. Here some of his famous sculptures can be admired, amongst them 'Kruger in exile', and the 'Bushmen hunter'. The Pretoria Museum has works on display of famous South African artists such as Frans Oerder, Anton van Wouw and Pierneef. Works of the latter artist, whose scenes of natural beauty often have a 'shock of recognition' effect on the spectator, also hang in the Pierneef Museum.

Near the Voortrekker Monument lie two old fortresses that were constructed in Kruger's day in defence of the city, but were never really used to that purpose. In Fort Skanskop the military history from the time of the *Voortrekkers* up to and including the Anglo-Boer War can be surveyed. Fort Klapperkop sheds light on the numerous events from the time of the Great War.

Just outside the city, in the Wonderboom (Miracle Tree) Nature Reserve, there is a twenty metres' high wild fig-tree which is more than 1,000 years old and extends its branches across a surface of almost half a hectare. From the air-roots, reaching to the ground, new stems sprout again and again. Pretoria lies in a hollow with a depth of a couple of hundred metres in the Transvaal Highlands, more than 1,000 metres above sea-level. This assures the city of a sheltered location. In winter the temperature fluctuates between 6 and 23 degrees Celsius and in summer between 15 and 28 degrees Celsius. According to official figures the number of inhabitants – of which by far the most are white – is more than three quarters of a million. However, outside the city lie large residential quarters of blacks.

The main industrial centres are located near Pretoria. Among them are the largest breweries in the southern hemisphere, an engine-assembly factory and the Yskor steel plants. Forty kilometres east of Pretoria lies the famous Premier diamond mine, where in 1905 the Cullinan diamond of 3,106 carats was found. This renowned gem was added to the British crown jewels, which are kept in the Tower of London.

The Voortrekker Monument

Every country has its myths, originating from important historical events. If one looks at the massive granite Voortrekker Monument on Monumentkoppie just outside Pretoria, the idea of myth-forming also arises. On the outside the sculptures of the *Voortrekkers* heroes have been applied and on the inside – on 27 giant panels along the four walls – the highlights of the Great Trek have been sculptured in marble. The impression that a myth is depicted here, is even more strengthened if one looks up to the highest point in the blue dome of the monument. Every year on 16 December – the day the *Voortrekkers* swore the oath – at twelve o'clock exactly a sunbeam falls through an opening in the vault onto a granite stone deep down in the monument. The words: 'Ons vir jou Suid-Afrika', from the national anthem of the Afrikaners 'Die stem van Suid-Afrika', are hewn in it.

Also due to these visual creations many visitors leave the Voortrekker Monument is left with a deep feeling of awe. In the first place for all those *Voortrekkers*, who were, with untamable willpower, despite innumerable hardships, on their way to their 'Land of Promise', that they eventually did not find after all. Moreover for the architect Gerard Moerdijk and the sculptors Peter Kirchhoff, Frikkie Kruger, Laurika Postma, Hennie Potgieter, Ernst Uilman and Anton van Wouw. The latter also designed the bronze sculptures of the *Voortrekker* woman and her children, standing in front of the monument.

At the corners of the monument are statues of Piet Retief, Andries Pretorius and Hendrik Potgieter. The fourth figure
▼ *represents the 'Unknown Voortrekker leader'.*

The woman-and-child statue in the façade symbolizes civilization and Christianity, which were kept in honour by the women during
▼ *the Great Trek.*

Panels of the frieze

▲ *This panel depicts the women leaving on horseback during the nightly Zulu attack on the laagers at Bloukrans in order to warn the remaining Voortrekkers.*

▲ *As a retaliation for the attack at Bloukrans Hendrik Potgieter and Piet Uys led a punitive expedition against king Dingaan. On 18 April 1838 Uys and his men are lured into an ambush. This panel shows Dirkie Uys trying to protect his father against the Zulu. In vain, both were killed.*

▲ *Voortrekkers-women encourage the depressed men to persevere in their quest for the 'Promised Land'.*

▲ *On 22 November 1838 Andries Pretorius joins the Voortrekkers in Natal. The new leader immediately starts to motivate his followers and reorganizes the Boer army.*

▲ *Gold Reef City, a reconstruction of Johannesburg at the time of the gold rush. The open-air museum houses, among other things, a brewery, a Chinese laundry, a hotel, bars, restaurants and a pharmacy in Victorian style.*

Gold Reef City

A trip through Johannesburg usually ends in the district where the old gold-diggers' town of the 1880s has been brought to life again. Gold Reef City was rebuilt on the site where once the richest gold-mine in the world, the Crown Mine, was active. It is possible to descend to a depth of 225 metres into mine-shaft number 14, which was in use from 1916 to 1977. Deep below the ground the people had to work in cuttings that, at the time, were no higher than 87 centimetres. Outside the mine-entrance groups of black dancers give traditional dance performances daily. During a walk through the streets of Gold Reef City the replicas of several old buildings can be observed. A number of labourers' and supervisors' cottages are reconstructed too. Around the houses grow old eucalyptus trees, which were fortunately saved during the construction of the 'city'.

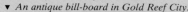

▲ *Performance of the Mine dancers.*
▼ *An antique bill-board in Gold Reef City.*

The main office of the Anglo American Corporation in Johannesburg. In the old conference room in Gold Reef City, at the time furnished under the directions of the founder Sir Ernest Oppenheimer, hangs a survey of the development of the gold-price:
1849:   16 dollars per ounce
1900:   20 dollars per ounce
September 1991: 344 dollars per ounce

Johannesburg, the commercial heart of South Africa

In Johannesburg, the commercial and industrial heart of South Africa, live almost twice as many people as in Pretoria. The population structure however is entirely different. Johannesburg houses more than one million blacks, 500,000 whites, 100,000 coloureds and 50,000 Asians. The wide three-lane road from Pretoria to Johannesburg is, like all main roads in South Africa, in excellent condition. En route to the city high yellow mountains of waste material from the mines are passed. Around Johannesburg are vast industrial areas and workplaces.

Johannesburg is an amazing metropole, surrounded by a number of small nature reserves, such as Harvey, the Wilds, Melville Koppies and Klipriviersberg. In the city itself a beautiful botanical garden can be visited. There are magnificent parks, for a part in and for a part outside the city, among them the 100 hectares' large Delta Park and the Johannesburg Lions Park. In the neighbourhood are splendid lakes, such as lake Florida and lake Victoria.

The city-centre of Johannesburg is dominated by a collection of skyscrapers closely packed together, which are surpassed in height by the 269 metres' high J.G. Strydom Tower. At the top of this building is a rotating restaurant. The skyscrapers are situated on the place where the tent-village of the gold-diggers used to be after the first gold finds had taken place in Witwatersrand in 1886.

Since that time the course of history has also left its traces in this biggest city of the country. Within four years the paltry tent-camp grew into a city with 100,000 inhabitants. At the end of that period tens of thousands of gold-diggers left. For, the deeper the digging had to be, the more impossible it was made by the rock-composition to extract the gold from the ground with the primitive means of

excavation then in use. After changing over to a new gold-winning method, using cyanide, the gold boom could be resumed. In the course of the twentieth century Johannesburg developed into the largest industrial area of South Africa: 70 percent of all industrial products are produced here. In contrast to Pretoria the historical buildings have nearly all disappeared. Looking around in the city-centre, the eye takes in a city mainly constructed of glass, alternated with colossal concrete structures. One of the most spectacular buildings is the main office of the Anglo American Corporation. The building is completely built of blue mirror-glass, divided into 58 facets, just like a diamond. The exorbitant increase in property prices has led numerous companies to settle down in the northern district of Sandton, also boasting a lot of luxurious houses. In the old city-centre only the town hall dating from 1915 and the post office in Rissik Street dating from 1897 are reminiscent of the past. In the city-centre one also passes the modern Carlton Centre, fifty stories high, housing offices, restaurants, shops and even a skating-rink. In the area around Diagonal Street are the stock exchange and the new Indian district Oriental Plaza. The pre-eminent shopping-centre, Hillbrow, with its own African characteristics, lies somewhat to the north of the centre.

Johannesburg has a number of very important museums. In the first place the Africana Museum, which, awaiting new accommodation, is still housed in the public library on the Market Square. The museum possesses a fascinating collection of historical paintings, prints and photographs. Besides this the library houses a geological museum. The Jewish Museum tells the history of the Jewish population group in South Africa. A true museological milestone is the Johannesburg Art Gallery and Sculpture Garden in the Joubert Park. Works of Dutch masters from the seventeenth century hang here among a collection of magnificent English and French paintings from the nineteenth and twentieth centuries. The African Museum in Progress owns an enormous number of ethnological and archaeological objects, pictures of rock paintings and traditional African objects. Finally, a visit can be paid to the highly interesting museum of social anthropology, which is specialized in objects relating to African population groups.

Soweto

In the south-west of Johannesburg lies Soweto, the 'South Western Township'. Soweto consists of a conglomerate of suburbs where in the past the black labourers, despite the homelands policy, gathered in the industrial heart of South Africa. In this respect Soweto does not differ a lot from similar housing areas on the outskirts of big cities in other African countries, in South America and in Asia. This concentration of black population groups in the residential town of Soweto originates from the history of South Africa. At the moment two to three million people inhabit the area. A large part of them lives in decent, albeit small, houses. These houses were especially built around 1970 according to deliberate housing plans of the Administration Board. A growing number of inhabitants, however, lives in all sorts of mixed constructions, called squatters' houses and shanty-towns. There are also luxurious houses, such as those in the districts of Pinville and Duba. Soweto has a large modern hospital with about 3,000 beds, providing work for almost 10,000 staff members; the treatment fees are very low. A number of travel-agencies, such as Welcome Tours, Springbok Atlas or Jimmy's Face to Face Tours, organize bus-trips through Soweto.

The luxurious Blue Train maintains the connection between Johannesburg in Transvaal and Cape Town in ▼ the Cape Province.

5

THE ENDLESS SOUTH-WEST

Portuguese, Dutch and English seafarers who called at the Cape of Good Hope in the course of the centuries, already were impressed by the marvellous and alternating landscapes in their days.
The interior of the Cape Province boasts just as variegated a plant and animal world. This southern tip of the immense African continent was once inhabited by the nomadic Khoisan peoples.

In this chapter several spectacular landscapes are given close attention, both along the 'coast of a thousand faces' around the Cape peninsula, and along the 'coast of the shipwrecks' on the southern Cape. The Garden Route takes in impressive beaches, lakes, forests and mountains. Around 1820 the British colonists hoped to find their 'Promised Land' in the region around the deep Algoa Bay.
In the interior beyond the southern coast the *koppies* landscape of the Little Karoo merges into the Great Karoo, the 'land of thirst'. Behind the legendary diamond city of Kimberley and the thundering Augrabies Falls in the River Orange, thorn trees and extraordinary tuber trees indicate the transition from the Karoo to the semi-desert Kalahari. In the extreme north of the Cape Province lies Kalahari National Gemsbok Park, which abounds with plant and animal species that have adapted to the arid environment. This semi-desert continues right up to the West Cape. Here, in spring, the apparently withered red soil changes like magic into a lush carpet of flowers. The surroundings of Cape Town also take on an ethereal beauty. In autumn the fascinating colours of the wine-regions of the Cape form a striking contrast with the indigo-coloured Franschhoek Mountains and the gigantic dome of the Paarlberg.

The routes between the north-east and the south-west

The connecting routes between the industrial heart of Transvaal and the peninsula of the Cape Province, where Cape Town is located, run straight across the south-western plain of the Transvaal and through the vast prairies of the Karoo. The N1 from Cape Town to Pretoria, which continues north to the border with Zimbabwe, is a very good motorway of about 1,600 kilometres. It connects Johannesburg with Bloemfontein, the capital of Orange Free State and leads via Colesberg and Beaufort West in the Karoo to Cape Town. Another big motorway, the N12, leads from Johannesburg via Potchefstroom along Orange Free State to Kimberley. A little to the north of Beaufort West, at the site where three *dolerite* rocks – the Three Sisters – rise from the plain, this road joins the N1. The main train-connection between Johannesburg and Cape Town also runs almost parallel to the N12 (and from the before-mentioned place parallel with the N1).

◀ *The majestic Table Mountain, symbol of the Cape Province.*

By Blue Train from Johannesburg to Cape Town

The railway between Cape Town and Johannesburg was finished in 1892 and ended in Bulawayo in what was then called Rhodesia. The famous Zambezi-express rode this railway around the turn of the century. In 1923 the blue Union-express, soon referred to as the Blue Train, was introduced on the section Johannesburg-Cape Town. After the Second World War broke out, it was decided to take this train out of service, but from 1946 onwards the by now legendary train has been in regular operation again. In 1972 two entirely new blue trains were built, provided with a special air-bag construction, so that the waggons seem to glide over the rails. The train is drawn by electric locomotives, except during the section between Kimberley and De Aar which is covered during the night. A diesel locomotive then takes over the task of drawing the train. The blue train numbers seventeen carriages, among them a kitchen, a dining carriage and a lounge-car with large panoramic windows offering a view of the interior of South Africa, which is transversed in about 24 hours. In the carriages are various types of compartments, varying from suites to bed-sitters with shower and toilet in the corridor.

▲ *Namaqualand in the north-west of the Cape Province is barren and dry for the main part of the year. After the first spring rains the earth is covered with a carpet of flowers.*

▲ *The Big Hole in Kimberley. The hole has a circumference of 4,572 metres and covers a surface area of eleven hectares.*

The statue of Cecil Rhodes in Kimberley. This son of an English country vicar was the mightiest and ▼ *wealthiest man in South Africa around the turn of the century.*

Kimberley

More than 60 million years ago a strange kind of blue-tinged stone, which had liquified due to enormous heat, welled up to the surface from the very depths of the earth, via volcanic 'chimneys', at the present-day Kimberley. The melted mass, called *kimberlite*, cooled down to a soft stone, with diamonds hidden in it: rock-hard crystallized carbon, formed in the kernel of the earth under an inconceivably high pressure. Every crater pipe nearly always contains several kinds of diamonds. These are sometimes scattered about the pipes, but it does occur that they are located in so-called potholes, where the diamonds lie more or less heaped together.

The first diamond was found by a boy near Hopetown, 128 kilometres south of Kimberley in 1866. The diamond looked like a glittering stone and appeared to be 21 carats (1 carat is 0.2 grammes). The stone was immediately called 'Eureka'. Another diamond was discovered in 1871 on the land of the De Beer brothers and, not much later, a pothole with diamonds was found in a *koppie* on the land, called Colesbergkoppie. Due to the fact that thousands of fortune hunters came flowing in and were granted claims, the gradually increasing Big Hole of Kimberley was formed.

A few years after the first finds the already wide hole, in which individual fortune hunters were using long hoists to get the *kimberlite* from their claims to the surface, resembled a peculiar kind of web with a black ant-heap in the middle. Fifty thousand mine-workers were active there in 1872! Within a short time the enormous hole had been dug to a depth of 400 metres. Finally it appeared that here, as in other places, only substantial mining companies were capable of digging 1,300 metres deep. After the activities were finished more than 25 million tons of *kimberlite* had been moved and from it 14.5 million carats of diamonds had been obtained, which amounted to 2,900 kilogrammes. Today diamond is still won in four 'pipes' in the area around Kimberley. Other diamond mines are located at Jagersfontein and Koffiefontein in Orange Free State.

In the Kimberley Mine Museum, comprising the Big Hole, are replicas of the old church, the saloon, Barnato's Boxing Academy and houses and shops of the former mining village. Besides this the private railway carriages of Cecil Rhodes and other directors of De Beers are on display too, as well as a collection of uncut and cut diamonds, among which the Eureka and the largest uncut diamond in the world of 616 carats. Finally there is an interesting collection of watercolours of the surroundings of the old Kimberley, painted by Philip Bawcombe who was commissioned by Cecil Rhodes.

In the vicinity are also two drive-in saloons, where gold-diggers entered on horseback to drink beer and whisky. The Duggan-Cronin Gallery owns a special collection of ethnological photographs. These were taken before the Second World War and shed light on the way of life of several African population groups. The William Humphrey's Museum houses a precious collection of South African art, besides Dutch, English and French paintings.

The surroundings of Kimberley

At Magersfontein, 30 kilometres south of Kimberley, the English army suffered one of its three defeats in the 'black week' of the Anglo-Boer War. During this war Kimberley was besieged by the Boers for four months. A 28-pounder, the so-called 'Cecil'-cannon is set up as a memorial at Magersfontein. The cannon was designed by an American engineer, who himself, however, was killed at the Grand Hotel by ammunition from one of the Boers' Long Toms.

West of Kimberley is the foothill of the Karoo and begins the endless Kalahari desert. The town of Olifantshoek, about 250 kilometres north-west of the city, is sometimes called the gem of the Kalahari. In the surrounding area one can hear the strange roaring produced by the dunes, built up from the so-called 'howling sand'. The curious sound is caused by friction of the

extremely dry sand-grains from which the hills are formed. This
is the most clearly audible in the southern part of the dunes.
Just north-east of Olifantshoek lies Kuruman, where the
Kuruman rises from a spring in the rocks. The spring, the 'eye
of Kuruman', supplies eighteen million litres of water a day and
is one of the natural wonders of South Africa. At this spot the
Moffat Mission, the 'source of Christianity in Africa', was
located. In 1820 dr Robert Moffat, who had been sent to Africa
by the London Missionary Society, arrived at Kuruman. He
preached to the Tswana, saw to the construction of the Moffat's
Sendingkerk (Missionary Church) and translated the bible into
the Tswana language. Moffat printed the bibles on his own
press. Shortly after the church had been finished, David
Livingstone also arrived in this region. He married Moffat's
daughter in the Sendingkerk and started his renowned
explorations from this region.
Often the missionaries' ideas were contrary to the existing
customs and traditions of the local population, which were based
on ancestor worship and *polygyny*. Not far south of Kuruman
evidence was found revealing that the San people lived in this
region as early as 10,000 years ago. In the 'Wonderwerk' (Miracle
work) Cave numerous rock engravings bear witness of their
presence.

Through the Great Karoo

At night the 'Blou-trein' (Blue train) travels through the vast
flat country south-west of Kimberley, crosses the wide Orange
and arrives at De Aar in the morning. In the early morning light
guenons (Cercopithecus spec.) here and there gaze at the train
dashing by. The traveller is then still only in the north of the
Cape Province, where the Central Karoo has few rivers and
which was rightly called the 'thirstland' by the Khoikhoi. Across
endless plains, which stretch out far into Orange Free State,
millions of antelopes and other hoofed animals have roamed
since time immemorial. When the Boers moved into the Little
and Great Karoo, they gazed in amazement at the infinite
numbers of springboks, (Damaliscus dorcas dorcas), gnus,
zebras, hartebeests and elands, when these animals crossed the
plain during their great migration movements. Herds sometimes
covered many square kilometres. If they were startled by
threatening danger, they went on the rampage in panic, during
which the springboks in particular made their metres' high and
often ten metres' far leaps into the air. It seems difficult to
imagine, yet in the course of the eighteenth and nineteenth
centuries the herds were decimated as a result of incessant
hunting. What was worse was that the wild animals were driven
back by the large numbers of sheep that were brought to the
Karoo and that caused overgrazing. Today attempts are being
made to keep sufficient numbers of the original hoofed animals
alive in the nature reserves.
Close to the spot where the railway starts to run parallel to the
N1 motorway the 'Three Sisters', high *dolerite koppies*, rise up
into the sky in the eroded flat landscape. Further on one of the
many 'blockhouses' can be seen. Such fortifications were erected
at numerous places in South Africa by the British during the
Anglo-Boer War in order to withstand the Boers' guerrilla
attacks.
Near Beaufort West lies Karoo National Park with a unique flora
and a lot of game. The train crosses the River Leeuw and then
Prince Albert Road. More than an hour later the train passes
Matjiesfontein, a village that has been completely restored. The
Victorian Lord Milner hotel is a good example of this. Soon the
train goes through the valley of the River Touw. Beyond the
Hex River Pass the broad Hex River Valley with its vineyards
against the slopes opens up. Along the railway track numerous
arums (Richardia africana) flower in September, the first signs
of spring. In the fields water-mills provide irrigation and
whitewashed houses with Dutch gables lie scattered across the
landscape. The wine-regions around Paarl offer possibilities for
a further exploration by car. As does the immediate vicinity of
Cape Town, the destination of the journey by the 'Blou-trein'.

▲ Surikats (Suricata tetradactyla) sit like small pillars on the plain of the Karoo. Surikats are not shy.
They live in colonies in holes dug by themselves.
Two hundred years ago herds of sprinkboks covered many square kilometres of the Great Karoo.
▼ Overhunting and overgrazing by sheep decimated the springbok population.

▼ The legendary Blue Train speeds on through the wine-regions around Paarl, en route to Cape Town.

Cape Town

No greater difference is conceivable than that between the garden city of Pretoria and Cape Town, a port which has kept its own character throughout the centuries. Cape Town still breathes an atmosphere of former days. This originates from a close tie with the open sea, in fact a tie with two world seas: the Atlantic and the Indian Ocean. There is also a feeling of safety in Cape Town, caused by the location at the foot of a mountain

ridge. This stretches from the Table Mountain to the area near Cape Point where it seems to sink away in the usually choppy ocean. The nostalgic character of Cape Town is also related to the simple houses, pubs and workplaces, which arose around the wooden fortress that was erected by van Riebeeck immediately after his arrival. Ten years later the wooden fortress was extended into a stone castle with five heavy bastions. The cannons were directed towards the bay in order to stop possible intruders.

The cosmopolitan atmosphere of the city is the result of the settlement of different black population groups and of large groups of people from Malay, Indonesia, Madagascar and India in the course of the seventeenth and eighteenth centuries. Moreover remaining groups of Khoikhoi, who had already lost the battle for grazing-land in the beginning of the Boers' migration to the interior, moved to Cape Town. And finally there are the reminders of the arrival of the British, who took their chance to settle permanently here in 1806. This signified the end of 150 years of Dutch supremacy in this outpost of the world. The British introduced a different life-style and adapted themselves to that of the heterogenous population groups already present. All this contributed to the fact that an interwinding of different ways of life can be observed in Cape Town.

A walk through the old city-centre

An exploration of Cape Town, in size the second city of South Africa, usually starts with a car-ride to the top of the Signal Hill. From the hill one has a splendid view across the city in all its glory. The entire coast of the deep Table Bay, with Robben Island at the entrance, unfolds itself. Already in the seventeenth century, when the battle for grazing land between the Dutch colonists and the Khoikhoi constantly flared up, rebellious Khoikhoi were banned to this island. Much later Nelson Mandela would spend the majority of his term of imprisonment there, just as numerous other prominent ANC members. By way of tradition a cannon is fired from the top of the Signal Hill at twelve o'clock daily. Viewed from the sea, the Table Mountain, flanked by the 'Leeukop' (Lion's head) and the 'Duiwelspiek' (Devil's Peak), offers a unique panorama. The contours of both steep peaks and the Table Mountain hemmed in between them, can also be admired from the Blouberg Beach, 25 kilometres north of Cape Town. In 1806 the English expedition army, which ended the power of the Batavian Republic, came ashore here.

A good point of departure for a stroll through the old city is the Tourists' Information Bureau of Captour. The beach was located at this height when Jan van Riebeeck landed on 6 April 1652. Names in the centre of the city like Waterkant (Waterside) and Strandstraat (Beach Street) bear witness to this. Today the statue of van Riebeeck and his wife stands at that particular spot. On the corner of the wide shopping promenade Adderley Street and the Waal Street is the Groote Kerk (Large Church), the mother church of the 'Nederduitse Gereformeerde' (Dutch Reformed) churches in South Africa. The church was consecrated in 1704 and later re-built. Opposite the church is the Cultural History Museum, which is housed in the former slaves' quarters of the V.O.C. Next to the Cultural History Museum one can see the snow-white parliament building. The building adjoins the Tuynhuys, which used to be the house of the state president and now serves as his office block. On the other side of the parliament building lies the South African Library. It possesses at least one copy of every book that has been published in South Africa. Near the library a statue has been erected in honour of the founder of the British empire in South Africa, Cecil Rhodes.

Not far from here is the Kompanjiestuyn (tuyn means garden), the site where the vegetable gardens were laid out at the time of the Dutch settlement. Today it is a botanical garden and promenade park with a special 'scent garden' for the blind. The Jewish Museum, housed in the oldest synagogue of South Africa

The Table Mountain

In the summer months the south-east wind blows humid sea-air across the Table Mountain and ensures that the mountain area does not dehydrate. Due to the fact that this wind full of moisture cools down, the spectacular phenomenon of 'the tablecloth' often arises: a blanket of clouds topping over the mountain during otherwise dry summer weather.

The Table Mountain can be explored in numerous ways. In the first place along various footpaths, which here and there offer breathtaking views. 'Leeukop' (Lion's Head) and 'Duiwelspiek' (Devil's Peak) can also be climbed, although on these mountains, as on the Table Mountain itself, some of the paths are dangerous. On the Table Mountain and on the summits live baboons, ibexes and 'klipdassies' (Procavia capensis).

The highlight of a visit to Cape Town is a trip by cable-railway, called 'sweefspoor' in Afrikaans, to the top of the Table Mountain. The gliding trip in the cabin to a height of 1,087 metres does not even last ten minutes. During fair weather views open up as if out of a fantastic dream: across the city far below, to the north along the foamy edge of the beach and in a southerly direction across the mountainous peninsula. The residential and office districts of Cape Town extend from Bantry Bay, on the western slopes of Leeukop, to beyond Bellville, near Paarl in the east; and from the Blouberg Beach in the north to Muizenberg on the False Bay in the south.

(1862), overlooks the Kompanjiestuyn. The adjoining impressive white synagogue dates from 1905. Opposite these buildings, on a rectangular pedestal, is the statue of Jan Christiaan Smuts, the man who served his country as a general during the Anglo-Boer War, as commander-in-chief in the Great War, as prime minister immediately afterwards, and during the Second World War. A few streets further on the South African Museum, the oldest museum of the country, is located, founded in 1825. The museum has beautiful dioramas about the old San people, an extensive collection of mammals, birds, fish, insects and reptiles and a famous planetarium.

About five million visitors find their way to the Victoria Basin in Table Bay harbour every year. It has grown into an entertainment centre with good hotels and attractive restaurants in old harbour warehouses, a museum and numerous other relaxation possibilities. The old Castle of Good Hope, behind the station, resembles all those other seventeenth century star-shaped pentagonal fortifications. Such fortifications were constructed at many places in the world, which once fell under the influence of the V.O.C., such as the former East Indies and Ceylon. Each stone of this fortress was brought in by V.O.C.ship that called at the Cape. In the seventeenth century the waves of the Table Bay still battered against the castle, where Dutch and later English governors resided. Now a part of the renowned William Fehr watercolour collection is on display there. Another part of this collection hangs in the eighteenth century Cape-Dutch manor Rust en Vreugd (Rest and Peace).

After having left the castle, one overlooks the Grand Parade, formerly used as a military parading ground, nowadays a large fruit-market and parking place. On wednesdays and saturdays there are animated flea-markets here.

In the neighbourhood of the Groote Kerk (Large Church) and the Anglican St George's Cathedral, near the Grote Parade, lies the former city hall. The classicistic building first served as a police station after 1905, but now houses the Michaelis collection of seventeenth century European painting.

In the Strandstraat, behind the station, lies the old dam, at the bottom of the Goue Akker (Golden Field) shopping centre. Wagenaer, van Riebeeck's successor, had it built along the beach that was situated there at the time. There one can take a look at a survey-map on which the outlines of the Table Bay in the seventeenth century are indicated. Behind the grounds of the dam the building of the Standard Bank, dating from 1892, forms a place of interest. The Koopmans de Wet House in the Strandstraat, dating from 1871, is equipped as a museum, with a collection of Cape-Dutch furniture and paintings. Diagonally opposite it, in the Waterkantstraat, the remarkable Lutheran Church rises up. The church has a beautiful pulpit with decorations by the sculptor Anton Anreith. The Martin Melckhuis is the former vicarage. The nearby Greenmarket Square, with its bumpy cobble-stones, its splendid trees and terraces providing a view of houses with Cape-Dutch gables, invites the walker to take a rest.

Somewhat higher against the Signal Hill lies the Malay district, also called Bo-Kaap, hemmed in between the Roos and the Waal Streets. What rests is merely a shadow of the original district, once known as 'Distrik Ses'. From the seventeenth century the descendants of thousands of slaves, who had for the major part been imported from Asia, have lived here. Most of these inhabitants are Muslims, which becomes apparent, among other things, from the mosques in the district. There are also houses that have had a certain amount of Dutch influence, with high steps and plastered walls, often decorated in warm colours. The interesting Bo-Kaap Museum in the Waal Street provides some further insight into the Muslim culture of the city.

Those who want to see the entire development of the Cape re-envisaged on old photographs, after having explored the inner city, can do so in the Cape Archive, near the Kompanjiestuyn.

▲ *The business centre of Cape Town at the foot of the Table Mountain.*
▼ *The South African Museum in Cape Town.*

▼ *A jumble-sale in the Green Market Square.*

The Kirstenbosch National ▶ Botanical Garden, situated on the eastern slope of the Table Mountain.

Groot Constantia, one of ▶ the famous wine-houses in the Cape Province. This oldest vineyard of South Africa was founded by governor Simon van der Stel in 1685. After a devastating fire the splendid mansion was completely restored and today it is a national monument.

The interior of Groot ▶ Constantia. Besides a wine-museum and a bar the estate houses two renowned restaurants.

The Cape peninsula: a paradise of plants and flowers

The 200 kilometres' long journey from Cape Town via Muizenberg and further, mainly along the coastline of the Cape peninsula, probably belongs to the most beautiful touristic routes in the world. At some places – especially along the Chapman's Peak route – one can clearly see the dividing-line between the old granite soil of the mountains and the sandstone layer on top of it, which was formed 50 million years later. During the Ice Ages the sea came and went and a part of the peninsula south of Fish Hoek even became an island.

During an Ice Age some tens of thousands of years ago the entire False Bay stood clear of the water. In those days, on the peninsula and on the virgin grounds from Cape Point to Cape Hanging Cliff in the east of the bay, gigantic Cape horses (Equus caballus) and buffaloes of a similar huge size grazed besides springboks and wildebeests.

Hippopotamuses (Hippopotamus amphibus) inhabited the fresh water streams in the region. Human beings also roamed here, but when the polar ice started to melt and the False Bay again filled with seawater, they withdrew to the higher peninsula. In the middle of the so-called Peers cave two amateur archaeologists, father and son Peers, found a complete human skeleton in 1927, which was considered to be about 15,000 years old. The find was called 'Fish Hoek man'.

From a botanical point of view the entire Cape peninsula belongs to one of the richest regions on earth. Hundreds of species of shrubs and bushes, denoted as *fynbos* (a kind of brushwood) cover the south in particular, where the Cape Good Hope Nature Reserve extends from the Indian Ocean to the Atlantic Ocean and ends at the end of the world: Cape Point.

In spring, in September and October, the flowers on the Cape provide an explosion of colour. The splendour of flowers can be very well observed in the Kirstenbosch National Botanical Garden, just outside the centre of Cape Town located along the major M3-road to Muizenberg. The garden was laid out in 1913 on Cecil Rhodes' old estate, who had legated it to the state in 1902. There is also a memorial on the estate to commemorate this founder of the British empire in Africa.

Not far from here is Groot Constantia, the house, built in 1685, of the Dutch governor at the time Simon van der Stel. He was presented with the estate of 800 hectares in 1683, due to his merits for the V.O.C. Van der Stel had thousands of trees planted and developed vines that yielded the famous Constantia wine.

Seal Island lies before Muizenberg, in False Bay, providing a habitat for at least 50,000 sea-lions (Arctocephalus pusillus) which can be observed from a close range. In summer it is possible to make a boat-trip to the island. Simon's Town, more to the south on the M4 to the Cape of Good Hope, breathes the atmosphere of an old English port. Small wonder, because for more than 140 years the headquarters of the South Atlantic British fleet were located here.

A large part of the Cape of Good Hope Nature Reserve can be reached by car. To the left and right *fynbos* extends, in a landscape that the British explorer Sir Francis Drake called the most beautiful cape in the world. In a comparatively small region to the north, east and south of Cape Town grow 7,300 species of *fynbos*. Five thousand of these species do not occur anywhere else in the world. The marigold (Calendula spec.) with 1,000 species, the iris (Iridaceae spec.) with 600 species and the lily (Leliaceae spec.) with 400 species belong to the largest families of the *fynbos*. The heather family (Erica spec. and Calluna spec.) is represented by 600 species, whereas in the rest of the world only 26 species of this family occur.

The coast of a thousand faces

▲ *The coastal road along Chapman's Peak. The marine sediments are clearly visible.*
▼ *Houses on St James' beach on the False Bay.*

The most southerly point of the Cape sinks abruptly into the swirling streams and foaming waves which assail the land. In the awe-inspiring space above the ocean, which extends southwards over a distance of 5,000 kilometres to Antarctica, numerous vistas open up, due to the constantly alternating capricious shapes and colours of the cloud masses and the sea. This is the territory of the giant albatrosses (Diomeda exulans), Cape stormy petrels (Procellaria aequinoctialis) and the giant stormy petrels (Macronectes giganteus).

To return to Cape Town one can choose between the M4 along the east coast, a meandering road across the peninsula, and the M6 along the west coast. At a height of 150 metres, on top of a perpendicular rocky wall, one drives on the M6 past the almost 600 metres' high Chapman's Peak. The crumbled coastline gradually changing into the beautiful bend of the Hout Bay can justifiably be referred to as 'the coast of a thousand faces'. Here the hard south-westers often caused shipping-disasters in the winter months. Just above the sand at Long Beach, for instance, the remains of the wreck of the Kakapo, which was wrecked in 1900, protrude.

In the past Hout Bay was bordered by vast forests, which have, however, for the majority found their way to the saw-mills. Finally the coastal road leads from Hout Bay to Cape Town along the capriciously shaped rock masses, known as the Twelve Apostles, through which the Table Mountain descends to the ocean.

Saldanha Bay

The coastal road to the north leads along the south-west bulge of the mainland, which starts on the Cape peninsula and ends near Stompneus Point north of Saldanha Bay. Millions of years ago this was the site of the estuary of the River Great Berg, which ran into a lagoon and formed a delta near the present-day Langebaan. Due to an elevation of the mainland the course of the River Berg altered, so that it flowed into St Helena Bay at Velddrif. The sea then came into the delta and caused a five to six metres' deep tidal gully. At that place one of the regions with the richest bird-life of the country developed.

The lagoons behind the row of dunes are the habitat of numerous sea and aquatic birds such as the mute coots (Fulica cristata), black foot penguins (Spheniscus demersus) and fledgling ducks (Anas undulata). Black-backed gulls (Larus dominicanus) and cormorants (Phalagrocorax capensis), but also ibises (Ibis ibis) and large flamingos (Phoenicopterus ruder) fly to and fro in enormous numbers. It was obvious that the region was destined to become a nature reserve, the West Coast National Park. The Panorama Hotel at Langebaan organizes informative boat-trips along the remarkably shaped tidal gully. Parts of this nature reserve are marked with buoys for watersports purposes.

In the hinterland, near Hopefield, skeleton parts of the Saldanha man were discovered, a Neanderthal type of man. Other fossils reveal that this early human being lived among animal species that have in the meantime disappeared from this region, such as sable-tooth tigers (Smilodon), elephants, lions and buffaloes. Some of the finds can be seen at the South African Museum in Cape Town.

The Saldanha water region used to be the site where Dutch and French seal-hunters disputed each other's possession of immense quantities of sealskins. As various islands in the bay were covered with a ten metres' thick layer of bird-dung, thousands of ship-loads of guano have been exported since the middle of the nineteenth century.

▼ *Whiskered tern with offspring in Saldanha Bay.*

Magical Namaqualand

The north-western part of the Cape Province is so dry that the soil makes a crunching sound beneath the feet. The roads cut through barren plains, hills and mountains. The fastest road to Namaqualand is the wide N7, straight across the big 'granary' of South Africa, the Swartland around Malmesbury and Moorreesburg. This latter town houses a museum, where the history of the grain cultivation is depicted.

The entire region is famous for its citrus cultivation. The road along the River Elephant provides lovely views across the water, the citrus plantations and vineyards up to Clanwilliam. In the background the curious rocky formations of the Seder Mountains are visible, which are still regarded as real wilderness. On the Groot Heksrivier Farm in Citrusdal stands an old orange-tree, which is rightly considered to be a natural monument. Citrusdal lies at the foot of the mountain with the same name, in the caves of which one can see primitive rock paintings of the old San people.

West of Citrusdal the Sandveld starts, forming the transition from the fertile region around Cape Town to Namaqualand. To the north the Sandveld changes into the area of the Kalahari, which extends into Namibia.

The Sandveld

The Sandveld, the most southern area of Namaqualand, was, just like the rest of the entire northern region, characterized as 'that dry and merciless land' by Jan van Riebeeck. Indeed, the whole of Namaqualand, deriving its name from the old Khoikhoi people of the Nama, lies in the semi-desert region. However, in spring the ground in these surroundings is hidden beneath an enormous splendour of flowers, which, so to speak, burst open after the first rains have fallen. Between Clanwilliam and Lamberts Bay lies one of these magnificent areas. The drought of winter has impeded the growth of the, in other places, omnipresent *fynbos* and has transformed the earth to sand and gravel. After the spring rains the apparently barren parts of land between all those thorny bushes are, like magic, adorned with millions of wild flowers. The most dominant is often the purple dew-flower (Drosanthemum hispidum), of which more than 100 species occur. They derive their name from the small lumps on the flower-petals, resembling dew-drops. Lemon-yellow 'duikerwortel' (Grielum humifusum) creeps among the blue, red and yellow rockplants, which in their turn overgrow the stony hills. Dark-yellow pigweed (Conicosia pugioniformis) beam forth from the light-yellow hearts of the flowers. The pink 'turkeys' (Gladiolus alatus) often stand in a solitary position between the innumerable white stars of the daisies (Bellis perennis) and the gold tails of the Lebeckia simsiana. In places the red blossoms of the 'geese' (Sutherlandie frutescens) draw the spectator's attention. Near the Clanwilliam dam in the River Elephant a concentration of all these flowers can be discovered. Clanwilliam was founded by Irish colonists, who had been allotted the land by the governor. The doors of several old houses in the town are made of the rare cedarwood. The splendid Dutch Reformed Church and the Anglican Church date from the 1860s, just as the old prison. Clanwilliam is the centre of the region where the famous 'rooibos' is cultivated. The very tasty rooibos tea is made of this plant, which does not contain detrimental tannin and is full of vitamins.

In the Bidouw Valley east of Clanwilliam amazing flower carpets also appear after the first spring rains have fallen. Besides the already mentioned species numerous *vijgies* (Dorothianthus spec.) grow there, as well as buttercups (Ranunculus spec.) and even proteas.

▲ Namaqualand. Bright orange-coloured daisies (Arctotis fastuosa) compete with tall, up-shooting yellow buttercups and blue daisies (Herschelia graminifolia). The penetrating colour effects could have inspired a Van Gogh.

▲ A variegation of flowers at the Clanwilliam Dam in the River Elephant.   The Ramskop Nature Reserve at Clanwilliam. ▼

▲ *Lamberts Bay is famous due to the fact that large colonies of Cape ganders have their nesting-places here.*

Information panel about the
▼ *Cape gannet at Lamberts Bay.*

Greeting ceremonies take place ▶
during the mating season and when
the partner returns to the nest.

Lamberts Bay

Lamberts Bay is especially well-known for its bird-island. This is not really an island, but a protrusion of the land behind the harbour. It is the breeding-ground of a cormorant colony and even far bigger colonies of gannets, seagulls and penguins. Particularly fascinating is the greeting-ceremony of bird-couples that, returning from their search for food at sea, stretch their long necks touchingly in each other's direction and rub them against each other. The Cape gannets (Morus capensis) that nest here migrate across distances of about 3,000 kilometres when they are young. The older birds usually stay in the vicinity of their nocturnal abodes, that is if there is sufficient food available. The River Elephant flows on north of Clanwilliam, along Klawer and Vredendal and discharges into the sea at Papendorp. The whole region along the river is renowned for its excellent wines. Behind Vanrhynsdorp, on the N7, the Knersvlakte (Kners plain) extends. East of it lies an impressive forest of tuber trees (Aloe dichotoma) between Nieuwoudtville and Loeriesfontein. The San marksmen used the fibrous wood as a kind of pin-cushion in which they stuck their arrows.

The Richtersveld

Past Vanrhynsdorp Namaqualand extends further northwards. Close to the River Orange, which forms the border with Namibia, Namaqualand changes into the most recent acquisition of the National Parks Board of South Africa, the Richtersveld, covering 75,000 hectares. The region is so barren that only *succulents*, such as euphorbias, can survive there. These plants are able to store a large quantity of moisture in their fleshy stems and leaves for a considerable time, allowing them to bridge a lengthy period of drought after an occasional shower. The very rare Pachypodium namaquanum, referred to as 'half-human', also grows in the Richtersveld. The plant has a long stem becoming increasingly more conical towards the top, crowned with few leaves. The leaves are always turned in a northerly direction and are shed during the summer months. From a distance it does seem as if human beings are standing in the landscape where these plants grow.

The Copper Mountains ·

The borderline of the spring flower splendour of Namaqualand lies near Springbok, once the region where the Khoisan people lived. In 1685 governor Simon van der Stel decided to head an expedition to the Copper Mountains in this region in order to discover copper. After a 57 days' journey in a carriage, drawn by six horses, from Cape Town to the Copper Mountains, van der Stel found a rich copper vein. Due to a lack of fire-wood the smelting-works could not be kept going. Moreover, it appeared that the distance to the nearest port was too far to exploit the copper mines in this region any further. The old remains of Simon van der Stel's mine are open to the public. In Springbok, Okiep and Nababeep, however, copper is still won.

◀ *The chimney of an old copper mine in the vicinity of Springbok, the capital of Namaqualand. In 1685 governor Van der Stel discovered copper in this region, but it was to take another two centuries before the exploitation of the ore-layers could be started.*

◄ *Pachypodium namaquanum ('half human'). About 50 percent of the vegetation in the Richtersveld is exceptionally rare.*

The vast Richtersveld in the north-west of the Cape Province is characterized by rock formations, sand dunes ▼ and a sparse vegetation.

The baobab

The undisputed king among the trees of South Africa is the baobab or monkey bread tree (Adansonia digitata). The baobab is a semi-*succulent*. During the rains the tree quickly forms foliage. The leaves of this giant tree can be consumed as a vegetable and the bread-shaped fruits are edible too. By roasting the seeds a tasteful coffee is obtained and rope can be made from the wood. A strong glue can be produced from the pollen of the flowers. Finally, the peel of the fruits contain tartaric acid.

The cavities in the trunk provide excellent nesting possibilities for all kinds of birds such as rollers (Coraciidae) and rhinoceros birds (Bucerotidae). The top branches form a lookout for large birds of prey such as hawks (Accipitrinae) and eagles (Buteonidae).

The life-span of a baobab amounts to circa 1,000 years. A strange thing is that when the baobab has reached its age-limit, the tree suddenly literally falls apart and the remains decompose to dust in a very short time.

The place of thundering din

Two hundred kilometres north-east of Springbok are the Augrabies Falls, the surrounding area of which has been declared a national park. The park has a varied plant and animal life. Here one can find, among others, 'tuber trees', the wild olive tree (Olea africana) and the Karoo 'Boerenboon' (Scotia afra angustifolia). The fauna consists of, for instance, black rhinoceroses, elands, baboons and klipspringers. The Augrabies Falls National Park can be reached both from Springbok in the west and from Upington, 120 kilometres more to the east. However, the most obvious way to travel to this distant region is by plane, for example by taking the 'Suid Afrikaanse Lugdiens' (SAL).

The multi-coloured high granite wall, where the water-masses of the River Orange plunge 60 metres down at several places, undoubtedly belongs to the most spectacular waterfalls in the world. The thundering violence with which the water crashes down was why the oldest inhabitants of this region, the Khoisan, called the waterfall 'Aukurebis' (place of thundering din). It is asserted that at the bottom of the 100 metres' deep pool lies a treasure of diamonds, which have been supposedly transported via the River Orange in the course of the centuries.

Several viewpoints offer a panorama across the fifteen kilometres' long gorge. High fences have been installed as a security measure. Yet there are always people who climb across the barrier in order to get an even better look at the horrifying abysses. Up to this day as many as twenty people have lost their lives due to such daredevilry. On both sides of the gorge a very barren landscape extends. To the north this gradually changes into the Kalahari desert.

▼ *Augrabies Falls, the 'place of a thundering din'. Here the River Orange plunges to a depth of 56 metres into a twenty metres' wide gorge.*

The Kalahari Gemsbok National Park

Although seas of dune-sand can be found in the Kalahari, just as in Namibia and Namaqualand, still this enormous area is not a real desert but a savanna, covered with grasses from which numerous thorn trees, especially acacias, emerge. That is why the San called the region 'Kgalagadi', meaning wilderness. North of Upington, where the Cape Province borders on Namibia and Botswana, lies the 'Nasionale Gemsbokwildtuin' (Gemsbok National Park). This largest wildlife park in the world covers one million hectares and extends, in effect, well across the border with Botswana. The most significant of the three overnight stopping-off places lies at Two Rivers, in the southern corner of the park.

Two rivers, the Nossob and the Auob, flow through the park, but they often dry up. Dozens of wells provide sufficient water. The hundreds of lions, leopards and cheetahs inhabiting the park prove that the region also houses immense numbers of hoofed animals. More than 10,000 springboks, but also thousands of elands, wildebeests, kudus and gnus roam the area, besides the numerous gemsbucks from which the park derives its name. The hoofed animals in the Kalahari Gemsbok National Park hardly need any rainwater during the lengthy periods of drought. For in that period they extract moisture from the ever-present tsama-melons and wild cucumbers (both of the Cucurbitaceae family). Only elephants, giraffes and zebras have failed to adapt to the circumstances in the region.

▲ *The huge nest of a colony of sociable weavers (Philetairus socius). Such nests are used for years on end by successive generations of birds.*

▲ *A San rock painting depicting a buffalo hunt.*

San descendants

Very few people live in the vast eastern regions of the Kalahari. About 10,000 of them are descendants of the legendary San. They trek through the wilderness, which forms a refuge for them and where they can still maintain their Late Stone Age culture. During the hunt the men use bows and poisonous arrows, the women search insects, roots and especially the unsurpassed melons. In chapter three it was already pointed out that the San people inhabited large parts of Africa before the arrival of the black and the white population groups.

▲ *Springboks (top) and gemsboks (below) in Kalahari National Gemsbok Park.* ▼

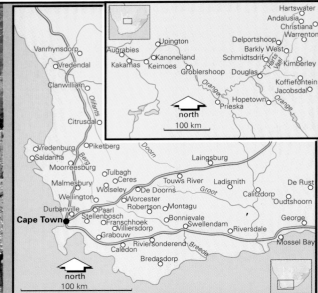

▲ *Wine-farm in the western Cape Province.*

The Cape Wine-lands

Several travel agencies arrange day-trips to the wine-regions. The good roads, however, make the West Cape region an ideal place to tour for a couple of days by (rented) car. Just like the well-known wine-castles along the French 'route du vin' and the German 'Weinstraßen', many famous estates provide the opportunity to get acquainted with the entire wine-producing process and to taste several wines. Various wine-houses also have good restaurants in combination with their companies. Famous restaurants are Buitenverwachting in the Cape Town suburb of Constantia and Boschendal in Franschhoek.

Along the Cape wine-routes are numerous other ideal places to stay. The wine-farms and their cellars usually have a construction of heavy whitewashed walls and are decorated with Cape-Dutch fronts. There is no lack of Victorian and Georgian architecture either. Many buildings have beautiful yellow wooden floors and roof beams. The interior consists of furniture of gleaming brown stink wood and the lighter yellow wood. In the well-kept gardens one can often have lunch under old oaks in summer-houses covered by vine-tendrils. Apart from the already mentioned production centres, the famous wineregions are located around Paarl, Stellenbosch, Durbanville, Tulbagh and in the Swartland. In the valley of the River Breed Worcester, Robertson and Swellendam are also well-known wine-districts. Finally several smaller wine-estates are located in the centre of the Cape Province, in the region of the River Orange.

The South African wine-regions have been respected in wine circles for years. At international exhibitions and wine-samplings, the South African wines regularly win the highest awards. In 1991, for example, in London the Simonsig Chardonnay 1989 was elected as the best white wine and the Cabernet Sauvignon 1986 carried of the palm as the best red wine. The wines of the Nederburg house have also won many gold medals in the course of the years. The best-known and appreciated wines on the international market are: Boschendal, Simonsig, Nederburg, Meerlust, Westhof, Bellingham de Laborie, Rustenberg, Buitenverwachting and Klein Constantia.

▼ *The Wine Museum in Stellenbosch.*

The Cape wine-regions

Whoever has visited the Cape Province, can, on returning, leave the N7 for a journey through Namaqualand past Citrusdal and drive straight to the Cape wine-regions via Tulbagh. The first part of the route leads through the 'granary' of South Africa, between Porterville and Gouda. Past Gouda the road twists through the Nuwekloof Pass to the town of Tulbagh, a wonder of restoration.

Tulbagh was called Tulpies Dorp (Tulip Village) when it was founded in the middle of the eighteenth century. The name was derived from the wild tulips then growing in the surroundings. Later the village was named after Ryk Tulbagh, one of the governors of the eighteenth century. After the earthquake of 1969, which destroyed a large part of the old town, the long main street, Church Street, was completely restored to its former state in the Tulpies Dorp of around 1900. At the beginning of Church street is the old church with its curiously shaped white gate. It was consecrated in 1750 and is now furnished as a cultural anthropology museum.

Coming from the Old Church Museum and looking into Church Street, the picture of a village of about 100 years ago enfolds: on both sides of the street is a row of white-plastered Cape-Dutch houses, nearly all of them provided with a high 'stoep' (doorstep) and crowned with the familiar gables. The steps in front of the houses can only be reached via narrow stone stairs. This method of construction was bound to the fact that in the eighteenth century taxes on property depended on the width of the steps at the entrance. The oldest house dates from 1754, when Church Street itself had not even been laid out. Adjoining is a house originating from the end of the nineteenth century. In the middle of the street stands one of the few remaining houses dating from 1800, which were built in an H-shape. The nearby construction consisting of two storeys is called Monbijou. Right at the end of the street is the old vicarage.

En route to Paarl

Through the valleys of the Witsenberg the road leads past Wolseley and via the magnificent Bains Gorge to the West Cape wine-regions. At the end of the gorge one has a unique view across the Berg River Valley, where Wellington is located. Behind it the 2,729 metres' high Paarl Rock in the Paarl Mountains looms up, a forebode of the Groot Drakenstein Mountains (Large Drakenstein Mountains). The peculiar dome-shape of this rock forms the remnant of the granite mountain ridge that covered the southern part of South Africa 500 million years ago. On this ridge itself soft rock layers were deposited up to a height of 1,000 metres. Due to the influence of wind, water and temperature fluctuations the soft stone has crumbled down during a period of millions of years. The granite Paarl Mountain and Gordon's Rock and Bretagne Rock behind it, have also been ground away by erosion into curious giant domes. In these intriguing mountains many caves arose through erosion. They formed ideal hiding places for run-away slaves in the eighteenth century. On the southern slope of the Paarl Mountains the imposing monument in honour of the African language can be seen.

At Paarl the famous Cape wine-regions start, lying in a 160 kilometres' long curve around Cape Town. Here wines are produced that can measure themselves with European wines. The grape cultivation started when Jan van Riebeeck, after some unsuccessful attempts, could note down in his diary: 'Heeden is Gode loff van de Caepse druyven d'eerste mael wyn gepaerst...' (Today, God be praised, wine has been pressed from the Cape grapes for the first time). The construction of vineyards was important for Van Riebeeck as red wine, just like fresh vegetables, has a high vitamin content, which could prevent scurvy among the sailors of the V.O.C. Simon van der Stel's vineyards in Constantia yielded such an excellent sweet dessert-wine at the end of the eighteenth century, that it was already renowned internationally at the time.

▲ *Tulbagh, the former Tulpies Dorp, was largely devastated by an earthquake in 1969. The Cape-Dutch houses have been scrupulously restored.*

◄ *Dwarf-eared owl (Otus scops) in the south-western Cape Province. The family of the dwarf-eared owls numbers 30 species, scattered over almost the entire world. The habitat of the large African eagle owl (Bubo capensis) is not limited to the Cape, but extends up to Ethiopia.*

Language Monument

The monument erected in honour of the African language on the southern slope of the Paarl Mountains, is a creation of the architect Jan van Wijk. It is dominated by a huge pillar, 57 metres high, as a symbol of the enrichment of Afrikaans by many influences from other languages. These influences are symbolized in the complex by three round shapes on a pedestal, three separate pillars next to the main pillar and a wall around a beautiful gallery with several steps. The rounded shapes represent the contributions made by the languages of the African population groups. The three pillars, which have been erected in the western part of the monument, express the influences of the western languages. The wall along the gallery represents the significance of the Malay language for the South African language. Next to the main pillar is a smaller one, as a symbol for the South African nation.

From Paarl to Stellenbosch

From Paarl, the biggest city of the region, a tour along the well-known wine-farms, such as Nederburg, Bachsberg, Villiers and Fairview can be made. Many wine-farmers' houses have a view of the three giant granite semi-spherical forms, which compel the spectator again and again to look upwards to the Paarl Mountains.

All building styles of the previous 200 years are represented in Paarl. In the Hoofstraat (Main Street) lies the 'Strooidakkerk' (Thatched roof Church) dating from 1805. The old Parsonage Museum accommodates a collection of French Huguenots' furniture, Cape-Dutch objects and attributes from former African cultures. The Co-operative Wine-cultivators' Society house in Paarl is located in a historical Cape-Dutch farm. Here all sorts of wine from the district are on offer.

Another 'pearl' of the wine-regions, Stellenbosch, lies south-west of Paarl. On the road leading to it, along the R310 in the Drakenstein Valley, lies one of the splendid wine-estates of South Africa: Boschendal. The plot of land was originally allotted to the Huguenot colonists. In 1812 the estate was bought by Abraham de Villiers and remained family property until it fell into the hands of Cecil Rhodes, the empire founder, in 1896. In Boschendal world-famous wines, meanwhile also much coveted in The Netherlands and England, are sold. One of the famous restaurants of the Cape Province, specialized in the French and Dutch cuisine, is situated beneath impressive oak trees.

From Boschendal one first passes the old missionary post Pniel before climbing the steep road to the Hellshoogte Pass and then descending to Stellenbosch.

A walk through Stellenbosch

When the enterprising Dutch governor Van der Stel set out to explore the wilderness behind Cape Town in 1679, he discovered the romantic valley of the First River, thickly overgrown with high trees, which gave way to ideal grasslands in the valley itself. The first houses of the settlement 'het bos van Stel' (Stel's forest) or Stellenbosch, were built close to the river. The Dutch Reformed mother-church in the Drostdystraat is a good starting point for an exploratory tour of the old town. The church was built in 1722, with a roof of grass and a high front and was later rebuilt, retaining the original walls for the main part.

Opposite the church is the old town district with restored houses, which represent several periods in the history of Stellenbosch. These buildings are called the Dorpsmuseum (Village Museum). It shows the first urban house of South Africa, built in 1710. It is the Schreuder House, with its earthen floor, reed and twig ceiling and a large open fire-place, as was common in Old Dutch seventeenth century houses. Adjacent to it is the Bletterman House with six facades, once belonging to a wealthy citizen. Now it has the solid Dutch oak cupboards on display, with their unique brown patina, which could only arise through an age-long careful treatment with wax. Grosvenor House also belongs to these buildings, furnished in the English style of around 1800. From the garden there is a surprisingly beautiful view of the church. In Church Street number 30 is the inn 'D'ouwe werf' (The old ship-yard), which has recently been restored and now houses a beautiful hotel-restaurant. The centre of the town is formed by the Braak, an open common green, once serving as festival and parade grounds. It is surrounded by historical buildings. The most remarkable of these is the Anglican St Mary's Church, dating from 1852, with its grass roof. The church looks out on the older Burgers House, today in service as a furniture and ceramics museum. Next to the Burgers House is the snow-white high gunpowder-house of the V.O.C., which nowadays accommodates a military museum.

Walking from the Marktstraat to the Hertestraat, one can see the former vicarage dating from 1815 and subsequently a whole row of smaller houses. The liberated slaves lived there in the

The Old Vicarage in Paarl ▶ houses a museum nowadays.

Old church at Pniel at the ▶ foot of the Hellshoogte Pass.

The garden of the ▶ Grosvenor House in Stellenbosch offers a splendid view of the Dutch Reformed mother-church.

▲ *The former Gunpowder house of the V.O.C. in Stellenbosch today houses a military museum.*

beginning of the nineteenth century. The Hertestraat ends in the long Dorpsstraat, with interesting old houses. They are overshadowed by high oaks, which provided Stellenbosch with its second name, 'Oak city'. One of the characteristic old shops of the town, 'Oom Samie se Winkel' (Uncle Samie's Shop), a fancy-goods shop, has virtually anything on sale. The magnificent, completely restored, gabled house 'Libertas Parvas', where general Smuts courted his beloved Sibella Krige, is situated in this district. It now houses the Rembrandt van Rijn Art Gallery, with, among others, works by Irma Stern, Anton van Wouw and Pierneef. The painter Pierneef managed to capture the stately wine-farms against the dramatic peaks of the Drakenstein and Jonkershoek Mountains in an unparalleled way. In the wine-cellar next to the art gallery the Stellenryck Wine Museum is accommodated.

At number 30 in the Dorpsstraat the Lutheran Church rises up, the Museum of Contemporary Art of the University of Stellenbosch, one of the old universities in South Africa. The main building is a national place of interest. The most beautiful Cape-Dutch house in the Dorpsstraat is 'la Gratitude', dating from 1798. Over the window in the gable 'God's all-seeing Eye' was depicted by the original owner himself.

There is another national memorial in the Van Riebeeckstraat: the first grain-mill of Stellenbosch. Close to the river the old Vrederust Farm is in use as a restaurant.

▲ *The interior of 'Oom Samie se Winkel' (Uncle Samie's Shop) in Stellenbosch. This second-hand shop in Victorian style dates from 1904.*

Via Franschhoek to the south coast

During the drive from Stellenbosch via Boschendal to Franschhoek one of the most spectacular landscapes of the West Cape wine-region is passed. Franschhoek was founded around 1690 by Huguenots, who were fleeing the fate that awaited them due to the withdrawal of the Nantes Edict. This region rightfully boasts important wine-producing centres such as Bellingham and l'Ormarins, where special wines of the district can be tasted and bought.

From Franschhoek the R45 leads southwards to the bridge across the Theewaterskloof Dam. From there the R321 leads past the Riviersonderend to Grabouw on the wide N2. Due to the mountains the route offers splendid views of the Groenland and the Hottentotten-Holland Mountains. West of Grabouw lies the fishing-port of Gordon's Bay, the starting point of a very attractive coastal road. It leads past the Koeël Bay and the Pringle Bay near Cape Hangklip, to Hermanus, located on the Walker Bay.

◄ *The Huguenot monument in Franschhoek in commemoration of the French immigrants who settled in this region between 1688 and 1690 at the invitation of the V.O.C.*

▲ *Shipwreck on the south coast. Painting from the eighteenth century in the South African Library.*

▲ *Lithograph by M. Bond: The wrecking of the steamship H.M. Birkenhead off the coast at Gevarenpunt (Danger point) at one o'clock in the morning of 26 February 1852. Collection South African Museum.*

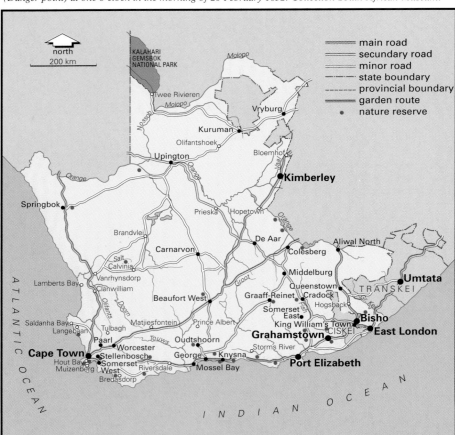

Hermanus is a fishing-port, from where the southern right-whales, which once lived in large numbers in the Walker Bay, were hunted for a long time. As this whale remains floating after it has been harpooned, the species was a favourite target for the whale-hunters. The name 'right' referred to that aspect. Today the bay is still the place where female whales bear their offspring. From the Marine Hotel on the coast one can survey the whole bay and regularly observe the spouting and high-jumping whales, sometimes very close to the rocky coast. Since 1935 the right-whale has been protected. Of the entire estimated whale-population in the world about a tenth live in the South African coastal waters.

The coast of the shipwrecks

From Hermanus one looks across the long cape ending at Danger Point, a most suitable name. In fact the entire southern coastal region is notorious for the shipwrecks that took place there. In the Shipwreck Museum at Bredasdorp the numerous remains of the circa 200 shipping-disasters are on display. The wreck of the Birkenhead near Danger Point on 15 February 1852 has even been elevated to a true myth. The ship carried, besides 131 crew-members, 487 soldiers and officers to Port Elizabeth. The soldiers were to be employed in the eighth 'border' war against the Xhosa. Furthermore there were seven women and thirteen children aboard. During the night the ship ran on a reef and was completely ripped open. Within half an hour it sank. At the last minute three lifeboats could be lowered. 'Women and children first!', the captain ordered. As soon as the boats touched the water, however, a number of soldiers jumped into one of them. The captain ordered this boat to remain at some distance of the ship, while the women and children were lowered down into the second boat. The third boat also received the order to sail away in order to prevent hundreds of men jumping into it, which would make it sink. All remaining men thereupon had to stand to attention on the quarter-deck. At that moment the Birkenhead broke into two and sank. Only 50 men managed to reach the coast, as did all the women and children. However, most crew-members got entangled in the treacherous seaweeds before the coast and were drowned. The tale that they had given their lives so as to comply with the order: 'Women and children first!', was the crux of the stories about this shipwreck that went around in the years succeeding it.
Along the R320 from Hermanus to Caledon groups of inhabitants from this region can be observed on Sundays, dressed in their Sunday attire, on their way to the Methodists' church. From Caledon, along the big N2, one first reaches Swellendam and then George, the starting point of the famous Garden Route to Port Elizabeth. En route to Swellendam a visit to the first missionary post of South Africa, Genadendal, only requests a slight detour on the R406.

Genadendal (Valley of Mercy)

In 1737 George Schmidt of the Moravian Brotherhood founded a missionary post at the foot of the Riviersonderend Mountains. He preached to the remaining groups of the Khoikhoi tribe, who had gathered in the Baviaanskloof (Baboon's Gorge). However, after seven years Schmidt was forced to return to Germany, as he was not qualified to baptize heathens according to the church authorities. Fifty years later his task was continued by three other Moravian missionaries. The village that arose was called Genadendal. Next to the church with its historical bell-tower is an interesting museum, devoted to the works of Schmidt and his followers. Today the village numbers about 5,000 people.

▲ The Dutch Reformed church in Swellendam.

▲ The splendid mansion Tokai Manor at Swellendam.

Swellendam

The bontebok had almost become extinct in the Little Karoo in the middle of the nineteenth century. Fortunately, at that time a group of farmers in the surroundings of Swellendam decided to cease hunting this gracious animal species. Somewhat to the south of Swellendam this antelope species is multiplying again in the park named after it: the Bontebok National Park. Swellendam, founded as an administrative centre for a wide and sparsely inhabited environment, originated circa 1750 around the *Drostdy*. The former office of the local administrator is now used as a museum. Originally it was a low Cape-Dutch building with a thatched roof, which was later rebuilt in Georgian style. At the end of the nineteenth century the Dutch Reformed Church found accommodation in the *Drostdy*. The former prison, where the prisoners learned a skill, is also part of the Drostdy Museum. In an annex one finds the oldest ox-waggon of the country, made in 1795, next to a replica of a mail-coach dating from the nineteenth century. Opposite the *Drostdy* lies the Zanddrift Farm, dating from 1768.

Through the Little Karoo

On the road from Swellendam to Oudtshoorn, just past the bridge across the River Groot, is a jojoba plantation. The nuts of the jojoba shrubs (Simondsia californica) form the raw material for exclusive oils, notably used in the cosmetics industry. Many psoriasis patients benefit from this wondrous oil. The jojoba plants are resistant to both ten degrees frost and lengthy periods of drought. In the Little Karoo it can occur that there is only rain once a year.
East of the River Groot lies Ladismith, which, just like the far better known Ladysmith in Natal, was named after the wife of an English governor, Sir Harry Smith. The town consists of a collection of old buildings, which are mainly concentrated in Church Street. Just outside the town lies the Toverkop, consisting of two high split peaks, dominating the entire landscape.
At Zoar, the location of a Dutch Reformed Missionary, one can take a special turning to the north. It leads between high-rising rock walls that have arisen due to erosion. The gorge is called Seweweekspoort. The road offers occasional views of a 2,300 metres' high peak in the Groot Swart Mountains. Beside the road, baboons, called *bobbejanen* here, often rummage about in the bushes.

▲ Two of the estimated 200 piebald-bucks in the Bontebok National Park near Swellendam.
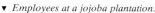
▼ Employees at a jojoba plantation.

▲ *In the Cango Caves at Oudtshoorn are huge stalactite and stalagmite formations.*

Oudtshoorn, the feather capital

On the road to Oudtshoorn it is noticeable that this centre of the Little Karoo is the land of the ostriches: the more than two metres' tall birds on their long, strong legs heave all over the landscape. In the years before the Great War 750,000 of these giants among birds lived here. As a result of the fashion of the time, ostrich-feathers were in heavy demand. Today about 100,000 ostriches inhabit the area. In the town several palace-like buildings bear witness to the period when the 'ostrich barons' were able to lead their lives of luxury here.

South of Oudtshoorn are two large ostrich farms, the Safari and the Highgate Farm, with, in the background, the blue silhouettes of the Outeniekwa Mountains. The Cango Caves with their underground world of stalactites and stalagmites are located at a distance of a good 25 kilometres from Oudtshoorn. Beneath monumental vaults the most remarkable formations have been shaped. One can see gigantic domes, pillars, towers and long needles, catacombs, figures resembling elephants and trees and curtains, which, if touched, resound like a drum. Imaginary names have been thought up for the many areas, such as: the rainbow room, the bridal room, the crystal palace, the ice-room, the devil's workshop and the devil's chimney. At several places in these caves the army of uninventive graffiti artists has left its mark. Some formations needed tens of thousands of years to come about, others 'grew' faster. In the caves, of which three are open to the public, two-hour-long guided tours are provided. The impressive Swartberg Pass north of the Cango Caves connects the Little Karoo with the Great Karoo. At the foot of the Groot Swart Mountains lies Prince Albert, a town with a nineteenth century atmosphere.

Ostriches

Halfway down the Cango Caves is the Cango Ostrich Farm, where the difficult process of breeding ostriches can be closely observed. A significant impediment in breeding these animals is the fact that ostriches have a strong individual preference in choosing their partners. They are extremely loyal and hardly ever change mates, which complicates selection. During the tour of the Cango Farm the manager said that it has more than once appeared that beautiful male specimens simply refused to mate with an exquisite female, because they were adamant about getting an insignificant female, laying only a few eggs. Another hampering factor is the relative high mortality among young ostriches due to the high sensitiveness these animals have as regards stress. These desert birds actually demand unlimited space and do not feel at home within the demarcated areas of the farms.

Not only the feathers but literally everything of the ostriches that are bred is put to use. The eggs, weighing about one kilogramme (about 24 chicken eggs) are a much desired raw material. Moreover, ostrich meat is tasty and beautiful bags and shoes are made of the skin.

The birth of an ostrich. After 40 days the chicks are hatched out ▼ and are able to run immediately.

The ostrich (Struthio camelus australis) is the largest bird in the world and can weigh as much as 150 kilogrammes. This huge ▼ cursorial bird can reach a speed of up to 50 kilometres an hour.

The Garden Route

Between Mossel Bay and the River Storms lies one of the most splendid coastal areas of South Africa: deep bays with long sandy beaches alternate with rugged cliffs, where the mountains descend steeply into the sea. Lagoons reach far inland. Rain forests extend in places close to the crumbled coast and just behind the coastline lies a series of saltwater lakes.
The so-called Garden Route runs through this unique coastal region. All travel agencies take their tourists here. Unfortunately the available time does not allow most travellers to catch more than a glimpse of the many fascinating sights in the region.

Mossel Bay, the landing site of Diaz

In 1488 Bartolomé Diaz landed in the bay that is now called the Mossel Bay. His sailors, in search of fresh water and profitable barter-trade, were greeted with a shower of stones by a group of angry Hottentots. One of the seamen pierced a Hottentot with an arrow from his cross-bow, after which the attackers withdrew. Diaz sailed on to the east. In the Algoa Bay he planted a wooden cross on the island of Santa Crux. However, his exhausted crew refused to travel further and Diaz returned to Portugal. At Kwaaihoek he placed a second cross on the coast. Nine years later Vasco da Gama did succeed in getting on friendly terms with the 'brown shepherds'. Many Portuguese after him used Mossel Bay as a revitalization spot. From 1500 onwards a large tree on the coast even served as a kind of curious post office. Sailors on their way to India or the Moluccas dropped letters in a boot, which was hung on this tree. The letters were taken back to Portugal by sailors who were returning home.

The wilderness of the brackish lakes

The lake district between George and Knysna can be explored in two ways. Most tourists drive by bus or rented car along the N2 past the town of Wildernis, with its golden beaches, and then via the lakes and the Goukamma Nature Reserve to Knysna. Romantics however go by steam-train! There is a railway from George through the lake district, along which the 'Outeniqua Choo-Choo' rides its puffing and steaming course. The views across the inlet of the River Kaaiman, the brackish lakes such as the Langvlei, Rondevlei and Swartvlei and the only freshwater lake, the Groenvlei, are breathtaking. Then the spectacular descent to the Goukamma Valley follows and after traversing the bridge over the Knysna lagoon the train arrives at the timber town of Knysna.
The town owes its name to a Khoikhoi word signifying 'steep descent'. With 'knysna' the so-called Knysna-Heads are denoted, two high sandstone rocks that seem to protect the entrance to the large Knysna Lagoon against the open sea. Knysna originated thanks to the rainforest at the foot of the Outeniekwa Mountains. Together with the Tsitsikamma rainforest this tropical belt extends along the coast over a length of 180 kilometres and a width of 20 kilometres. Enormous yellow wood (Podocarpus falcatus) and stinkwood trees (Ocotea capensis) grow besides Cape chestnuts (Calodendrum capense) and saffron trees (Crolus sativus). Some reach a height of 30 metres. In the hinterland rises the patriarch among the yellow wood trees, the king Edward tree. It is over 700 years old and stretches its heavy trunk 46 metres upwards, before ending in a labyrinth of branches. In the middle of the forest a separate wood of large fern trees (Filices spec.) flourishes. Hundreds of elephants used to live in the Knysna forests, of which just a few have survived. They are the subject of several stories among the population in the neighbourhood. Knysna is also a centre for the production of splendid furniture, made from the durable yellow, stink and black timber.

◄ In the line of the tradition of the 'post-office tree' this curious stone bin can today be found at the Mossel Bay. One is advised not to deposit envelopes with valuable contents in this 'letter box'.

The Outeniqua Choo-Choo crosses the Kaaiman Bridge en ▼ route from Knysna to George.

◄ Name-sign of the Jonker furniture factory in Knysna. The British immigrant George Rex laid the basis for the wood industry in Knysna in 1804.

▲ *The rugged rocky coast at Tsitsikamma National Park.*

Tsitsikamma National Park

After leaving Knysna the N2 leads across the foothills of the Tsitsikamma Mountains to Plettenberg Bay. At this place, with its remarkable long beach, the sun shines 320 days a year. A renowned hotel is nowadays situated on Beacon Island off the coast, once the site of a large whaling station.

Tsitsikamma National Park was founded at the spot where the River Storms has cut its canyon through the mountains and the heavily eroded mountain ridge dives steeply into the sea at many places. Only now and then is the rough coastal region broken by a narrow beach. The park extends over a length of 80 kilometres and a width of merely one-and-a-half kilometres. The adjoining sea region, up to a distance of 800 metres off the coast, also belongs to the national park. Scuba divers and skin-divers can explore a fascinating underwater world at several places. However, one has to realize, that, as at other places on the south-east coast, sharks occur here. In this remarkable nature reserve walks can be undertaken, varying from one hour to five days. For the enthusiastic hikers the 'ottertrail' has been laid out. They can especially enjoy the rich bird-life in the park. More than 200 bird species have been observed in Tsitsikamma National Park. The rare clawless otter (Aonyx capensis) hunts underwater for fish, crab and octopuses between the mussel-covered black rocks.

Port Elizabeth

The Garden Route ends at Storms River. Whoever follows the N2 further eastwards, will reach Port Elizabeth after travelling more than 150 kilometres. The city, named after the wife of the first governor Sir Ruffane Donkin, lies at the foot of the hill on which Fort Frederick is situated. This fortress is the oldest stone building in the eastern part of the Cape Province. In the old district, known as 'Upper Hill Street', several houses have been completely restored.

In the middle of the city lies Donkin Reserve, offering a beautiful view across the city and the Algoa Bay. In the north this green borders on a row of terraced houses built in early Victorian style. In front of the city hall, which was rebuilt after a fire, is a replica of the Diaz cross that was placed at Kwaaihoek in 1488. The pyramid in Donkin Reserve was erected in commemoration of Elizabeth, governor Donkin's wife, who died in India. Next to the pyramid is an old lighthouse, housing a military museum. The campanile (bell-tower) at the entrance to the docks measures 52 metres in height and offers a possibility for an orientation of the wide surroundings.

The King George IV Gallery houses a collection of English and South African paintings and art objects. The Oceanarium with dolphins, reptiles and tropical birds attracts a great number of visitors throughout the year. The main building displays the famous Boskop-skull of a prehistoric man, who was closely related to the Cro-Magnon man, an early form of Homo sapiens. In honour of the *Voortrekkers* leader Piet Retief a monument was erected on the former site of his Strandfontein Farm.

The land of the setlaars

After every war, poverty and unemployment are rife among the losers and the conquerors. Thus was the situation in Europe at the beginning of the nineteenth century after Napoleon's defeat. Taking Australia as an example, the English government decided to offer a large number of people the chance to settle as colonists – in Afrikaans called *setlaar* – in the region around Grahamstown. Ninety thousand pioneers, the majority of them unemployed people who dreamed of a free and prosperous life, applied for this opportunity. However, the 21 sailing vessels only offered room for 4,000 colonists. They embarked in the bitterly cold month of January 1820. After a journey of three months the first ship, the Chapman, sailed into Algoa Bay and the 270 immigrants saw Fort Frederick on the top of a hill. They were transported by sloops to the beaches and English soldiers carried them through the breakers. They pitched their tents on the beach for the night. With their scarce luggage on their backs and on waggons, they travelled through the coastal region to the site of the present-day Grahamstown.

There they faced an enormous task: first of all reclaiming and cultivating the land, which was completely unfamiliar labour to most of them. Moreover the attacks by the Xhosa, living east of the Fish, had to be braved. Their grazing grounds were located in the present-day Ciskei and they felt threatened by the *setlaars*. In the 1820s the Xhosa were systematically flooded by Nguni refugees from the north-east, such as the Mpondo and the Mfengu, who were driven southwards by the armies of the Zulu king Shaka. Beyond the Fish the Boers and the English *setlaars* brought them to a halt.

In 1834 thousands of heavily-armed Xhosa warriors raided the colonists, killing some fifty of them and setting fire to many newly-built farms. However, they were repelled by the determined core of the immigrants, who adhered to the devise: 'take firm root or die'. The first option appeared to apply to many of them; their landing site Port Elizabeth expanded steadily.

◀ *Thomas Baines: the first settlers ship the Chapman; landing of the 'setlaars' in Algoa Bay in 1820. Collection 1820 Settlers Memorial Museum in Grahamstown.*

Grahamstown

In the course of the years many *setlaars* left their farms and became proficient in trade and service-rendering in Grahamstown, which grew into a real city. The impressive Settlers Monument stands on Gunfire Hill. In the Memorial Court 24 panels have been installed, on which Cecil Skotnes depicted the arduous beginning years of the *setlaars*. The Settlers Memorial Museum is situated at the bottom of the hill that is also the site of the old Fort Selwynn, which once controlled the city with its cannons. On the top floor of the museum the growth of Grahamstown is depicted by historical photographs. The Albany Natural History Museum shows numerous aspects of the Xhosa traditions, a collection of fossils and African objects dating from prehistoric times.

The inner city is dominated by the imposing Anglican Cathedral of St Michael and St George. The construction started in 1824 and took more than 100 years. The churchyard in front of the cathedral is surrounded by magnificent nineteenth century buildings, for the majority in use as shops. Grahamstown boasts another 39 churches, which have given the town the name 'city of the saints'. The townhall has a special bell-tower, constructed in honour of the *setlaars*.

Addo Elephant National Park

Addo Elephant National Park, comprising 8,600 hectares, is located between Port Elizabeth and Grahamstown. The thick growth mainly consists of 'spek' trees (Portulacaria asra), the favourite food of elephants, other low trees, thorn bushes and climbers. The fenced-in region is the habitat of 21 rare black rhinoceroses, dozens of buffaloes, elands, kudus, bushbucks (Antelope silvatica), grey divers (Sylvicapra grimmia), forest swine (Hylochoerus meinertzhageni), porcupines (Hystrix africaeaustralis), jackals (Canis aureus) and desert lynxes (Felix caracal). However, the 170 elephants are by far the most important inhabitants.

Around 1900 about the same number of elephants lived in this region. The animals caused such extensive damage to the crops of farmers in the neighbourhood, that they called on the government for help. For a decade hunters tried to decimate the number of elephants, but the thick growth in the territory proved a good protection for the animals. In 1919 a big-game hunter, major Pretorius, who had just made his honourable return from the Great War, was assigned to kill as many elephants as possible. After he had killed 120 specimens within a year, a mere fifteen remained.

In 1931 the decision was made to found Addo Elephant National Park. Yet the escapades of the elephants onto the surrounding agricultural land remained unacceptable for the farmers. It was attempted to keep the elephants within the boundaries of the park by regularly laying their favourite fruit, oranges, at fixed places, yet the effort was insufficient. The habit even proved to be dangerous to the visitors of the park. Two tourists once got the shock of a lifetime, when they drove into the park with a big bag full of oranges. Suddenly a colossal elephant appeared, coming straight at the car. The incident took place so quickly, that the tourists failed to drive off. The giant started to push the car across the road. Both passengers panicked to such an extent that they jumped out of the car and fled into the park on foot by way of a sand-path. The elephant then started to tear the car apart systematically, until he managed to reach the oranges. Fortunately the two terrified tourists were taken care of by a ranger. After numerous vain attempts Graham Andrews managed to design a fence that could keep out elephants. It consisted of railway tracks, stuck deep into the ground, with heavy cables in between, which were once used to lower lifts into mining shafts. Thereafter the elephant population gradually grew again. The current number of 170 is already close to the limit which the surface-area of the park sets.

There are plans to extend the park considerably. The most important motive is the genetic necessity to bring the herd to a size of at least 500. For that purpose, however, a park is needed that is much larger than the existing one. As long as the neighbouring farmers obtain good profits from the wool of their angora goats (Capra hircus angorensis), they constitute an impassable impediment for the expansion of the park.

And what good is it then if a born writer like Carmen Bernos de Gasztold is so enthralled by the Addo elephants that she created the following 'Prayer of the Elephant':
'Lord, it is me, the Elephant, Your creature,
who is talking to You.
I am so embarrassed by my great self
and, truly, it is not my fault
if I spoil Your Addo Park a little with my big feet.
Let me be careful and behave wisely,
always keeping my dignity and poise.
Give me such philosophic thoughts that, wherever I go,
I can rejoice everywhere I go in the lovable oddity of things.'

In the beginning the elephants were very aggressive as they still remembered the years of persecution. Especially 'Hapoor' (Bitten Ear), the largest bull the park has ever known, intensely hated human beings all his life. Addo Elephant National Park offers the possibility to see elephants at close range between the low bushes and the water-pools. The animals have, in the meantime, grown completely accustomed to cars driving about. When, after a heavy shower, one drives past the place where a high sand-hill descends to the fence, one can observe how 'human' the behaviour of elephants sometimes is: for deep sliding-tracks reveal that the elephants use this hill as a kind of slide or 'ski-run'.

There is so much to see in the park that a stay of a couple of days is advisable. There are, for instance, around 170 species of birds to be observed. The lookout near the reservoir offers an opportunity to watch not only birds but also nocturnal animals.

▲ *Historical facades in the charming city of Grahamstown.*

Hapoor

In his younger years a hunter had shot the largest elephant of Addo Elephant National Park straight through its left ear, a hole which had been torn into a big 'bite' from his ear in the course of the years. That is why the elephant was called Hapoor (Bitten Ear). From 1944 to 1968 he was the leader of the growing herd. Only once was his leadership disputed: in May 1955 a young bull, called Bellvue, felt so strong that he entered into the battle for Hapoor's females. However, he had to pay the challenge with his life.

Years later though, in 1968, Hapoor, who had grown considerably older, was dethroned, after a horrible fight with the strong bull Lankey. The casting out of the herd and the subsequent life as a solitary elephant appeared to be unacceptable for Hapoor. He managed to break down a part of the two metres' high, heavy fence and climb over the rest. Then the warden had to decide to have him shot, as Hapoor had become a threat to the surroundings. His stuffed head now hangs on the wall in the restaurant of the park.

Gondwanaland • Graaff-Reinet • Mountain Zebra National Park

The gem of the Karoo

About 250 kilometres north-west of Addo Elephant National Park lies Graaff-Reinet, the oldest city in the eastern part of the Cape Province. The city can be reached via Somerset East on the R63, in a region full of farms with sheep and angora goats. Graaff-Reinet, founded in 1786, was named after the Dutch governor of the Cape, Cornelis van der Graaff and his wife Ester Reinet.

The city is known for its well-restored houses and churches. In the first place the Reinet House, a parsonage at the beginning of the previous century, which was completely restored to its nineteenth century state. It is equipped as a museum, housing a great part of reverend Murray's original furniture. It also boasts a collection of dolls, which were made here during the Great War. Another beautifully restored building is the old *Drostdy*. Today this is the Drostdy Hotel, where one can spend the night in the antique cottages, known as 'Stretch's Court'. The Anglican St James Church possesses many objects which are relics of the Anglo-Boer War.

South-west of Graaff-Reinet a mountain of *dolerite* rises up in Karoo Nature Reserve. Between the uprising heavily eroded rock colossuses one looks down on the Valley of Desolation, which gradually merges into the endless plains of the Karoo. In the distance lies a remnant of *dolerite* stone, called the Spandau Kop because a German immigrant thought it resembled the Spandau castle near Berlin.

Mountain Zebra National Park

Near Cradock, 100 kilometres east of Graaff-Reinet, a national park that was founded in 1937 safeguards 200 Cape mountain zebras (Equus zebra zebra) from an almost complete extinction of this rare species. Only five stallions and one mare lived here in 1930. Mountain Zebra National Park, called Nasionale Bergkwaggawildtuin in Afrikaans, is, just like Addo Elephant National Park, too small. Yet, for zebras there is also the genetic necessity to bring the herd up to a number of about 500.

The park is also famous for its rich bird fauna. The rare Cape eagle owl (Bubo capensis) and the dwarf eagle (Hieraaetus pennatus) still occur here, besides the equally rare kite (Circus aeruginosus). There are several camping possibilities in the park. Besides this a dozen cottages and an old farm offer accommodation to tourists.

The charming town of Cradock along the banks of the Great Fish River was a military outpost on the border of the Cape colony and the Xhosa territory around 1800. The former tensions can still be traced during a visit to the Great Fish River Museum. On the River Kat, 77 kilometres north of Grahamstown, lies Fort Beaufort, also a former outpost of the British. A historical museum is now housed in what used to be the old officers' mess. Besides a range of fire arms and a unique collection of historical books, one can admire some fascinating paintings by Thomas Baines, the great painter of nineteenth century South African landscapes.

East of Fort Beaufort, just on the border with Ciskei, the Amatola Mountains rise. This is the place of the various landscapes that enthralled Thomas Baines artistically. He was very much attracted by Hogsback, reminiscent of villages in the hilly parts of England. The road from Fort Beaufort to King William's Town leads straight across Ciskei. Cattle breeding and agriculture form the means of livelihood in this region.

▲ *The Valley of Desolation near Graaff-Reinet. Behind the eroded rocks a dolerite koppie rises up out of the landscape.*

Gondwanaland

Hundreds of millions of years ago, when Antarctica, Australia, India and South America were still attached to the continent of Gondwanaland, a large part of the African interior consisted of enormous mountain ridges and plains, with imposing volcanoes rising from them. This landscape disappeared due to erosion and as a result thousands of metres of earth layers were deposited in South Africa.

A long period began during which the southern hemisphere was covered with ice and therefore became lifeless, while the northern hemisphere, which was very warm at the time, teemed with life. About 220 million years ago the ice-masses in the heart of South Africa melted. Temperatures rose to a tropical height, probably as a result of a toppling of the earth's axis. The era of the dinosaurs, which was to last for more than 100 million years, had arrived. Thick earth-layers formed in which evidence of the presence of mighty forests was found. These layers contain many fossils of dinosaurs and amphibians. During the period when the dinosaurs were the supreme rulers, the crumbling away of the continents – about 190 million years ago – started, which reduced Gondwanaland to the present-day Africa.

In the central plains of South Africa volcanic eruptions occurred at many places. From the depths of the earth magma, mainly consisting of *dolerite*, flowed over old layers. When this magma cooled down, all kinds of folds of exceptionally hard stone arose in the landscape. The remnants of these rise up from the flat, meanwhile eroded, landscape in the interior of Orange Free State and the Cape Province as *koppies* and pinnacles. Again there were volcanic eruptions and this time thick layers of basalt were deposited – often to a height of more than 1,000 metres – in a large region of southern Africa. At several places the hard *dolerite* rocks wrenched their way again between the softer basalt layers. In the millions of years that followed these basalt masses were shaped into the extraordinary figures of the Drakensberg Mountains by water and wind erosion.

◄ *Burchell zebras (Equus burchelli) live, among other places, in the Mountain Zebra National Park near Cradock, in Karoo National Park at Beaufort West, in Oviston Nature Reserve near the Hendrik Verwoerd Dam and in the Rolfontein Nature Reserves on the Le Roux Dam.*

East London and surroundings

The port of East London is reached the quickest via King William's Town, known for its Kaffrarian Museum and its Missionary Museum. A detour on the N6 past Happy Valley, Cathcart and Stutterheim offers the possibility to get to know the artistic handicraft of this region. Many women in the villages occupy themselves with weaving and spinning; beautiful pottery is also available. The villages lie among splendid landscapes. East London is situated on the River Buffalo and is the only river-port in South Africa. The town used to be a small trade settlement, named after a trader, George Rex. Five thousand German immigrants arrived here around 1858, who were alotted plots of land in the interior. Towns like Berlin, Hamburg and Potsdam are reminiscent of these new *setlaars*.

In the long Oxford Street is the East London Museum, famous because of the fact that the 'coelacanth' can be admired here, which was caught off the coast in 1938. This almost two metres' long fish had strange belly-fins, which seemed to enable it to walk on the bottom of the sea. The coelacanth (Latimera chalumnae) was only known as a fossil and was supposed to have been extinct for 50 million years. It appeared that these predatory fish live at a depth of 150 to 250 metres. Scientifically the find was of great importance, as it concerns a species from which the first land-dwelling animals are supposed to have evolved long ago.

Both to the south-west and to the north-east of East London beautiful coastal areas extend, with sandy beaches, lagoons and hills as far as the eye can see. Numerous traditional huts of the African population draw the visitor's attention. Rare shells can be found on the beaches. The interior of East London is cut by a large number of rivers and has a rich bird-life. Morgan's Bay,

◄ *Statue in commemoration of the Anglo-Boer War, next to the town-hall in East London.*

south-west of the River Great Kei is one of the beautiful resorts along the border with Transkei.

The Apple-Express, a romantic survival of the steam era, rides from Port Elizabeth through the Long
▼ *Kloof Valley to Loerie. A trip on the narrow-gauge train is a real 'must' for steam-train enthusiasts.*

6

THE EXOTIC EAST

Natal, a world of contrasts. The rough subtropical east coast offers a variety of cliffs, creeks, lagoons and golden sandy beaches. In the west the peaks of the Drakensberg Mountains rise up like enormous dragonteeth. In the north this smallest province of South Africa borders on Swaziland and Moçambique and in the south on Transkei. Once the hilly midlands were the scene of bloody battles.

The territory of Natal is characterized by alternating landscapes, a wide variety of plant and animal life and monuments bearing witness to a turbulent history. Transkei also has a varied natural scenery and a rich past. Between the Drakensberg Mountains in the west, the Ubombo Mountains in the north, the hills of Transkei in the south and the Indian Ocean in the east, innumerable hills extend, with *rondavels* of the Zulu surmounting them. Natal also comprises the regions known as KwaZulu. In the valleys of the mountains and hills the echoes of battle cries from a distant past still seem to resound. Nearly all groups that met in the course of time in Natal felt an embittered enmity towards each other and fought bloody fights. It may be true that not as much blood by far was shed here as on the European combat fields in the twentieth century or during the same period in several other African countries, but the conflicts were often just as ruthless. The hills of Natal are cut by rivers, of which some discharge into giant lagoons and estuaries. The mountains, the underwater world along the exotic coast and the wildlife reserves in the north house a great diversity of flora and fauna.

From Transkei to Natal

The N2 from East London in the Cape Province runs straight through Transkei to Port Shepstone in the province of Natal. At several places this route offers the traveller the possibility to get acquainted with the Nguni population that has lived here for hundreds of years. Along the roads the Xhosa women in their traditional clothes attract attention. They usually wear big rings around their ankles, are often draped in beautifully embroidered blankets, and wear turban-like bandages on their heads. En route to the capital of Umtata one passes Butterworth, the oldest city of Transkei, founded in 1827. In Umtata traditional buildings juxtapose modern building-blocks. Close to the city are the Nduli Game Reserve and the Luchaba Nature Reserve. In the city itself the famous Izandla pottery school can be visited. From Umtata it is not very far to the so-called 'wild coast', which extends between the mouth of the Great Kei to Port

Edward on the north-eastern border of Transkei. There is no road along the 'wild coast' itself. The only way to explore the 280 kilometres' long coastline is by undertaking a six days' walking-tour.
A curious freak of nature is located somewhat south of the Coffee Bay, at a spot where a long cliff protrudes into the sea. Due to the force of the waves that have beaten against it in the course of time, the large 'hole in the wall' has arisen. A boat could sail through this opening. Long ago a ship loaded with coffee was wrecked in Coffee Bay. Many coffee-

Traditionally clothed Xhosa
▼ *women in Transkei.*

◄ *In a manner compatible with modern times medicine-men, fortune-tellers and bone-throwers still play a mediating role between the worldly and spiritual domains. The enormous adaptability of traditional religious views confirms their viability and profoundness.*

▲ Reconstruction of
Mgungundlovu, Zulu king
Dingaan's kraal.

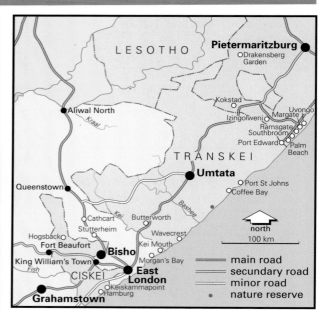

beans ended up ashore, where they sprouted. However, it
appeared that the wild coffee plants could not maintain a
durable existence here.
Another journey which one can take along the R61 from
Umtata to the coast, ends at the vast sandy beaches of Port
St Johns. The N2 from Umtata to Port Shepstone leads past
Kokstad in Natal. Here one finds the grave of Adam Kok III,
the last king of the Griqua. In the middle of the city is
the impressive Roman-Catholic cathedral.
Via the hilly border region, where the white walls and dark
thatched roofs of *rondavels* abound, Port Shepstone in the

south of Natal is finally reached. From this city one can make
a tour through the extreme south of Natal. The Oribi Gorge,
located in an imposing nature reserve, is one of the places
of interest. For more than 40 kilometres a good coastal road
leads to Port Edward on the border with Transkei. Along
the way the river Ivungu is passed, which flows into a
beautiful lagoon at the coast. The road leads past a series of
broad sandy beaches, with in the hinterland sugar cane
fields, mango and banana plantations. From Port Edward
one can drive through the Maringo plains to Izingolweni,
where the N2 leads back to Port Shepstone.

Along battlefields and monuments

In the heart of Natal are numerous former battlefields. An
enterprising travel agency such as Welcome Tours & Safaris
organizes several trips along these historical battle scenes.
The Mgungundlovu Museum, north of Melmoth on road to
Vrijheid, lies on the spot where the *kraal* of Dingaan used
to be. Here Piet Retief and his companions were murdered
on 6 February 1838. The sizeable, restored, Zulu town gives

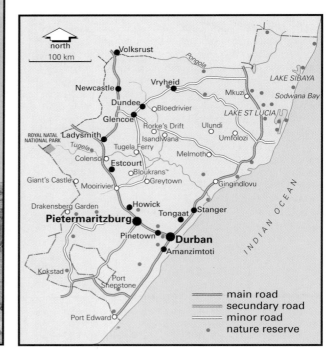

Piet Retief's fate

Discord among the *Voortrekkers* caused Piet Retief and his men
to climb the Drakensberg Mountains in 1837 and to move into
Natal in search of their 'promised land' over there. After initially
having reached an agreement with the Zulu king Dingaan, in
which Retief would have been granted the right to have a large
Zulu area grazed by the Boers' cattle, Dingaan broke his
promise. He had Retief and his party, 70 volunteers and their
non-white *agterryers*, killed in his *kraal* in East Natal. Eleven
days later there was a Zulu attack on the Boer camps at
Bloukrans, during which 500 women, children and older men
were killed. The remaining men of the *Voortrekkers* were so
discouraged by all this adversity, that they wanted to retreat
over the Drakensberg Mountains. However, the women
appealed to the men not to end the migration to the promised
land, because otherwise too much blood would have flowed for
nothing. It was decided to ask Andries Pretorius, a much
respected and wealthy Boer living in the east of the Cape
Province, to act as their leader in Natal. Pretorius agreed and
subsequently formed a 'commando' of about 500 men. They all
took a solemn vow to build a church together, the so-called
'Geloftekerk' (Church of the Vow), if they would be victorious
in the coming battle.

The grave of Piet Retief and his men at the entrance to
▼ *Mgungundlovu.*

▲ Piet Retief and king Dingaan
sign a treaty. Panel in the
Voortrekkers Monument at
Pretoria.

▲ The murder on Piet Retief
and his men.

▲ This panel depicts the Zulu
attack on the laagers at
Bloukrans, during which 500
Boers were killed.

▲ The taking of the vow under
the leadership of Sarel Cilliers
on 9 December 1838.

▲ *This tableau of the Bloukrans Monument depicts the murder of the Voortrekkers in 1838.*

a good impression of king Dingaan's might.
On the N3 from Durban to Ladysmith, nineteen kilometres past Estcourt, one can take a side-turning to Bloukrans. After the murder on Retief his remaining followers were assaulted there. At this site an impressive monument was erected in remembrance of that night of horrors on 17 February 1838. East of Dundee the Blood River flows. Here Andries Pretorius and his commando drove king Dingaan's warriors into the Ncombi, revenging the murder of Retief and his companions. At this spot another imposing monument was erected. The 64 bronze ox-wagons, representing the Boer *laager* that proved to be a fatal ambush for the Zulu, are set up in a circle.

▲ *The Bloukrans Monument in commemoration of the Voortrekkers who were killed by king Dingaan's warriors.*

▲ *Battle at the Blood River on 16 December 1838. On this panel in the Voortrekkers Monument at Pretoria, the fleeing Zulus, who are being pursued by the Voortrekkers, are depicted.*

The battle on the Blood River

Pretorius' commando with 64 ox-wagons, 900 drawing-oxen and 500 horses moved into the region where Dingaan had quartered his central forces. Dingaan mobilized an army of 10,000 Zulu warriors, who were trained at King Shaka's warrior schools. When Pretorius received the message that this enormous mass was coming at him, he chose a strategically located defence site. Near the place where the river Ncome (which would later be called Blood River) and a deep dry ditch, a *donga*, joined, he formed a *laager*. All ox-wagons were positioned in a circle and tied together with strong bunches of thornbushes. At the back of this *laager* lay the *donga*, where an army could not quickly pass through.
In the early morning of the sixteenth of December 1838, when the nocturnal mists had hardly lifted, the *Voortrekkers* saw, from their ox-wagons behind the battle-line, the Zulu regiments setting up their feared 'bull's head' formation. The main force of the Zulus came straight at them, while on both flanks rapid runners formed the so-called 'horn' formation. The 10,000 attackers, who stormed forward in serried ranks, did however not reckon with the destructive effect of the two small cannons which had been set up by the *Voortrekkers* between the ox-waggons. Another unexpected element was the fatal accuracy of the Boers' muskets, fired from a short distance, as was the fact that a number of Pioneers on horseback suddenly threw themselves on their attackers from the *laager*. Despite its numerical advantage the Zulu army had to cease the attack and withdraw. Whereas the Boers only counted four injured men, among whom Pretorius, who had received a stab-wound in his hand, they counted 3,000 dead among the Zulu warriors after the battle. Thus the murder on Retief and his men and the attack on the *Voortrekker* women and children at Bloukrans had been revenged in a horrible manner. Subsequently the 'Geloftekerk' (Church of the Vow) was built in Pietermaritzburg.

The Blood River Monument. This reconstruction of Andries Pretorius' laager consists of a circle ▼ *with 64 life-size bronze ox-waggons.*

▲ *Voortrekkers Monument in Pretoria: the building of the Church of the Vow. The architect of the Monument, Gerard Moerdijk, modelled for the man on the left of this panel.*

The Church of Vow that the Boers built after their victory, is located in Pietermaritzburg. The church, imposing due to its simplicity, is now equipped as a *Voortrekkers* museum. The house 'Welverdient', where Andries Pretorius lived, forms part of the museum. In front of the church are the life-size statues of the city's namegivers: Piet Retief and Gert Maritz, another Boer Leader, who was also killed in 1838.

The Church of the Vow ▶ in Pietermaritzburg, today a museum with a collection of memorabilia dating from the time of the Voortrekkers.

▲ *Memorial stone in commemoration of Gert Maritz, chairman of the 'Trekkers'-council.*

▲ *The Victorian townhall of Pietermaritzburg with its 47 metres' high bell-tower.*

En route to the coal-mining town of Dundee one first passes Colenso and then Ladysmith. There the Anglo-Boer War, which had started in 1899, was almost ended. For the Boers were besieging Ladysmith, while the British general Buller suffered a severe defeat near Colenso. This defeat gave Redvers Buller his nickname Reverse Buller.
Before the general finally relieved Ladysmith, owing to an enormous military advantage, he made a second blunder, this time at Spioenkop. Despite the bad experiences of the British in occupying high hills, as at Majuba in 1881, general Buller decided to capture the Spioenkop in the night of 23 January 1900. The following morning his troops were subjected to such heavy fire from the Boer snipers situated on a nearby hill, that they had to withdraw. Viewing the landscape from the mainly barren Spioenkop, it is as if the tragedy, connected with the death of hundreds of young English soldiers, can be felt.

Sign near the entrance road to ▼ Spioenkop.

▼ *Spioenkop. The Boers inflicted a defeat on the British army on this hill on the 24th of January 1900.*

▲ *Woman in KwaZulu, on her way to the market. Many women in Zululand still dress traditionally.*

Through the heart of KwaZulu

From Pietermaritzburg the R33 leads to Greytown and from there via Keate's Drift, Tugela Ferry and Pomeroy to Elandskraal and Fugitive's Drift. This journey conducts the traveller through the central part of KwaZulu. During the trip many beautifully decorated Zulu huts are passed. The people, especially women, often wear colourful traditional clothes.

After the N33, the R68 and the N11 lead along the coal-mining town of Newcastle and the historical town of Volksrust. Then the R23 leads via Standerton, on the bank of the Vaal, to Johannesburg. This route, which is more attractive than the wide N3 from Pietermaritzburg to Johannesburg, passes through a splendid landscape and past picturesque villages and hospitable farmhouses.

On the way back from Pietermaritzburg to Durban, just before the turning at Catoridge, one sees the Natal Table Mountain, which strongly resembles the one on the Cape. Past Catoridge the R103 meanders through the Valley of a Thousand Hills. On the slopes of a ravine at PheZulu lie very beautiful Zulu huts, where traditional tribal dances are performed twice a day.

By following the R103, a spectacular vista opens up from the Kloof Waterfalls road in Kranzkloof Nature Reserve. On the edge of the ravine one has a view of the perpendicularly plunging waterfall. In the reserve many birds of prey, red, blue and grey divers (Cephalophinae spec.), bushbuck antelopes (Tragelaphus scriptus) and forest swine

▲ *Waterfalls in the Karkloof Valley, a game reserve nineteen kilometres outside Pietermaritzburg.*

Zulu girls during a welcoming ceremony in the museum village of PheZulu. Twice a day traditional
▼ *tribal dances are performed here.*

▲ *Isandlwana, the hill with the sphinx head.*

The drama of Isandlwana

David Rattray accompanies his guests to the Sphinx hill, where he gives an expert account of the Isandlwana drama. En route to the strangely shaped hump, rising from an undulating plain, cut through by dongas, Rattray recounts in a gripping manner the causes of the Anglo-Zulu War against Cetshwayo, the descendant of the grand king Shaka.

On arrival at Isandlwana David Rattray draws his guests' attention to the stones in the plain. Dozens of white-washed heaps of stone lie on the site where the flower of the British army, 1,329 men, suffered a severe defeat against the army of 20,000 Zulu warriors. Standing on the slope of Isandlwana Rattray gives a description of the terrible battle: 'In the early morning of 22 January 1879 the commander-in-chief, Lord Chelmsford, made a fatal decision on this spot. He had received the message that a reconnoitring detachment had spotted a force of 2,000 Zulu men in the south-east, at a distance of twenty kilometres from the main camp. Assuming that the enemy's main forces were also located there, Lord Chelmsford and 2,000 of his men, somewhat more than half of his total forces, went to the site concerned in the hills near the Mangeni.

Later in the morning another group of scouts on horseback reached a deep gorge in the north. When they looked down into the canyon, they got the shock of their lives. As far as they could see, the crouched figures of Zulu warriors sat against the slope of the ravine. At first there was an ominous silence, then a loud order from the warriors' leader followed 'Usuthu!' (Attack!).

The chieftain's cry surged to a roar that seemed to come from the throats of 1,000 lions. Immediately the Zulus lined up in their 'horn' formation and while the British trumpeters blew the 'retreat' signal, 20,000 warriors armed with assegais stormed towards the British troops. The soldiers were lined up in squares, their backs towards each other, and could first resist by aiming their deadly gunfire at the attackers. But not for long. Almost to the last man they were pierced by the Zulu assegais from a short range. When Lord Chelmsford – meanwhile warned – returned to the Sphinx hill in the evening, the Zulu warriors had already left the camp.

In a letter to his father one of the few survivors wrote later: 'You could not put one foot before the other without touching a dead body. Oh, father, never in my whole life have I seen such a sight. I could not help bursting out in tears'.

Memorial at Isandlwana in commemoration of the British troops who were defeated here ▼ by a Zulu army in 1879.

The stone on which the Zulu in Isandlwana sharpened their spears. ▼

(Hylochoerus meinertzhageni) can be seen.

In the heart of KwaZulu (Zululand) lies Isandlwana, the hill with the sphinx head. Here the war of the English against the Zulu started with a dramatic defeat of the British army in 1879. At the 100 metres' deep gorge of the Buffalo, in an imposing natural setting at five kilometres' distance from Isandlwana, David Rattray has set up a comfortable Lodge. Rattray tours his guests around the land of the former farm, which is now destined as a nature reserve.

Near the Buffalo River is the site of the tragic history of two young lieutenants, Melville and Coghill, who had been given the assignment to save the British flag after the battle at Isandlwana. Together with a dozen fugitives, they immediately rode to the river, where at that moment the water had risen very high. They jumped into the water on horseback and managed to reach the other shore, while around them other soldiers were drowned. During the desperate struggle in the stream Melville let go of the flag. When the two lieutenants climbed out of the ravine, they were stabbed to death by hostile Zulu. On the spot where they fell a snow-white monument has been erected. The Queen's colour was later retrieved by the British on the bank of the Buffalo River. Since that time this site has been named Fugitive's Drift.

The Isandlwana drama was one of the worst colonial defeats ever suffered by England. Later there was also a nightly assault of the Zulu on Rorke's Drift on the Buffalo, where 149 men had stayed behind. Next to the missionary post the defenders built a barricade out of biscuit tins and bags of maize and withstood the assaults until auxiliary forces arrived in the early morning.

It was to last until the end of May 1879 before an overwhelming British force defeated the Zulu army at

Fugitive's Drift, the site on the Buffalo River where lieutenants Melville and Coghill jumped into the water on horseback in order to ▼ save the British flag during a desperate flight.

◄ *Hotels along the palm boulevard of Durban, a paradise for watersports enthusiasts.*

Ulundi, during which king Cetshwayo was taken prisoner. Finally, in 1887, the British government annexed the whole of Zululand.

Durban

The capital of Natal seems to have concentrated on the beach and the subtropical warm water; along the wide bay the hotel-fronts are turned towards the sea. Shark-nets lie off the coast over a distance of four kilometres, offering sufficient protection against the 'terror of the sea'. The surfers and skindivers glide swiftly with the long waves of the Indian Ocean. They sometimes even jump with their surfboards into the sea from the end of the long Vetch's Pier. From the pier fishermen also cast out their lines.

Durban. The statue of Dick King, who made a journey of 960 kilometres together with his Zulu companion Ndongeni in 1842 in order to get reinforcements in Grahamstown when his camp was ▼ *besieged by the Boers.*

At the beginning of autumn, June-July, the famous sardine-rush takes place in this bay, as at other places along the east coast of Natal; hundreds of millions of sardines are then on their way along the coast from Cape Town through the cold Benguela current and the warm Agulhas current to their spawning places in the coastal waters off Moçambique. In a belt of some hundreds of kilometres from Port St Johns to Durban the fish are caught in great masses.

During a one-day or a half-day tour one gets a good impression of Durban. Welcome Tours, Public Tours and other travel agencies first lead the tourists past the busy harbour and the gigantic docks. This is the site of three large sugar silos, where this main agricultural product of Natal is stored for export.

On the Victoria Embankment, opposite the old High Court of Justice, is the statue of Dick King, who rode on horseback over a distance of 1,000 kilometres to Grahamstown in 1842 in order to get help for the British forces who were besieged

The neo-classicistic townhall of Durban, which houses, besides the public library, two ▼ *museums as well.*

The Krishna Temple in ▶ Durban. The city boasts many Hindu Indians among its inhabitants, descendants of the nineteenth century contract labourers.

Churchill's escapades in South Africa

As a war correspondent during the Anglo-Boer War in 1899 Winston Churchill rode, at his own request, on an armoured train. The British army used this train to explore the region south of Ladysmith, which was besieged by the Boers. The train was forced to a halt due to the fact that the Boers had broken up the track at Chievely. The incident was followed by fiendish shooting by commandos who had hidden themselves in the nearby hills. During the panic that arose, Churchill proved to be a true leader. Amidst a shower of bullets and shell splinters he gave directions, as if he were a commander. After the Boers had stormed the train, Churchill was taken prisoner and transported to Pretoria. He managed to escape by crawling under a barbed-wire fence in the night and subsequently covered the distance of 450 kilometres to the Portuguese Delagoa Bay as a stowaway in a goods carriage.

After his return to Durban by boat, he delivered a flaming speech in front of a large audience, who greeted him as a war hero. Standing in front of the city-hall, without his hat, his hair hanging down on his forehead, he incited the population to a greater patriotic disposition. Back at his post as a war correspondent of the Morning Post, he expressed serious criticism on the British war-management in his articles. Apart from that he spoke with admiration about the Boers. 'The individual Boer on horseback can take a stand against three to five British soldiers. The only way to face up to these Boers, is to deploy people with a similar character on our side, or a mass concentration of regular troops.' This latter advice was followed, but it would still take years before England won the war.

Plaque in remembrance of ▶ the speech delivered by Winston Churchill in front of the townhall of Durban in 1899.

in Natal by the Boers. The imposing new town-hall houses a natural-history museum and an art gallery. Nearby is the town-hall dating from 1885, which is nowadays in use as a post-office. Opposite this national monument is a plaque on a socle, with on it a statue of the young war correspondent Winston Churchill, shortly after his escape from Boer imprisonment.

In Durban many people of Indian origin live and work, the descendants of the Indian labourers who were recruited in the 1860s for the sugar cane plantations. A great number of them eventually ended up in trade and service-industries. The Muslims among them can be proud of their beautiful Juma Mosque, the largest mosque in the southern hemisphere. The Indian district and the Indian bazaar seem to move the tourist to a district in an Indian city. The Hindu Krishna Temple of Understanding in the suburb of Chatsworth is an unusual building on the outside, on the inside it resembles a huge mysterious treasure-chamber.

The African Art centre is located in the Guildhall shopping-arcade, where numerous handicrafts are offered for sale. The history of the city comes alive in the Museum for Local History in the Aliwal Street. The Old House Museum in the St Andrew Street has several pieces of furniture and objects from the houses of the first *setlaars* on display. The botanical garden houses, among other things, a fine orchid nursery. Twenty kilometres north of Durban, near Umhlanga Rocks, lies a second beach area, protected by shark-nets. These are, just like the shark-nets off the dozens of other beaches along the coast of Natal, regularly checked and maintained by the Natal Anti-Shark Measures Boards. It is the only council of its kind in the world. The main building of the council, situated between Umhlanga Rocks and Edgecombe and where thorough research is done into the way of life of sharks, can be visited.

The 'holiday coast' of South Africa, with sunshine the whole year round, extends to the south between Durban and Port Edward on the border with Transkei. A train-journey from Durban to Port Shepstone leads past wide sandy beaches, lush vegetation, quiet seaside-resorts, fishing waters, hotels, casinos, golflinks, and five subtropical nature reserves just beyond the coast.

◄ *Black residential district outside Durban. In the housing districts KwaMashu and Umlazi live an estimated 850,000 people. Durban itself has about 800,000 inhabitants.*

◄ *The interior of the Temple of Understanding in Durban.*

◄ *Exotic vegetables at the Indian market in Durban.*

◄ *Spices, curry restaurants, perfume and incense provide the aroma of the Orient.*

Shakaland

From Durban two main roads lead to Johannesburg and Pretoria. The N3 forms the direct connection via Pietermaritzburg in South Natal and Harrismith in the east of Orange Free State. The indirect road leads on the N2 along the east coast of Natal up to the southern border of Swaziland. Via the capital of Mbabane the southern entrance of the Kruger park in Transvaal is reached. From there the N4 leads back to Pretoria and Johannesburg. Most travel agencies and individual travellers follow this longer, but more scenic, route. Highlights are Shakaland, the game reserves in North Natal, the drive through Swaziland with a stay at Mbabane, Krugerpark and an optional visit to the private game reserves west of Krugerpark.

To the north of the Umhlanga Rocks the almost infinite sugar cane plantations begin, that have left their clear mark on life in Natal. In the surroundings of Tongaat and Stanger the agricultural Indian community is concentrated, where Mahatma Gandhi practised his ideas for twenty years on end. In this area Gandhi founded the Phoenix community farm. Near Stanger Zulu king Shaka was killed by his two half-brothers, Dingaan and Mhlangane in 1828.

On the bank of the Tugela stands an old fig tree, the Ultimatum tree, under which the British governor handed the ultimatum to Zulu king Cetshwayo in 1878. This act was the signal for the Anglo-Zulu War. Close to the mouth of the Tugela lies Fort Pearson, the spring-board for the British in the final stages of the Anglo-Zulu War.

At Gingindlovu the R68 bends away from the N2 to Shakaland. Eshowe, the location of king Cetshwayo's *kraal*, is the centre of the sugar industry nowadays.

Near Eshowe king Shaka's main *kraal* used to be situated. Just beyond the city Shakaland was built on behalf of the tourists. The huge Zulu *kraal*, among several other beehive-like huts, had a central function in the film Shaka-Zulu which was for the main part shot here. On the grounds the Protea chain exploits guests' quarters in the form of beehive huts.

In the open space in front of the huts the visitors to Shakaland are received. An interpreter explains about Zulu culture, their clothing, dancing and way of life. The contents of this explanation are, apart from other sources, based on the research of the socio-anthropologist Barry Leitch, who, together with Kingsley Holgate made a study of Zulu culture. This study was also the basis for the film Shaka-Zulu.

During a tour one can see two 'witchdoctors' and a pupil sitting on the hard tamped earth, surrounded by magical attributes. In the chief's huge *kraal* lively Zulu dances are performed. The *kraal* is a holy site, which according to the Zulu is protected by the ancestors' spirits. The ingeniously constructed giant hut is supported by long heavy tree-trunks.

▲ *In Shakaland an attempt is made to imitate an authentic Zulu community, including 'magicians' and 'ritual' dances.*

In Shakaland one can observe how women in traditional costume ▼ *produce Zulu handicrafts.*

Warrior in the kraal of PheZulu, a Zulu village also laid out as a ▼ *'living museum'.*

The floor was hardened by using the tamped soil of termite hills. On top of that cow-dung was smeared, providing a smooth finish. Dances are also performed around a flaming wood-fire with, in the background, the beautiful lake in front of the dam in the Umhlatuzi. In Shakaland one can also observe how colourfully dressed women produce the traditional Zulu handicrafts.

The game reserves of North Natal

The well-meant chemical operation, aimed at annihilating the tsetse fly, very nearly also destroyed the majority of the wildlife in North Natal. The action was concentrated on the Umfolozi Game Reserve, the most southern in a chain of wildlife parks. In 1940, the spraying by means of aircraft sparked off an ecological disaster on this territory measuring 47,500 hectares. Almost 100,000 wild animals lost their lives. Fortunately nature managed to recuperate from this catastrophe. Today there are again more than 50 species of mammals, 40 species of reptiles and at least 400 species of birds.

Only half of the wilderness in Umfolozi can be visited by car, along a narrow road. The southern part can only be explored on foot, as if in the tracks of the hunters of Zulu leader Shaka. During hunts they drove large number of game into camouflaged pitfalls. The traps had been set up at the site where the Black and White Umfolozi meet in the south-east of the game park. The Natal Parks Council organizes two and three days' hikes through the wilderness.

In Umfolozi Game Reserve a spectacular operation took place in order to safeguard the survival of the almost extinct white rhinos. This rhinoceros with its broad lips was described as 'wide-lip renoster' by the Boers. The word 'wide' was corrupted to 'white', explaining the strange name for the animal that certainly has not got a white skin. The rescue operation caused the rhino population to increase from some dozens to thousands! The animals have multiplied to such an extent that in the meantime 3000 have been taken to other regions.

Umfolozi houses the same animal species as Kruger Park. As in the whole of Zululand, the lion was extinct in this area. However, in 1958 a solitary male specimen from Moçambique arrived here. After years of solitude a female joined him. After some period of time a hundred of lions were living in Umfolozi. From 1985 elephants have been introduced from Kruger Park. Four shelters at drinking-places and rivers offer good opportunities to observe the game.

Umfolozi Game Reserve borders on the Hluhluwe Game Reserve which is only half as big and extends along the river of the same name to the vicinity of the N2. In Hluhluwe one finds – in a hilly landscape – reasonably passable paths. During heavy showers, especially in the beginning of the summer period, the rangers in their landrovers sometimes have to come to the rescue of car-drivers, as the roads, due to their low location, then change into shallow pools. Besides the animal species that live in Umfolozi, giraffes and black rhinos can also be seen in Hluhluwe. A distinction from the white broad lip rhinos is that the black rhinos have a pointed mouth, more suited to eating foliage. The black rhino is, in contrast to the peaceful white rhino, aggressive by nature. It is therefore wise always to keep a distance from these animals.

North of Hluhluwe, also close to the N2, lies the savanna landscape of the Mkuzi Game Reserve. The great diversity of animal species here is characteristic for the north of KwaZulu. In this region one can find, among others, wart-hogs, klipspringers, elands, waterbucks, mountain-reedbucks (Redunca fulvorufula) and saddle jackals (Canis mesomelas). Besides large numbers of black rhinos there are many nyalas in the reserve. Just like kudus they have vertical stripes on their flanks, however the shape of the head and

The way to an elephant's heart is through his stomach

During the safari through Mkuzi Game Reserve an extraordinary thing happened: an elephant-couple was standing in the shade of a few high trees. The male was seemingly excited by the proximity of the female, because he had a marked virile appearance. His figure became more and more impressive, when he went over and stood close to the female. Meanwhile we wondered how these tyrants actually couple. But at the 'moment suprême' the female grasped a heavily leaved branch in front of her, tore it down without any visible exertion and...offered the tasty bite in a graceful gesture to her partner! The latter accepted the branch just like that and started to grind it away. In the meantime the female took two slow steps forward and then we saw that apparently the way to an elephant's heart is through his stomach. Peacefully the two elephants walked on and disappeared in the shadows of the thick thorn bushes.

▲ *Behind these rhinos, accompanied by the inevitable oxpeckers, a large termite hill is visible.*
▼ *Nyala at a pool in Mkuzi Game Reserve.*

▲ *Snorting hippos; hippo-bulls can reach a weight of up to 3,000 kilogrammes.*

▲ *Pink flamingos in St Lucia Lake.*

The terror of St Lucia

Besides the elephant, the crocodile belonged to the most hunted animals in the past. Over the past 30 years at least three million crocodiles have been killed in Africa. The crocodiles are not only threatened by hunting but also by the use of fishing nets, in which they can get entangled and then drown. That is why their numbers, in South Africa as well, have decreased at an alarming rate.

However, in the aquatic paradise of St Lucia the species survives well. It is strictly prohibited to swim in the water of the lake or the estuary or to be out on the water with a rubber-boat or canoe. Even putting a hand into the water, let alone dangling one foot overboard, is explicitly dissuaded by the rangers.

Although this dangerous protozoic animal incites sympathy among very few people, the crocodile fulfils a useful ecological function. If this animal becomes extinct, the omnivorous barbels (Barbus spec.), forming the crocodiles' staple diet, would decimate the other fish. Consequently the existence of at least 40 species of birds, such as the gracious fish-kingfishers (Alcedininae spec.) and the herons (Ardea spec.) would become jeopardized.

It is amazing how carefully the female crocodiles handle their young. The males have no part in this. In contrast, they sometimes behave like cannibals, even towards their own offspring. In the mating season, when the strongest among them have as many as five females within their territories, there are terrible fights between the dominant male crocodiles. With a blood-curdling roaring and loud clapping of their long jaws, they sometimes jump up high from the water. When they fall back into the water, the water-surface, lashed by their tails, transforms into foam.

After the mating season the females lay their eggs in holes of about 40 centimetres deep, which they dig themselves. Then they cover the nest with soil and sand. For a period of about 90 days they then guard their nesthole against predators. After that time the young crawl from the eggs and immediately start producing a loud clamour, resembling the sound of crying. Subsequently the female digs up the nest with her front legs. With incredible precision she very carefully picks up the young one by one with her sharp teeth and transports them to a quiet spot between the water plants. Here the baby crocodiles immediately start hunting for insects, snails, tadpoles and small frogs. They grow very rapidly: from a length of a few decimetres at birth to about four metres when they are adults. Their weight increases from 125 grammes to about 500 kilogrammes, that is up to 4,000 times their original weight!

the horns of the male specimens differ strongly.

On the coast, south of the Mkuzi Game Reserve, the Mkuzi broadens into a huge lake with a length of 60 kilometres. Already at the end of the previous century the area was labelled as Game Reserve. St Lucia Lake is a pleasureground for more than 350 bird species. Sailing on the shallow lake and the long gully into which it discharges, one often sees ibises (Threskiornis aethiopica), pink pelicans (Pelicanus onocrotalis) and pink flamingos (Phoenicopterus ruber roseas). From open spaces in the infinite reed-lands ducks make their drumming sounds across the water, rising up in flocks that resemble clouds. On the banks and on the islands in the lake several species of antelopes, impalas, reedbucks and divers live. Here and there a group of hippos lie close together in the shallow water, only the huge heads are visible. Sniffing and consequently producing a fountain of water drops, an inquisitive specimen now and then emerges. Among the reed on the islands lie crocodiles. These masters of camouflage are often hardly visible.

St Lucia is the mecca for nature lovers and fishermen. Along the lake several walks can be taken, guided by parkkeepers. Resting camps, hotels and apartments in the town of St Lucia offer accommodation to the visitor.

To the north of the four large game reserves in Maputoland, as North Natal is also called, lie several other smaller reserves, such as Sodwana Bay National Park, Kosi Bay Nature Reserve and Ndumu Game Reserve. These parks form ideal biotopes for leather tortoises (Dermochelys coracea) which can reach a length of two metres and a weight of 500 kilos. Here the animals come ashore to lay their eggs. Sodwana Bay National Park is renowned for its coral reefs and water basins that fill up at high tide. Sea-fishing is especially popular in the region. Kosi Bay Nature Reserve, near the border with Moçambique, also boasts a rich fauna. In the reserve live, besides leather tortoises, among others hippos and crocodiles. About 247 species of birds have been spotted in the reserve, among them the swifts (Cypsiurus parvus), herons (Gorsachius leuconotus) and plovers (Dromas Ardeola). Ndumu Game Reserve on the border with Moçambique houses 416 species of birds besides innumerable small and large mammals. A breeding station for crocodiles is also located in Ndumu. In Maputoland, 40 kilometres from the Sodwana coral reefs on the coast, the latest game reserve of Natal, Phinda, has recently been opened to the public. For a long time the 14,000 hectares' large area was the missing link between Mkuzi Game Reserve and Sodwana Bay National Park. Rare nyalas and even rarer suni, dwarf antelopes weighing no more than four kilogrammes, and several other well-known species of game, roam here through a varied landscape.

At the initiative of the owner of the Londolozi Game Reserve a 'conservation corporation' was founded. This institute aims at getting the surrounding population involved in the interests of nature preservation. They are allowed to chop wood and cut grass on the grounds of the park and are allotted the game that has to be shot. Several animal species that had already disappeared from this region, have been brought back to nature in Phinda.

The lofty world of the Drakensberg Mountains

In the Drakensberg Mountains landscapes have arisen that seem to belong to a phantasy world. This capricious freak of nature can be called lofty in two senses. In a distant past this extraordinary roof of South Africa was shaped out of a series of basalt layers. The basalt was pushed upwards in a liquid form from breaches in the earth's crust by volcanic forces. The layers were kept together by a stone-hard skeleton of *dolerite*. The softer basalt was broken down and ground away in the course of time due to erosion. What rested are the more than 1,000 metres' high flattened walls, with sharp rocks protruding from them as the most fantastic sculptures of nature. Due to a combination of sunlight and cloud shadows the entire mountain range with its gorges is often mysteriously coloured. In the summer months the thunder-clouds accumulate. While heavy thunder makes the ground tremble, flashes of lightning now and then strike down onto the mountain peaks and illuminate the landscape that had been covered in half-darkness. When the sun already starts to shine on one mountain ridge, new castles of thunder-clouds arise in the violet distance and the rumble of thunder resounds.

In former days the valleys and gorges were the hunting grounds of the San people. During their hunts they found shelter in caves, the walls of which proved to be an ideal underground for their imaginative rock paintings. The black hunters and warriors climbing the endless mountain crest, compared it to a world of dragons. The Boers who, in their turn, crossed the 1,000 kilometres' long mountain ridge, copied this well-chosen name. In letters they made mention of the fact that these gigantic mountain edges conveyed a sense of oppression. After the *Voortrekkers* families had wrestled their way to the top in their wagons, made of stone-hard stink wood and drawn by extremely powerful oxen, they were often overcome with a deep sensation of triumph. When, today, one stands on one of the peaks of the Drakensberg Mountains and looks down below, where vast hills and valleys extend up to the horizon, one is overwhelmed by this grand nature. A journey through the Drakensberg Mountains is a highlight in the long series of indelible impressions the tourist experiences in South Africa. The best time for such a journey is in spring and in the beginning of summer, that is to say between September and November. When, after the dry winter period the first abundant summer rains have drenched the gorges and valleys, the earth reveals her gratitude. Everything comes alive: between the light-green tendrils on climbers hang wall-flowers (Dierama pendulum); pink river-lilies (Schizostylis)

shoot up along the banks of mountain streams and, from cracks in the basalt, hanging orchids bloom. The lower mountain slopes are transformed as by magic into variegated carpets of daisies. Golden proteas are surpassed in beauty by fiery orange-coloured aloes (Aloe arborescens).

◄ *Orange-red aloes at the foot of a slope of the Drakensberg Mountains.*

The southern Drakensberg Mountains

Near the border of Natal with Lesotho are three regions, which can be considered as belonging to the panoramic highlights in the southern Drakensberg Mountains. The comparison of some mountain peaks to castles was the reason why the game reserve, measuring 34,000 hectares in surface-area and founded west of Estcourt in 1903, was called Giant's Castle. All around the highest point in this game reserve, the 3400 metres' high Njesuthi Dome, the high mountain walls were elevated here and there by turrets and fortresses of basalt and *dolerite*. Along the Bosjesman River an unforgettable walk can be taken. At other places the area is also cut through by paths. For the elands, the largest species among the antelopes, this region is an ideal resting-place. In several caves rock paintings of the San are to be found. In the most significant cave along the Bosjesman the walls are covered with as many as 500 paintings.

South of Giant's Castle lies the lovely Drakensberg Garden, an ideal region for a rest after some days of strenuous trips along the sights. Dozens of apartments offer views of the capricious mountain ridges, through which a river, teeming with trout, flows in the summer months.

A literal and symbolical highlight in the southern Drakensberg Mountains is formed by the amphitheatre in the Royal National Park of Natal. There is a steeply rising mountain wall at that spot between two 'watchtowers', which are called 'the sentry' and 'the eastern pillar'. From a deep gorge in the 'pillar' a long sharp rock rises up, the Devil's tooth. On the slopes of 'the sentry' grows one of the rarest plants in the world, the small pink Protea nubigena, which only occurs on this apparently inhospitable mountain tower. Behind the amphitheatre lies the highest mountain peak of the park, the Mont-Aux Sources, given that name by two French missionaries because in this region several rivers rise. These rivers plunge down in waterfalls at various places. The most famous are the Tugela Waterfalls in the Tugela River; at the largest of them the water drops down over a depth of 600 metres.

These western regions of Natal form an ideal entrance-gate to the heart of South Africa, the Orange Free State.

Paradise-bird flower (Strelitzia regina). The flowerbud consists of a pointed, green sheath from which orange coloured flower petals point upwards. Each of these petals has a blue, oblong protrusion with a ▼ *gland excreting nectar at the bottom. Honey-birds suck up the nectar by drilling holes in these protrusions.*

7 THE LEGENDARY CENTRE

Hemmed in by two huge rivers, the Orange and the Vaal, the sun-drenched Orange Free State forms the heart of South Africa. In the tracks of hunters, traders, Voortrekkers and missionaries, the visitor can get acquainted with this hospitable province, surrounded by land.
In the east lies the mountainous world of the independent kingdom of Lesotho.

New diamond cities are arising in the west of Orange Free State. In the eastern part of the province, on the border with the 'kingdom in the sky', Lesotho, the traces of the *Voortrekkers*, who left deep marks in history, can be recovered in the landscape. In the Drakensberg Mountains, where the Orange rises, the artistic heritage of the San archers has been preserved in numerous rock paintings. The sagas and legends of their descendants still lead their own lives there.

Lesotho, the 'kingdom in the sky'

The kingdom of Lesotho was declared independent by England in 1965. It is a 'kingdom in the sky', because there is not a place in the country that has an altitude below 1000 metres above sea level. The Thabana-Ntlenyana, the highest mountain of southern Africa, reaches to a height of 3482 metres.
The interior of Lesotho is a desolate mountainous world, alternated by vast hills and plateaus, once the habitat of dinosaurs and other giant reptiles. Their fossil footprints can be found at Butha-Buthe, in the north of Lesotho. In the rocks in the vicinity of Ladybrand, among other places at Teyateyaneng, Mafeteng, Moyeni and Ralebona, the San left their paintings. The Basotho kingdom of the wise king Moshesh was established here at the beginning of the nineteenth century.
Thirty kilometres from the present-day capital of Maseru, Moshesh had a sheer unassailable fortress built, on top of the 200 metres' high, flattened hill Thaba Bosiu. The king called his fortress 'The mountain of the night'. From there he and his Basotho repelled many attacks by Zulu and Ndebele and here he gathered a large group of displaced persons around himself, victims of king Shaka's victories. Moshesh's might was jeopardized by attacks of the Griqua, who possessed guns and rode on ponies. The Griqua had been driven to the north-east by the advancing Trekboers, who were in search of grazing land for their herds. The followers of the king managed to defeat the Griqua and soon the Basotho also developed into a 'nation on horseback', amply supplied with guns. Today many Sotho still move about through the country on horseback in their bright attire. The cool climate has caused a beautifully coloured blanket to be an important article of clothing.
Moshesh managed to resist the continuous attacks of the Boers from Orange Free State by calling in the help of the British, who subsequently annexed 'Basotholand' in 1868. On the hill Thaba Bosiu are the remnants of Moshesh's fortress and his grave. A statue of him can be found in Maseru.

◄ The Golden Gate Highlands National Park owes its name to the high sandstone formations on both sides of the western entrance road to the park.

◄ Orange river lily (Crinum bunbispermum), one of the most beautiful flowers of the Highveld.

In the south lies another mountain that was, for a long time, an unassailable fortress. It marks the site of the famous chief Moorosi's fortress. It took until 1879 before the British managed to conquer this bulwark. This occurred in the night of 19 and 20 November during an assault, launched by 400 men of the 'Cape Mounted Rifles'.

Qwaqwa

Qwaqwa lies hemmed in between Natal, Orange Free State and the north of Lesotho. One can make an adventurous journey through the region from the summit of the Mount-aux-Sources in Natal to the eastern entrance to the Golden Gate Highlands National Park in Orange Free State. The capital of the mountain kingdom is Phuthaditjhaba, which has a modest arts industry. Among other things mohair and sheep-wool tapestries, hand-painted porcelain, brass-ware, baskets and cane-furniture are produced here.

Straight across Lesotho

The places of interest in mountainous Lesotho are often difficult to reach. For some routes with a bad road-surface a rented Avis landrover is advisable. Both trips from Maseru to Moorosi and along Thaba Bosiu to Marakabei in the heart of Lesotho, are unforgettable. The traditional round and rectangular stone *rondavels* with their grass roofs lie scattered across the hilly landscape and artistic crafts are on sale in several villages.

The influences of generations of missionaries are still present

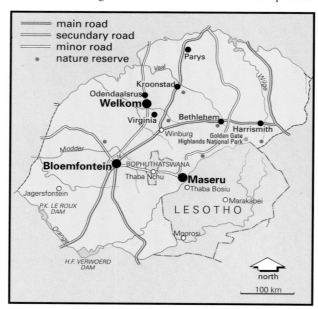

Hartebeests. Before the arrival of the Boers these hoofed animals migrated across the Highveld and the Karoo in ▼ huge herds.

in many places. In fact one can find a mixture of Christianity and ancestor worship in Lesotho, as is the case elsewhere in Africa. Belief in heaven and hell is combined with the age-old San concept that death is a rebirth into the world of the ancestors' spirits.

Medicine-men still have an important role here, such as for instance in tracing the causes of disease and adversity, in predicting secrets that lie hidden in the future, in protecting houses against lightning and invoking rain after a long period of drought.

There are initiation rites, just as in Swaziland, for both girls and boys. The girls then dress in sheepskin aprons, with plaited grass around their waists and a veil of grass and beads in front of their faces. At new moon they have to run to a river where they symbolically wash away their childhood. The boys are circumcised, after which they remain in an initiation-hut for the period of one month.

Orange Free State

If ever rivers can determine the face of a country, that characteristic can certainly be attributed to the Vaal and the Orange. Together they form the northern, western and southern borders of Orange Free State. This province of South Africa used to be an independent Republic. Just like Transvaal, the *Voortrekkers* state was recognized as a 'Boer Republic' by the United Kingdom in the middle of the nineteenth century.

The Orange rises in the Drakensberg mountains, flows straight through Lesotho and then forms the border between Orange Free State and the Cape Province. At the spot where the Caledon flows into the Orange from the north, a huge 100 kilometres' long lake arose at the Hendrik Verwoerd Dam. The dammed up water in front of the 90 metres' high dam is used to irrigate large parts of the dry interior region and to generate electricity. In the Hendrik Verwoerd Dam Nature Reserve live, among others, large herds of springboks, wildebeests and red hartebeests (Alcelaphus buselaphus caama). The reservoir boasts a rich stock of fish and offers a great number of possibilities for watersports enthusiasts.

The region north of the Orange, including Bloemfontein in the heart of the province and Boshof in the west, is called Transgariep. This name is derived from the Hottentot word 'Gariep', denoting the Orange.

The *Voortrekkers'* traces across the prairies were partly obliterated in the nineteenth century by those of the thousands of fortune-hunters, who searched for scarce fortune in the diamond mines at Jagersfontein and Koffiefontein. At Koffiefontein the open diamond mine has meanwhile been excavated to a depth of 240 metres. During the Second World War some of the terrain of the De Beers mines was adapted for use as internment camps for German civilians, Italian P.O.W.s and pro-nazi Afrikaners.

▼ *Herd of springboks in the Hendrik Verwoerd Dam Nature Reserve.*

Bloemfontein, city of roses

In the north of Transgariep lies the provincial capital of Bloemfontein. Roses grow everywhere in parks, along streets and in private gardens. The arrival of summer is celebrated for ten days by the Rose Festival. Bloemfontein has a particularly rich and splendid architecture. President Brandstreet, named after the fourth Free State President, is the only street in South Africa that is declared a national monument in itself. The official residence of the former Free State Presidents, built on the land of the old Bloemfontein farm, is situated along this street. The Fourth 'Raadsaal' (council chamber) , a stately Victorian building dating from 1885, is the architectonic gem of Bloemfontein. Here the Legislative Assembly of the Orange Free State first gathered. The oldest monument of Bloemfontein is the First 'Raadsaal', with a thatched roof and a floor of stamped dung. It was built in 1849, when the *Voortrekkers* settled around the Hartebeest house of Johannes Nicolaas Brits. The statue of the hero of the Boer War, general Christiaan de Wet, seated on his beloved horse Fleur, stands in front of the Fourth 'Raadsaal'. A number of personal belongings of Christiaan de Wet, state president Marthinus Steyn and photographs of the rebellion of 1914, have been collected in the Military Museum of the Boer Republic in Church Street. The National Afrikaans Literary Museum, devoted to the rise and development of the African language and literature, can also be found in President Brandstreet.

At the foot of the two hills south of Bloemfontein the poignant National Women's Memorial was erected, in commemoration of the 26,370 Boer women and children who perished in concentration camps during the Anglo-Boer War. The monument, dating from 1913, consists of a 36,5 metres' high obelisk and a socle with two women on it: one is carrying a dying child in her arms and the other gazes across the plains of Orange Free State. At the foot of the monument Emily Hobhouse's ashes have been interred. She was the great advocate of the constantly increasing opposition in England and other countries to the existence of concentration camps in South Africa during the Anglo-Boer War. It is less well-known that these ink-black pages in British history also contain the fact that, besides the 116,000 whites in the 40 concentration camps, a similar number of black women and children had to live in 60 separate camps. Of the latter category 14,000 died. The reason for their detention was that they, just like the whites, provided assistance to the commandos of the Boers.

There are two beautiful churches in Bloemfontein: the Anglican cathedral dating from 1850 and the Twin-spired Church, the only 'Nederduitse' Reformed church with two spires in South Africa.

The 'Riemland'

The north-eastern part of Orange Free State was called the 'Riemland' of old. This name was derived from the belts that were cut from the many hides, which game-hunting in these regions yielded in the second half of the nineteenth century. Unfortunately the large populations of elephants, lions and springboks that had their territories here were exterminated systematically. Today the landscape is dominated by sizeable landed estates, which yield an important part of the South African grain production. In many old *Voortrekkers'* villages, such as Heilbron, Reitz and Vreede, the farms lie in the middle of fields in which cannas (Canna indica) are cultivated. In the summer months the landscape is transformed into a fantastic colour-mosaic formed by these flowers. The region offers several possibilities to spend a hospitable farm holiday. In the east of Orange Free State lies the route that the *Voortrekkers* with their creaking ox-wagons took during the

◄ *This relief on the National Women's Memorial at Bloemfontein depicts the sad trail of the Afrikaner women and children to the British concentration camps during the Anglo-Boer War.*

◄ *Statue in the centre of Kroonstad: taking the Vow by Sarel Cilliers on 18 December 1838.*

◄ *Fields full of blooming cannas colour the landscape orange-yellow in the north-east of Orange Free State. This flower-reed originates from tropical regions, but is nowadays cultivated as a decorative plant all over the world.*

▲ *The black eagle has its domain, among other places, in the Drakensberg Mountains and, while hovering over the fertile valleys, searches for preys, such as cliff badgers, dwarf antelopes and young baboons.*

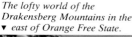

The lofty world of the Drakensberg Mountains in the ▼ *east of Orange Free State.*

Great-Trek to Transvaal. After having left Grahamstown and Graaff-Reinet, they crossed the Orange and went on northwards up to Thaba Nchu in the present-day enclave Bophuthatswana, east of Bloemfontein. From there a group migrated to Transvaal via Winburg. Others journeyed across the Drakensberg Mountains to Natal.

Winburg itself, located on the great N1 to Johannesburg, seems to be drenched in the history of the *Voortrekkers*. The town, which has hardly changed, became the first capital of Orange Free State in 1842. Near Winburg stand the five columns of the Voortrekkers Monument. They symbolize the five great trekking journeys of Louis Trichardt to Transvaal and the Delagoa Bay, of Andries Hendrik Potgieter to North Transvaal, and of Piet Retief, Gerrit Maritz and Piet Uys to Natal. As in Pretoria, a Voortrekkers Museum has been installed here too.

The 'golden gate to Natal'

The highland route runs from Zastron in the south-east of Orange Free State to Harrismith in the north-east. The R26 from Ladybrand via Ficksburg to Bethlehem offers marvellous views of the spectacular Maluti Mountains in Lesotho. At Fouriesburg one can take a left turning to Bethlehem in the fertile valley of the river Jordan, with its splendid recreation areas. Leaving Bethlehem, Harrismith is soon reached, close to the border with Natal and situated on the N3, about halfway between Johannesburg and Durban.

On turning right at Fouriesburg, in the direction of Clarens, one reaches the 'golden gate to Natal'. A visit to this park, the Golden Gate Highlands National Park, forms a glorious

conclusion of an exploratory journey through South Africa. At the western entrance of the park are two heavy sandstone 'pillars'. When the sun shines on them, they function as a golden gate to the rough sandstone formations in the more than 6,000 hectares' large nature reserve beyond.

The *Voortrekkers*, who considered Natal as their 'promised land', went through this gate. Here they discovered a true hunters' paradise. The region teemed with antelopes and as a result also with lions and leopards. During the journey through this part of the Drakensberg Mountains, the *voorlopers*, who walked in front of the cart oxen, had to explore the road with their guns at the ready.

In a later period seven farms were established in these highlands. On the grasslands numerous antelopes were shot successively in order to retain more grass for cows and goats. All predators were ruthlessly killed. When this wonderful region was declared a National Park in 1963, a start was made with bringing back most game species that had once inhabited the region. Today large numbers of gnus, zebras, 'blesbokken' (Damaliscus dorcas philippsi), hartebeests, 'klipjagers', rare oribi antelopes (Ourebia ourebi) and elands, the giants among the antelopes, roam the region again. However, lions were not brought back, as the park was deemed too small.

The Golden Gate Park is a treasure-trove of nature. It can be partly transversed by car or by walking-trips, varying from half an hour to a day. The rivers offer excellent trout fishing. The starting point for all of this is the main resting-camp Brandwag. A second resting-place is Glen Reenen camp, with *rondavels* and a caravan park, annex open-air swimming-pool.

Extraordinary sandstone formations and ravines can be

◄ *High in the sky above the Golden Gate Park the lammergeyer circles around. This species has almost become extinct in South Africa; the remaining population only consists of some dozens of pairs. The lammergeyer consumes the remains of carrion left by other vultures.*

reached on foot within ninety minutes. From a hill above the Echo ravine one overlooks the Drakensberg Mountains in all their splendour. Opposite the main camp the 'Brandwag pillar' rises from the surrounding hilly landscape like three yellow turrets melted together. Rock paintings by the San stimulate the spectator's imagination to envisage the life of the small archers and their families, who were at one with nature. The surrealistically shaped Cathedral Cave proves to be a cavern, formed by wind and water in a prehistoric past.
During the exploration of the Golden Gate Highlands Park one should cast one's eyes upwards now and then.

Sometimes a black eagle (Aquila verreauxi) hovers against the clear blue sky or the cloud masses. Lammergeyers (Gypaetus barbatus), the rarest birds of prey in South Africa, often also wheel their symmetrical circles in the sky. Unfortunately their numbers are much fewer than in the regions where predators are present. They mainly feed on carrion, which happens to be less prevalent here.
On leaving the Drakensberg region and returning to the civilized world, one realizes one has been in close contact with the still active, extremely versatile, creative process of nature. It is especially this process that makes South Africa a unique experience for tourists.

Between Bethlehem and Ficksburg steam-train enthusiasts can enjoy
▼ *impressive views.*

ECONOMIC PERSPECTIF

Recent political reforms are propelling South Africa into a new political, social and economic era. The country faces a future of great challenge and opportunity. South Africa can now take its place in the world economy unfettered by the extraordinary handicaps of recent years.

In this chapter the economical prospects of South Africa are discussed in more detail and viewed realistically against the background of several future expectations. The South African economists Nico Czypionka and Thomas Scott present their visions. The adjacent frame shows Clem Sunter's contribution, entitled: 'South Africa at a turning point in its history'.

Political reform has lifted the apartheid straitjacket from the economy. No longer will apartheid laws invade individual freedom of choice about where to work, spend and invest and thus interfere with the efficient allocation and distribution of resources in the economy; no longer will there be a need for wasteful duplication of public administration or a large military establishment.

Furthermore, the ending of international sanctions against South Africa, together with the political changes in other parts of the world opens the way for a return to traditional export markets and provides access to major new potential markets for exporters. The end of sanctions also means the end of obstacles to foreign investment and intellectual exchange as well as unimpeded access to the new technology necessary to make industry and commerce competitive.

For South Africans the challenge of the new era is to build a just and stable society which can meet the reasonable aspirations of its people. The country's considerable strengths and resources must be harnessed and use must be made of the new possibilities to right the wrongs of the past. For the foreigner the ending of apartheid brings interesting opportunities, such as access to new markets and investment prospects in a country with a significant growth potential, a wealth of natural resources and a well-established industrial infrastructure. All the more since the country is well-positioned on international trade routes serving Europe, Asia and America. Finally foreign investors are offered the possibility of a stake in a country poised to take a leading role in the economic rebirth of Sub-Saharan Africa.

The face of South Africa's economy today: a study in duality

A visitor flying to South Africa would enter the country through Jan Smuts International Airport in Johannesburg, the biggest of the country's 37 major and minor airports served by scheduled air services. From the moment of arrival impressions crowd in. It does not take very long for the

South Africa at a turning point in its history

South Africa is at a turning point in its history. Despite the violence, the country possesses a sufficient reservoir of good will for agreement to be reached on a new constitution in he near future. It is likely to be something akin to the American constitution: a multi-party system, a Bill of Rights, a two-chamber parliament, an independent judiciary, restricted presidential powers and devolution of authority to regional and locally elected bodies.

South Africa has four great strengths which can power its economy up to a growth rate between five and ten percent. It has one of the most modern infrastructures of any developing country in the world. The roads, railways, telecommunications network, electricity grid, harbours and airports are first class. Its mineral resources are still enviable despite more than a century of intense mining. It is potentially the tourist mecca of the southern hemisphere, possessing a unique floral kingdom (*fynbos*) in the Cape and an amazingly wide variety of flora and fauna. Finally, like Britain has its shopkeepers, South Africa has its entrepreneurs: from those who are prepared to bet their companies on mining ventures to those responsible for a growth rate in manufactured exports of twelve percent per annum during the second half of the 1980s. Heroes from the informal sector have brightened many disadvantaged communities by turning them into hives of entrepreneurial ingenuity.

Just like Singapore, Korea and Taiwan with their rapidly increasing export and conquest of the world markets are called Asian 'dragons', symbols of prosperity in the Orient, South Africa can, with a little bit of help from its friends, become the first 'African Dragon' of the 21st century.

C.L. Sunter,
chairman of the gold- and uranium division of the Anglo American Corporation of South Africa.

◄ *Avenue with jacaranda trees in the business centre of Pretoria.*

◄ *South Africa is an important supplier of gold and other precious minerals. Just like gold-winning in the mines, casting gold ingots is done by means of sophisticated methods.*

Johannesburg, the commercial heart of South Africa. ▶

Stone containing emerald. South Africa has a wealth of precious stones and minerals such as garnet, manganese, malachite, topaz and turquoise. ▶

complexity, and contradictions of South Africa to register on the visitor. At every turn new sensations add detail to the tapestry.

The first idea one gets is that of a modern industrial country. And South Africa certainly has those characteristics. The drive into the inner city of Johannesburg is on a crowded, modern multilane freeway system, part of the country's 181,000 kilometres' long road network carrying nearly five million passenger and commercial vehicles. The route into Johannesburg passes kilometres of airport service industries, modern industrial parks and neat residential suburbs. In the distance, between two ridges nestle the concrete and glass skyscrapers of the city – some of the buildings well over 30 storeys high. To be found in South Africa's city centres and in the satellite office and shopping centres which surround them, are characteristic elements of a sophisticated western economy. Hundreds of thousands of square meters of high quality office accommodation, international five-star hotels and busy modern indoor shopping complexes, some of them among the larger in the southern hemisphere. Besides this there are modern financial institutions using state of the art technology to provide full range international and local banking services to corporates and individuals. They have, for example, a countrywide electronic banking network of some 4,600 terminals. A strong core of well-trained and globally respected professionals offers its service in the fields of law, finance and engineering. On travels around the country the visitor would use the modern microwave-based telephone system which has 4,5 million telephones; could watch television beamed from one of the approximately 460 transmitters on one of the 2,6 million television sets; and read some of the 23 daily newspapers published in the country.

A journey across the country takes the visitor on good national roads over a wealth of mineral reserves, still in the ground, and past many mines producing a vast array of minerals. The list includes four precious metals, fourteen metallic minerals and twenty six non-metallic minerals. South Africa is a mineral treasure trove – estimated to have 47 percent of world gold reserves, 69 percent of world platinum group metals reserves, 24 percent of world diamond

◄ *The neo-classicistic office of the Anglo American Corporation in Johannesburg. Anglo American is the largest mining corporation of South Africa.*

reserves, 55 percent of world chromium reserves, 82 percent of world manganese reserves and 33 percent of world vanadium reserves to name but a few. Mining and metallurgical technology are well-advanced. South Africa has the world's deepest mines, such as the ERPM gold mine at 3,585 meters below surface. One of the world's largest coal export facilities is located at Richard's Bay. The visitor's journey could continue past some of the world's largest modern coal-powered power stations which, together with a nuclear power plant feed a 202,000 kilometres' long national power grid. This carries 60 percent of the African continent's electricity. The interested visitor could continue his journey past the industrial complexes of the land containing in excess of 17,000 factories. They produce iron, steel and other base metal products, synthetic fuels, industrial chemicals, pulp and paper. They beneficiate the country's natural resources and manufacture and assemble a wide range of goods from locally manufactured and imported inputs. A host of other industrial and consumer goods including such diverse goods as consumer electronics, motor vehicles and maxi-ocean racing yachts made from advanced composite materials, also leave the plants. Major international motor marques are exporting components and have recently started to export finished vehicles into the world market. Of interest is the fact that South Africa, with a long history and reputation as a wine producer is also a significant beer producer and consumer. The country has a higher per capita beer consumption (including sorghum beer) than the United Kingdom and United States of America and has the seventh largest beer producer in the world within its borders. South Africa has recently entered the beer export-market and is already the world's tenth largest beer exporter, shipping to some 47 countries in Africa, Eastern Europe, South America and the Far East.

On his journey the traveller will pass large tracts of farming land owned by commercial farmers. Owing to low rainfall, much of the land, nearly 80 percent of it, is natural grazing supporting commercial herds of cattle, sheep and goats. Closer to the metropolitan areas large feedlots and battery style cattle, pig and chicken farms can also be seen. Dairy and poultry products, red meat, tans and hides, wool and

◄ *Gold stocks in the Central Bank. Besides gold South Africa possesses large stocks of lead, copper and chromium ore.*

◄ *Diamonds that have been cut split the light into a broad colour spectrum and thus cause the characteristic glittering. The clearer the crystal, the stronger the glittering.*

Sugar-cane, the main crop ▶ on the eastern coast of Natal.

mohair are produced in abundance. On the remaining twenty percent of the commercially farmed land-surface a wide range of field crops and horticultural produce is grown, such as maize, wheat vegetables, deciduous and citrus fruits, grapes, sugar cane, tea and coffee. South Africa is a food surplus country and is a significant food exporter.

On the traveller's road he will also pass through forests. Although South Africa has never had much indigenous forest, it is now virtually self-sufficient for timber needs and for a number of years the country has been a net exporter of forest products. This has been made possible by the planting of over one million hectares of exotic hardwoods and softwoods. Amongst the products delivered by large sawmills and factories for export and domestic use are sawn timber and laminated beams, treated poles, mining timber, pulp and paper.

To a citizen of the 'first world' these impressions of South Africa strike a strong chord. There is more than a semblance of familiarity in the patterns of life in the cities and factories and on the farms. However, there is also another South Africa and one every bit as real. It is experienced by many millions of black South Africans – it is an urban and rural reality of 'third world' Africa. A world of underdevelopment and poverty, of rapid population growth and inadequate housing and health care, unemployment and pressure on available resources. A strong contrast to the 'first world' of South Africa.

▼ *Sisal plantation in Giyani (North Natal).*

▼ *Wood processing industry in Knysna.*

The legacy of apartheid

Around South Africa's modern cities the legacy of apartheid becomes visible. In the first place there are the black working-class satellite towns with inadequate infrastructure, amenities and services for the number of people they serve. Secondly there are the *plakkerskampen* (squatter settlements), housing the rural poor who have drifted to the cities to find work. The black 'homelands', in contrast to the well-tended white farming areas, are overpopulated and underdeveloped because of the high birth rate. Far too many people try to eke out a rural subsistence existence on small landholdings. In fact they rely heavily on remittances from relatives in the cities for survival. Rural poverty and pressure on the environment are characteristics South Africa's 'third world' shares with other countries in Africa and the developing world.

For many years the western 'first world' and the underdeveloped 'third world' were separated in South Africa. Government apartheid policies and a range of other legislation aimed at regulating industry, commerce, and public amenities on a western standard were responsible for this state of affairs. However incremental political and economic reform from the early 1980s onwards has progressively removed impediments to the mingling of these two worlds. Consequently, a visitor to South Africa today, is confronted early on with the 'first world/third world' duality of the country. In city centres, the visitor will see the informal 'third world' sector functioning in parallel with the formal sector. The two complement one another providing a continuum of goods, services and employment for a wide socio-economic and cultural spectrum. Traders 'set-up shop' outside city stores, in some parts of the cities forming a corridor of wares on the pavements. Swarms of private minibus taxis serve the needs of mainly black commuters. They keep a cost-effective and comprehensive countrywide rural and urban transport network in operation, improving on public transport. This interaction of the two worlds was the direct result of a government policy to deregulate the economy in order to stimulate employment creation and informal sector development.

The duality of South Africa's economy has its roots deep in history and has a development backlog from colonial times, which worsened during the apartheid years. Under apartheid the gap between South Africa's 'white' first world and 'black' third world widened. The share of resources made available for the development of the black community simply fell short of their rapidly growing needs. A core problem was, and is, that South Africa's third world population is increasing at a fast rate. At the same time systematic discriminatory legislation limited opportunities and handicapped black South Africans in a variety of other ways. Consequently, South Africa today has inherited a racially skew distribution of wealth and resources, a skew distribution of opportunity and a major development backlog in the black community with shortfalls of social and physical infrastructure. Moreover the country faces a large unemployment problem, serious rural poverty and rural overpopulation amongst black people, and a poor standard of education for the majority of the people when compared with first world standards. However, it must be said that, in some respects, South Africa's third world community is better off than the population in many developing countries. The new South Africa is faced with an inheritance that will present the country with enormous problems in the future.

▲ *The township Khayelitsha arose in the eighties as a residential town for the many homeless labourers in Greater Cape Town. Building ground and basic provisions were supplied and house-construction was deregulated, so that informal settlements could be formed. Today more than 300,000 people live here.*

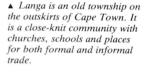

▲ *Langa is an old township on the outskirts of Cape Town. It is a close-knit community with churches, schools and places for both formal and informal trade.*

The unemployment, underdevelopment and poverty in the ▶ *'homelands' will confront the future governments of South Africa with large problems.*

South Africa's strengths and the future ahead

▲ *Just redistribution of property and chances requires a tangible improvement of life conditions, notably in the rural regions.*

▼ *In order to achieve economic growth, productivity will also have to be stimulated in the agricultural field.*

The future goal for South Africa is the building of a just, stable society. A society which can meet the aspirations of its people in the future. Reshuffling of political power brings with it rising expectations for redistribution of wealth and opportunity. People expect tangible improvements in standards of living and conditions of everyday life. The only way to achieve this is through sustained economic growth. Any meaningful redistribution of property and opportunity needs on-going creation of wealth and employment if it is to be continued.

The task is a large one but fortunately South Africa starts off well-equipped to meet the challenge. The economy survived the handicaps and adversity of the apartheid years and this in itself is evidence of its inherent strength. The country has many specific strong points. A well-developed infrastructure and sophisticated western economy, relying on abundant natural resources, large pools of unskilled workers and a core of highly skilled management, technical and professional manpower. Besides this South Africa has a modest infrastructure of respected primary, secondary and tertiary educational and research institutions. South Africa is geographically well-placed to serve markets in Africa and has a convenient location on established trade routes for accessing markets in Europe, the Far East and the Americas. Finally, the country has a good standing in world financial markets and is internationally underborrowed.

South Africa's future task can be translated into achieving rapid economic growth at the same time as redressing the skew distribution of wealth and opportunity. In short, the challenge is the setting-up of a 'virtuous cycle' of economic growth and redistribution. Rapid economic growth, however, needs a revitalization of the economy. Progressive stagnation occurred over the 1980s specifically because of the high cost of maintaining the apartheid state, economic and financial sanctions. Additional factors were the inefficiencies in the economy arising from apartheid distortions and from efforts to become self-sufficient, episodic droughts and weakening international commodity prices. Real economic growth turned negative on a per capita basis. Several causes can be indicated such as the fact that fixed investment in the economy dropped to very low levels, the public sector expanded to absorb too great a share of available resources and used them inefficiently. South Africa became a significant net capital exporter as it honoured foreign debts despite international restrictions on lending. Furthermore, low growth exacerbated the structural unemployment problem the nation had.

Achieving rapid economic growth depends on two conditions: an acceptable degree of political stability and the right economic policy environment. Current developments are encouraging. The Codesa-negotiations for a new democratic constitution show promise of eventually delivering a realistic compromise which can be sold to the majority of the people. Furthermore, the mediating talks themselves are helping to establish a culture of negotiations and give and take in the country. This bodes well for the second condition for rapid economic growth, namely an economic policy regime which stimulates welfare. Major political groupings, the business sector and organised labour all perceive the central importance of economic policy in shaping the future South Africa. Most also appreciate the urgency of arriving at an agreement to remove obstacles to getting the economy going. Various groups across the spectrum have already called for an economic policy-forum to produce a 'contract' between entrepreneurs, unions and the major political parties. This contract will define the approach to restructuring the economy to meet the challenge of growth and redistribution.

Although various groups have different ideas on economic policy, there is growing convergence owing to pragmatic consideration. The necessity to reach a compromise is obvious for all parties. South Africa can not afford to take a turning that ends in slight economical growth. Pursuing a strong socialistic policy-line, advocating redistribution of goods and property as a starting point for the rebirth of South Africa, could cause a situation like that. The mainstream black opposition parties are increasingly conceding the flaws in such an approach. Given international experience and pressure from the world community, hard logic, and the reasoned arguments of the South African establishment (i.e. government, the corporate sector and those who have some stake in the economy), they increasingly realize that such an approach can impair the capacity and incentive to create wealth. A virtuous cycle of wealth and redistribution would then not be sustainable. Fortuitously, the holders of economic power in South Africa also realize that their long-term interests are best served by promoting a sustainable redistribution of riches and opportunity in the country. The corporate sector for instance is already committing substantial resources and effort to community development and upliftment and advancement programmes for the underprivileged. The differing perceptions of the two main groupings are thus on a converging path. As time passes the convergence becomes more and more evident.

Economic policy: an important shaper of the business environment

Business opportunities flow from the nature of an economy and the shape of economic policy. South Africa's future economy and the possibilities for business will be shaped by the policies and 'contracts' negotiated between political parties, business and organized labour. Already certain features are clear. Policy will be driven by two major imperatives: the need to have a rapid economic growth and, as a result, increasing employment and a redistribution of wealth and opportunity, so that a just society is established and political pressure from the newly enfranchised is dissipated. The convergence in thinking and the balance of power between the major groupings suggests that the economy will remain market-based, although a greater degree of state intervention to facilitate redistribution is inevitable.

Economic policy is likely to focus on three areas. Firstly, the promotion of economic growth in the modern, 'first world' sector. This will mean focusing on restoring foreign and local business confidence, encouraging savings, and stimulating the supply side of the economy.

The second policy-theme will undoubtedly be the promotion of economic development. Two specific objectives are likely to be pursued: drawing in a greater proportion of the population into the modern sector in order to stimulate urbanization, rural development and the growth of the informal sector; the release of institutional funds for development and infrastructural spending, while encouraging the private sector to mobilize funds for development activities.

In the third place the policy will focus on a redistribution of wealth and opportunity in the economy to place disadvantaged communities on a better footing. At the very least this will entail the equalization of opportunity through a variety of mechanisms. This policy leg would have to address at least four areas. A first important point is to ensure that no racially based barriers to ownership and opportunity exist in society. Secondly racial per capita parity in public spending should be guaranteed. In the third place a programme of land reform has to be instituted to return agricultural land to black people dispossessed at the high tide of the apartheid resettlements. Finally, a programme of socio-economic spending aimed at addressing historical

backlogs in housing, education and health care has to be put into effect.

Axes of business opportunity in the future South Africa

South Africa's new economic and political environment and the likely shape of the economy in coming years define clear areas of opportunity for local businessmen and foreign investors alike. These chances can be grouped into three areas. Firstly, opportunities which arise from the disappearance of international sanctions against South Africa and from political changes in the international 'arena'. Secondly, business opportunities which arise from the changed domestic political scene with its associated shift in government policy emphasis. Thirdly, opportunities which arise from the underlying characteristics of the country such as its natural resource endowment, geographical position and market growth potential.

South Africa's new found political acceptability together with changes in the world-order has gained it access to a large number of new trading areas which were either previously closed, or which it could only exploit on a limited, clandestine basis. Amongst these are the former Eastern Bloc and Soviet Union, a large number of African countries, and various countries in the Middle and Far East. Today, even the People's Republic of China is open for trade with South Africa. All these potential new markets hold promise of two-way trade. It should be noted that South Africa's strategic position and local knowledge qualifies it well to supply African markets with goods, infrastructure and services. This is particularly interesting as Sub-Saharan Africa seems to be slowly moving into a new era with changes in economic policy thinking taking place. These could result in a rebuilding of their economies in coming years. Foreign entrepreneurs wishing to serve African markets would do well to do it from a base in South Africa, using a country with a sophisticated infrastructure and good living conditions as a springboard into the continent. A further aspect of market access is that political barriers to the country's traditional markets in Europe, The Americas, and the Far East are coming down. These markets are now much less difficult to reach. Another aspect of market access which provides prospects for foreigners is that South Africa's political acceptability makes it possible to invest and trade openly in South Africa again. This obviously generates possibilities in the domestic marketplace as well.

As a result of the lifting of economic sanctions import and ▼ export are increasing again.

After the political changes policy emphasis will be focused on: promoting urbanisation, achieving racial parity in government spending, meeting backlogs in particularly social but also physical infrastructure, land reform, promoting employment creation and developing the rural sector. The promotion of urbanisation will stimulate demand for urban infrastructure and utilities. Furthermore as people move into the city environment their needs change and they consume more goods and personal services than they would have living in the country. Policies aimed at addressing backlogs in housing, education and health care also offer business prospects in the building of the infrastructure and provision of goods and services. Achieving racial parity in government spending opens up interesting business possibilities. Limited state funds mean that the level of provision of some services previously provided on a high standard to whites by the public sector will be downgraded. An opportunity therefore opens up for the private sector to fill the gap. The demand for private provision of high quality education, health and security services and some public utilities is likely to grow strongly in the coming years.

Any policy which changes the distribution of wealth brings business opportunities. A redistribution of wealth in favour of low-income people implies major growth potential in the consumer markets. Lower-income groups generally spend a higher proportion of their income on goods and services than the higher income groups. Demand will accelerate first for essential basic consumer goods. The market for basic needs goods is expected to show strong growth in coming years. Later, as incomes will increase, the demand for more sophisticated consumer goods will rise as well.

The intrinsic characteristics of the country will also provide business opportunities in coming years. The beneficiation of minerals, agricultural produce, fish and forestry products all provide substantial chances for local and foreign investors to supply domestic, African and international markets with a wide range of products. South Africa's geographical situation also points to business possibilities. On the tip of Africa on a sea-route connecting Europe and the Americas with Australasia and Asia, the country is well-positioned to be a central supply and manufacturing base for a great number of world markets. Furthermore, Africa and much of the Indian Ocean Basin are a South African natural market and are likely to come into its economic influence sphere. South Africa's growing population is another intrinsic characteristic which points to future business opportunity. The demand for consumer goods and services and for urban and rural infrastructure will rise as the population grows. As economic growth enhances employment, incomes will rise and translate this latent demand into attractive markets for local and foreign business. A gradual improvement in the distribution of wealth in the country mentioned in the preceding paragraph will strengthen this effect even further.

Travelling

All important South African centres can be reached by train. It is possible to travel both first and second class and sleepers are available on the long distances. The famous Blue Train rides between Johannesburg and Cape Town. Since 1992 the similarly renowned Pride of Africa, known as Rovos-Rail, has also covered this section.

The transport company Autonet is responsible for the motorways, connecting the rural and urban centres across a distance of 181,000 kilometres. About 82,000 kilometres of the road network is asphalted and in excellent condition.

The surrounding regions of the big cities can very well be explored by coach. There is a scheduled service of comfortable coaches between Cape Town, Durban and Johannesburg. Such services are operated by City-liner, Inter-Cape-Express, Inter-city, Trans-city, Translux and Trans-State.

Motor-coach companies organize special coach tours to the popular places of interest in, for instance, East Transvaal (including Kruger National Park), Natal, the Cape Province and Transkei. These companies are, among others: Afro Venture Safaris, Connex Travel Coach Tours, Grosvenor Tours, Rand Coach Tours, Springbok Atlas Safaris, Trans Africa Safaris and Welcome Tours and Safaris. Moreover it is possible to rent a car in all cities at the airports rom internationally known companies such as Avis rent-a-car, Budget rent-a-car and Imperial Car Rental (of which Hertz is a daughter company).

The South African Airline company (SAL), the main one on the southern hemisphere, has played a major role in the South African tourist industry since its foundation in 1934. In the country itself there are 600 weekly flights between the main cities. An option here is the economical 'Airpass-tariff': five home flights within one months for an extremely low price. SAL has developed into the largest airline company on the African continent, calling at eleven destinations with a frequency of 37 flights per week.

During the apartheid period of 1963-1991 some African companies compelled the company to fly to Europe via an alternative route along the west coast of Africa. From June 1991 onwards SAL has been granted permission again to fly over a number of West African countries (Mali, Mauritania and Morocco). Since September of that same year the eastern corridor via Sudan and Egypt has been opened too.

The international network of SAL comprises scheduled services to nine European cities (to London even on a daily basis), to America and Australia (after an interruption between 1986 and 1991), to Israel, Taipei, Hong Kong, Rio de Janeiro, Singapore and Bangkok and, recently, Tokyo.

Comavi, Giyani Airways, Link Airlines, Mmabatho Air and Transkei Air also provide home flights. These companies operate from Johannesburg. From Cape Town and Durban, Air Cape and City Air respectively maintain several connections. International flights are also carried out by British Airways, KLM, Lufthansa, Luxavia and Sabena. The airline companies, including charter companies such as Transavia and Martinair, have focused their attention again on the 'country of many faces'. Together they provide regular flights to Johannesburg, Cape Town and Durban. KLM in particular has recently adapted its activities. This has resulted in non-stop flights and the addition of a third weekly flight from Amsterdam to Johannesburg. They also fly to Cape Town twice a week.

The business centre of Johannesburg.

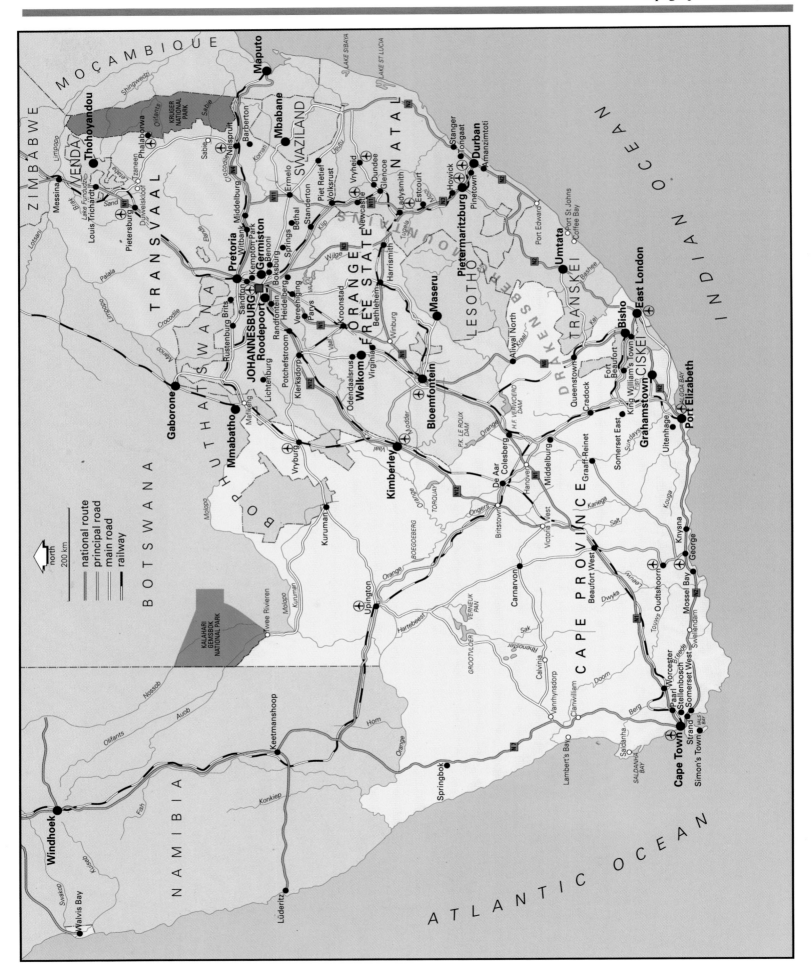

ILLUSTRATION SOURCES

The visual material in 'South Africa in focus' was contributed by the persons and institutions mentioned below.
The denotations behind the names refer to the pages where the pictures can be found.

Africana Museum: 15, 16 right and bottom, 17 left, 18, 30 left, 39 top and bottom, 40 middle, 41, 42 top, 45 top, 48 top, 112 middle

Albany Museum, Grahamstown: 116 bottom

Anglo American Corporation: 11 bottom, 143 top and bottom

ANP: 28

Willem Drechsel: 16 l.top, 17 right, 24, 30 r.top, 31 top, 54 top, 55 r.bottom, 57, 64 bottom, 65 left and bottom, 66 r.top, 68, 69 left, 70 middle, 71 top, 72 top and middle,74, 75 top, 79 top, 80 top, 81 top, 82, 83 right, 87 bottom, 89 middle, 91 right and bottom, 100 middle, 104 middle, 110 bottom, 122 left and bottom, 123 l. bottom, m.bottom and r.middle, 124 l.bottom, m.top and r.bottom, 126, 127 l.bottom, 128 middle and bottom, 130 middle, 131 top and middle, 137 top, 145 bottom, 146

Londolozi Game Reserve: 11 top, 65 r.top
Liesbeth Matser: cover: 'impressive monuments', 12, 25 top, 26, 40 top and bottom, 44 bottom, 61, 66 l.top, 69 right, 71 bottom, 79 bottom, 83 left, 84 top, 92 bottom, 111 right, 113 bottom, 114 l.bottom, 115 bottom, 124 middle and l.bottom, 144 r.bottom

Consul Pillay: 127 r.bottom

Rovos Rail: 63 middle and bottom

South African Airlines (Sal): 147-148

South African Tourism Board (Satour): large cover photo: 'unique fynbos vegetation' and 'fascinating fauna', rear cover, photo next to colophon, 4-6, 8, 9 top, 20 bottom, 22 bottom, 31 middle and bottom, 34-35, 37-38, 39 middle, 42 bottom, 44 top and middle, 55 top, 56 bottom, 58, 60, 63 top, 64 top and middle, 66 middle and bottom, 67, 70 top and bottom, 72 bottom, 73, 75 middle and bottom, 76 top and middle, 78 top and bottom, 80 bottom, 81 bottom, 85-86, 87 top, 88, 89 top and bottom, 90, 91 m.top, 92 l.top and middle, 93-99, 100 top and bottom, 101-103, 104 top and bottom, 105-109, 110 top and middle, 11 left, 113 top and middle, 114 top and r.bottom, 115 top and middle, 116 top, 117-121, 122 top, 123 bottom, 124 r.top, 125, 127 top, 128 top, 129, 130 bottom, 131 bottom, 132-136, 127 middle and bottom, 138-141, 142 top and bottom, 143 middle, 144 top, 149, 151-152

South African Communication Service: 9 bottom, 29, 45 bottom, 46-47, 48 bottom, 56 top, 76 bottom, 77, 80 middle, 84 bottom, 92 right, 142 middle, 144 l.bottom

South African Museum, Cape Town: cover: 'archaeological treasures' and 'artistic traditions', 36, 43 top, 49-53, 54 bottom, 55 l.bottom, 59, 78 middle, 145 top and middle

Eli Weinberg: 27

P. Westra: 112 top

Illustrations
History of South Africa by W.J. de Kock: 21 right, 23, 25 bottom
Memories of a game-ranger by H. Wolhuter: 62 top
Missionary Travels by D. Livingstone: 62 bottom
Uncle Paul by M. Juta: 19 middle
The Star of Johannesburg: 33
The Pretoria News: 72 middle
South Africa's history in pictures by dr E.C. Godée-Molsbergen & J. Visscher: 13, 14, 16 l.middle, 19 bottom, 20 top and middle, 21 top, 22 top, 30 r.middle and r.bottom

The objects, prints and paintings depicted in this book have been published with the permission of the museums in South Africa concerned.

Cartography: DataGraphics, Tiel
Large cover photograph: Waterbuck (Kobus defassa)
Photograph back: Zulu woman
Photograph colophon: Ndebele boy

The elegant crowned crane (Balearica pavonia regulorum) is a ▶ coveted 'prey' during photo-safaris.

GLOSSARY

Abakhwetha boys during their initiation period [Xhosa]
agterryers non-white servants of the Voortrekkers

Bittereinder stayer, go-getter; Republican who kept on fighting until the end of the war
bobbejanen baboons
boma space surrounded by branches

Caldeira funnel-shaped crater in a volcano; large bowl-shape brought about by the partial or complete explosion of a volcano

Difaqane period of battle and migration at the beginning of the nineteenth century [Sotho]
dolerite early vulcanic stone, extremely solid rock with green or grey color
domba initiation ritual of Venda girls
donga dried-up river bed; deep dry ditch
Drostdy administrator's office, in the seventeenth, eighteenth and nineteenth century judicial civil servant and administrator in the countryside

Fynbos [maquis or macchia], low growth consisting of several species of erica, proteas, restio (reed-like plants) and a large group of bulbous and tuberous crops.

Hensopper defector; Cape loyalist
hominids early anthropoids; family from the order of primates, to which both modern and fossil man and the anthropoids belong

Impi Zulu regiment
Incwala largest ceremonial feast of the Zulu, celebrated annually during the first new moon
inkundla the space between the large house and the stable, meeting-place for men [Xhosa and Zulu]
izindlu collection of huts, generally numbering ten or twenty, set up in a semi-circle around a central cattle pen [Xhosa and Zulu]

Kgotla meeting-place for men in a village [Tswana]

kimberlite bluish igneous rock; mother stone which may contain diamond
koppies hills
kraal fenced-in space for cattle; walled inner court and farmyard of black population

Laager [lager] camp; army camp of the Boers, in which the ox-carts were lined up in a circle
lapa front part of a walled inner court belonging to a family's house in a Sotho settlement
lobola dowry

Malopo cult of obsession with the Sotho and Tsonga in Transvaal at the beginning of the twentieth century
matrilineal system of kinship in which an individual becomes a member of the mother's descendants group
Mfecane period of battle and migration at the beginning of the nineteenth century [Nguni]
murundu special hut in which Venda boys undergo circumcision

Naturel aged term for black person

Patrilineal system of kinship in which an individual becomes a member of the father's descendants group
plaas farm
plakkerskamp informal settlement; slum
polygyny marriage in which one man is married with two or more women at the same time

Rondavel [rondawel] round hut or one-room house with a thatched roof

Setlaars colonists
sibaya cattle pen [Xhosa and Zulu]
spoorsnyer scout, tracker
spruit small river, brook
succulents plants that store moisture that they use during dry periods; among others cacti, crassulae and euphorbias

Therianthropes figures combining human and animal characteristics

▲ *Mountain baboon (Papio anubis), also called 'bobbejaan', in the Cape of Good Hope Nature Reserve.*

Vijgies mesembryantheumum; small creepers
voorloper leader of a team of oxen; scout
Voortrekkers people who migrated from the Cape colony in the period between 1834 and 1840 in order to built a new subsistence

BIBLIOGRAPHY

Chapter 1

Africa at a glance, Pretoria 1992: African Institute of South Africa
Annual Report, Pretoria 1992: Satour
Doing business in South Africa, 1990: Ernst & Young
Investment in South Africa, Johannesburg, Pretoria and Cape Town 1990: K.P.M.G. Aiken & Peat.
Race Relations Survey 1991/2, Johannesburg 1992: Research Staff South African Institute of Race Relations.
South Africa 1991/1992, official Yearbook of the Republic of South Africa 1991/1992, 17th edition: Publication department of the South African Communication Service
South Africa 1992, South Africa Foundation.

Chapter 2

History

Böeseken, A.J., *Slaves and free Blacks at the Cape 1658-1700*, Cape Town 1977.
Cameron, T., and Spies, S.B. [ed.], *Nuwe geskiedenis van Suid-Afrika in woord en beeld*, Cape Town 1992, 2nd edition.
Cohen, R., a.o., *Repression and resistance: Insider account of Apartheid*, London 1990.
Elphick, R., Giliomee, H. (eds), *The shaping of South African Society 1652-1840*, Cape Town 1989, second edition.
Esterhuyse, W., Nel, P., *Die ANC en sy leiers*, Cape Town 1990.
Kannemeyer, J.C., *Die Afrikaanse literatuur 1652-1987*, Pretoria 1988.
Kenney, H., *Power, pride and prejudice. The years of Afrikaner Nationalist rule in South Africa*, Johannesburg 1991.
Muller, C.F.J., *Die oorsprong van die Groot Trek*, Pretoria 1988 second edition.
Ploeger, J., *Die lotgevalle van die burgerlijke bevolking gedurende die Anglo-Boereoorlog, 1899-1902*, 5 volumes, Pretoria 1990.
Schutte, G.J., *Nederland en de Afrikaners: adhesie en aversie*, Franeker 1986.
Schutte, G.J., *Zicht op Zuid-Afrika*, Amsterdam 1981.
Van Jaarsveld, F.A., *Afrikaner-geskiedskrywing: Verlede, hede en toekoms*, Johannesburg 1992.
Van der Ross, R.E., *The rise and decline of apartheid. A study of political movements among the coloured people of South africa 1880-1985*, Cape Town 1986
Worden, N., *Slavery in Dutch South Africa*, Cambridge 1985.

Sociology

Kane-Berman, J., *South Africa's Silent Revolution*, Johannesburg & Halfway House 1990: SAIRR/Southern.
Lijphart, A., *Machtsindeling: de oplossing voor Zuid-Afrika?*, Haarlem 1978: Becht.
Mathiane, N., *Beyond the headlines: Truths of Soweto Life*, Johannesburg 1990: Southern.
Smith, K., *The changing Past: Trends in South African Historical Writing*, Johannesburg 1988: Southern
Van Doorn, J.A.A., *Een kwestie van overleven: Notities over Zuid-Afrika*, Amsterdam 1991; Meulenhoff.

Chapter 3

Biesle, M., *Shaken Roots*, Johannesburg 1990: EDA Publication.
Cameron, T. & Spies, S.B. (eds), *An illustrated History of South Africa*, Johannesburg 1986: Jonathan Ball.
Elphick, R., *Kraal and castle: KhoiKhoi and the founding of White South Africa*, New Haven 1977: Yale University Press.
Hall, M., *The Changing Past*, Cape Town 1987: David Philip.
Inskeep, R.I., *The peopling of southern Africa*, Cape Town 1978: David Philip.
Klein, R.G. (ed), *Southern African prehistory and palaeo-environments*, Rotterdam 1984: A.A.Balkema.
Lye, W.F. & Murray, C., *Transformations on the Highveld: the Tswana and Southern Sotho*, Cape Town 1980: David Philip.
Mellars, P. & Stringer, C. (eds), *The human revolution*, Princeton 1989: Princeton University Press.
Tobias, P.V. (ed), *The Bushmen*, Cape Town 1978: Human and Rousseau.
West, M., *Abantu. An introduction to the black people of South Africa*, Cape Town 1976: Struik.
Younge, G., *Art of the South African townships*, London 1988: Thames & Hudson.

Chapter 4 up to and including 7

Afrikanerbakens (Gedenktekens en Monumenten in Zuid-Afrika): Federasie van Afrikaanse Kultuurvereniginge 1989.
Bulpin, T.V., *Southern Africa: Land of beauty and splendour*, London 1977, third edition.
Cameron, T., Spies, J.B. (ed), *A new illustrated History of South Africa*, Cape Town and Johannesburg 1991, second edition: Southern Book Publisher & Human and Rousseau.
Gordon, R., and Bannister, A. (ed), *Off the Beaten Track*, Cape Town 1988: A.A. The Motorist Publications Ltd.
Kench, J., *The Coast of Southern Africa*, Cape Town 1987: Struik.
Livingstone, D., *Missionary Travels and Researches in South Africa*, 1857: John Murray.
Meintjes, J., *The Anglo-Boer War 1899-1902*, Cape Town 1976: Struik.
Reynierse, C. (ed), *Illustrated Guide to the Southern African Coast*, Cape Town 1988: A.A. The Motorist Publications Ltd.
South Africa, a World in one Country, Travel Guide, Cape Town 1992: Satour.
Stevinson-Hamilton, J., *South African Eden*, London 1952, second edition: Cassell and Camp Ltd.
Wannenburg, A., *The Natural Wonder of Southern Africa*, Cape Town 1978: Struik.
Wolhuter. H., *Memories of a game ranger*, Johannesburg 1948: The Wild Life Protection Society of South Africa.
Zuid-Afrika, land van wilde dieren en safari's, Cape Town 1990: Satour.

INDEX

Besides the geographical denotations, historical periods, personal names and names of population groups, the key words on top of the pages have also been incorporated into this index.

index